THE DEAN KOONTZ COMPANION

Martin H Greenberg, Bill Munster,
Ed Gorman

HEADLINE

British Library Cataloguing in Publication Data

Koontz Companion
I. Greenberg, Martin Harry
813.54

ISBN 0-7472-0830-1

Typeset by Keyboard Services, Luton

Printed and bound in Great Britain by
Mackays of Chatham PLC, Chatham, Kent

HEADLINE BOOK PUBLISHING
A division of Hodder Headline PLC
Headline House
79 Great Titchfield Street
London W1P 7FN

Contents

PART I
Interview with Dean Koontz
by Ed Gorman

EARLY YEARS

Q: A few years ago you remarked that your parents 'always thought books were a waste of time and money,' and discouraged you from reading as a child. Tell us about your early life.

A: Well, you have to understand we were poor. Books cost money. And they weren't essential to existence, the way food was. They were essential to *me*, you understand, but that's a difficult concept to get across in a household where fifty dollars a week was a *huge* cash flow.

We were so poor we thought hamburgers were what rich people ate when they flew to Paris to celebrate making another gazillion dollars. We ate a lot of grilled-cheese sandwiches, bologna and cheese sandwiches, cheese and cheese sandwiches, macaroni and cheese, macaroni and cheese sandwiches, tomato soup, tomato soup with macaroni. We probably would've eaten *piles* of tomato-soup sandwiches, too, except for the mess. My mother – a wonderful woman in most regards, gentle, kind – was obsessively clean; she kept an immaculate house, so food had to be both cheap and *neat*.

We also ate a lot of game meat because some of my uncles and other relatives were hunters. For a large part of the year, there were rabbits, squirrels, and venison, which were prized because they were free. By the time I was an adult, I was so sick of game meat – associated it so intimately with being poor – that to this day I can't tolerate any meat with a 'wild' taste, including lamb. I've even been known, on rare occasions, to get physically ill from the smell of it.

I remember helping my Uncle Ray to 'dress' a deer carcass on more than one occasion – which does not mean dolling it up in high heels, a dress, and a pillbox hat. That might have been fun. 'Dressing' a dead deer means gutting, skinning, and butchering it. If you're smart, you do it in your underpants because of all the blood and less delightful bodily fluids that are an unavoidable bonus of the process. Let me tell

3

you, there's no male-bonding experience more moving, more emotional, more downright *spiritual* than standing in a drafty basement with your cousin and uncle, a big doe or buck hooked to the rafters, all of you in your skivvies, smeared from head to toe with the unspeakable substances from the cadaver of a cloven-hoofed animal. (When I say 'all of you in your skivvies,' I do not mean to include the deer, of course; deer don't wear underpants, which is something you learn when you live in a rural environment; they don't wear neckties, either.)

My uncle Ray Mock was one of the sweetest guys who ever walked the earth, sentimental as all get-out. As a practical matter, he had to hunt and dress deer in and out of season to help supplement his own family's food budget, but he didn't have the heart for killing and butchering, so Uncle Ray always drank a few beers before we stripped to our skivvies and got started. And he kept putting away the beers – Rolling Rock or Iron City – all through the butchering. My cousin Jim would have a beer or two, as well, even when he was only twelve or thirteen, but I was always too young to be allowed one. As bonding experiences, skiing weekends and camping trips and river-rafting excursions *pale* compared to standing in a drafty basement in your skivvies with your uncle and your cousin, everyone spattered with blood and bits of deer fat, everyone with sharp knives, your cousin a tipsy and giggling adolescent, your uncle more than tipsy and, as often as not, teary-eyed with remorse over what had been done to the noble wild creature hooked to the rafters.

Occasionally there would be talk about making amends for this savagery. Plans were laid to haul bales of hay and bags of oats out into the woods as an apology to the entire deer nation. An appetite for venison was declared repulsive. It was announced with great sincerity that the current carcass would be given to the poor. Soon, however, we realized *we* were the poor, so the only thing to be done was open another beer and get on with it.

From the time I was born until I left home for college, we lived in Bedford, Pennsylvania, and from my fifth year we lived in a four-room house my grandfather built with his own hands. He was a good man, always kind to me – but, bless his heart, he should have been a concert pianist or a cardiovascular surgeon, anything but a house-builder. The tar-paper roof leaked. The whole house was heated by a coal-fired furnace with a single in-floor register in the living room, under the theory that heat would rise to warm the two rooms on the second floor, but there was never enough heat to warm more than the living room. We were always having flue fires, however. No heat in the house but wild gouts of flame shooting out the top of the chimney, which is something you want to avoid with a tar-paper roof.

Water was heated by a kerosene burner under a small tank in the basement. By the time I was ten, one of my chores was to walk to the nearest service station once a week and get five gallons of kerosene. Do they still sell kerosene at service stations? It sounds so ancient. Like saying, 'Once a week I walked to Caesar's stables and bought dung briquettes from the master of the horses, to burn in the fire pit of our hut.' By the time I was twelve, it was also my chore to refill the glass jug that hung upside-down over the wick ring, replace it, make sure it was dripping properly, then re-light this insanely dangerous Rube Goldberg device. I was always absolutely certain that I was going to set myself and the entire house on fire, and sometimes I used to stare at that jug for ten or fifteen minutes to get up the courage to do what needed done. Until I was nine or ten, we had no indoor plumbing, just a dilapidated outhouse at the end of the backyard, which was frigid in winter and acrawl with spiders in summer. We bathed in a galvanized tin washtub in the basement, which we filled with a hose connected to a spigot on the hot-water tank. Drawing a bath and cleaning up afterward were a laborious process. There was a hand pump on the kitchen sink, not faucets, and I can still clearly recall the sound of that device and the sudden gush of cold water that would come just when I thought my effort wouldn't be rewarded.

Even as a little boy, I remember worrying about being nuked by the Russians, and I always figured I would survive by hiding out in the big coal bin at one corner of the cellar. Somehow I had faith that my dear grandfather's spit-and-prayer house would withstand a direct thermonuclear strike. Oh, the second floor would go, sure, and the first floor would be a mess, but the cellar would surely be untouched. It never occurred to me that the Soviets might have more important targets than a farm-center town of four thousand people in the rural hills of central Pennsylvania. Instead, I envisioned a sky full of hurtling missiles and bombs, all zeroing in on Bedford in general and on the Koontz house in particular, while fat Russian dictators chortled evilly in faraway bunkers. Even then my imagination spun like the wheel on a perpetual-motion machine.

Somehow we came into enough money to put in a bathroom with a tub, a kitchen sink with hot and cold running water, and a few other amenities. However, we retained that kerosene-bomb water heater, as if the concept of electrically-heated water was just too scary to contemplate. It might have been one of those rare periods when my father held a steady sales job; he was a good salesman when he wanted to be. Or maybe he got lucky at cards and my mother managed to get some of it away from him before he lost it all back again.

Q: Your father, Ray, was quite an influence on your life – though in a negative way – wasn't he?

A: My father never met a vice he didn't like, and sometimes it almost seemed that he took pride in the fact that he succumbed to every temptation. He was a diligent alcoholic who could as easily become violent as maudlin when he was drunk. My earliest memories include his rampages and my fear that he would kill my mother and me. He lost more than one job because he took a punch at a boss or showed up drunk at work – or both.

He ran around on my mother with a series of women. Oddly enough, while my mother was a slender and attractive woman, my father generally chose to cheat on her with large *unattractive* women. One of these was a female wrestler. Now, this was back in the 1950s, when female wrestlers were extremely rare, and most of them were *nothing whatsoever* like women wrestlers and mud-wrestlers these days. They didn't wear bikinis. There was no demand for them to wear bikinis, no demand at all, zero, nada, zip. Women wrestlers in those days looked more like *male* wrestlers in those days, and male wrestlers in those days weren't 10 per cent as cute as male wrestlers today. I guess what I'm trying to tell you is that the average female wrestler at that time looked like the actor Edward Asner in a bad mood, and this was the type of woman on whom my father spent what money he earned instead of bringing it home.

He was a gambler. Cards and horses were primary interests, and he would think nothing of betting the week's grocery money on a single hand of cards – then expect my mother to feed us somehow. Those were days when you hoped there was a damned deer that needed to be dressed!

He was frequently in bar fights – which he always lost. This habit continued well into old age. Once, in a barroom, when he was sixty-five, he made an obscene suggestion to a young woman who was in

6

the company of a thirty-year-old man. My father was on the shorter side, five-feet-six, a hundred and sixty pounds, very blocky – but this young guy was six-two, two hundred plus pounds. When he objected to my father's comment to the woman, my father made an obscene suggestion to *him* and challenged him to a fight. Good old Dad was knocked out in one punch. Subsequently he decided to file a civil suit against this young man to obtain compensation for his injuries!

Suing people was as big a pastime for him as drinking, gambling, and woman-chasing. He had a profound faith that he was going to get rich through one suit or another, and he was capable of having three different ambulance-chasing attorneys at work on different cases at the same time. Over the years, while driving under the influence, he totaled five cars that I can remember – the number of fender-benders is beyond counting; we're talking only of *totaled* vehicles – and in *every* case he sued the innocent party. Once, in the 1950s, he received a $16,000 settlement out of court – which, pre-inflation, equalled maybe $100,000 today. Years later, his own attorney still expressed astonishment that the other side settled, considering the floor of Dad's car had been littered with empty beer cans. We were always amazed he never killed himself or anyone else; he had a weird dark luck.

He wanted me to be a sports star. He'd tell people, 'Yeah, Dean's on the small side now, but he's going to grow up to be at least six-two, two hundred-twenty pounds, and play for the Steelers.' I mean this literally. That is *exactly* what he'd say. That was bad enough; it put a lot of pressure on me. But then he'd add, 'He sure *better* get some meat on him, 'cause he's not going to amount to anything the way he is.' He was a real confidence-builder. My father was about five-six, and I grew up to be five-eleven, weighing about one fifty-five – but that leaves me three inches and sixty-five pounds short of his minimum requirements for a son. To say nothing of the fact that I've yet to play for the Steelers! Can you see me on a football field, up against the guys who play it these days? *Huge* guys. League rules don't allow the use of Tae Kwan Do, and I don't think my skill with language would wow defensive linemen into letting me slip past them!

I could go on about him for hours, and a lot of it would seem amusing – but, believe me, none of it was amusing to live through. Even if he hadn't been such a threatening, hot-headed figure at

7

home, living with him would have been intolerable if only because of all his other faults.

Q: What about your mother?

A: Her name was Florence, but many people called her Molly. She was a gentle person, more selfless than she should have been, far more selfless than I've ever managed to be. She had a hard life. Her father, John Logue, was a lovely man, but her mother was something of a dragon. They weren't poor, but they didn't have much, either. In high school, my mother was a first-rate musician, and a couple of her teachers thought she might have a real future in music. But there was no money for college or advanced lessons. It was the Great Depression, after all. Then she made the biggest mistake of her life and married my father.

She died young, fifty-three, and I know the strain of living with him shortened her life by *at least* a decade. She was too submissive by nature, and those were the days when divorce was nearly unthinkable, especially in small-town Pennsylvania; but I still wonder why she endured so much for so long. From things she said to me in her final days, I know love had died early on, so it seemed to be more duty that kept her with him than anything, duty and the mores of the times – which she took seriously even though he did not.

The last fourteen years of my father's life, long after my mother was gone, Gerda and I supported him in an apartment of his own, here in California. Because of what she put up with, my wife has earned a place in heaven. When Dad was in his late sixties, he was diagnosed as a lifelong borderline schizophrenic with tendencies to violence, complicated by chronic alcoholism. The psychiatrist told me Dad was 'sociopathic and a pathological liar.' I knew as much already, but it was a relief to hear it in clinical terms. The psychiatrist told me that men of this type are *extremely* dangerous when drunk and that I was fortunate to have survived childhood with little physical abuse. My survival was largely my mother's doing, of course; she was brave as well as kind, and protected me even when afraid for herself.

During the last three years, before he died at 81, long-term heavy drinking began to exact a greater toll; he suffered from degenerative alcohol syndrome, in which hollow spaces develop in the brain where there shouldn't be any. His violent episodes became increasingly extreme. Twice he attempted to stab me. In the second instance, taking a knife from him was a hard struggle. It occurred in front of witnesses, and someone called the police. He spent some time in a psychiatric ward and then a nursing home. It's so sad to say, but I cannot remember a single pleasant moment involving my father from over forty years of memories. They're all dark.

* * *

Q: In spite of that childhood, some of your strongest characters are bright, optimistic, well-adjusted children. Do you see any contradiction there?

A: Not really. In spite of it all, I've wound up a reasonably well-adjusted person. Aside from my habit of dressing like Helen of Troy at *any* opportunity, the five attempted assassinations of major figures in the professional-clown community, a compulsion to shout the word 'knockwurst' in church as many as two hundred times during a single service, and my obsession with building an accurate replica of the entire city of Bayonne, New Jersey, out of toothpicks and chewing gum, I'm a perfectly ordinary guy. I *do* like to wear jackets made out of live tarantulas stitched together with wire, but that's not eccentric; it's a simple fashion statement. Likewise the shoes made out of seedless watermelons and the linguine neckties.

Seriously, one thing that's central to my work is the idea that we are *not* necessarily doomed to lives of fear and neuroses because of terrors we experienced as children. Half our reader mail comes from kids, some of whom have suffered abuse. They're willing to tell me about it, without knowing my background, because from the novels they sense I've had similar experiences. I get mail from adults who, having endured terrible childhoods, find hope in my novels just by reading about abuse survivors who nevertheless grow up to be happy and successful. I always tell them that to surrender to despair is to hand victory to the abusive person who made their lives hell; it isn't easy, but you have to get past blaming that person, get past feeling negative about yourself, learn to open yourself to the world, and go on. The worst thing I could do would be to let my childhood taint the rest of my life – because I'd be letting my father *win*. And it's a mistake to think you have to 'forgive' the offender. Hell, no! If he or she deserves your anger and contempt, you have to learn it's all right to hate when there's a logical reason for it – then put that hate behind you. If some of my books, in some small way, help people to find the will and strength to get past the effects of disastrous childhoods, that alone makes writing worthwhile.

Q: Aside from your home life, is there anything about your childhood that still bothers you?

A: Well, as a kid, you never really think to tell people just how *much* you love them, maybe because you don't have the words yet, maybe because it's embarrassing when you're a kid, but also because, as a kid, you just don't have a sense of how tenuous life really is. People pass away, and after you're grown up, you wonder if they really understood how important they were to you, how very much they meant to your life. I think about that, sometimes, about all the love never adequately expressed, and it makes me feel as if I was a shallow and self-centered little snot. When I get in a mood like that, I know I'm being too hard on myself, and I figure it's probably something that most people feel when they look back, but I still brood about it sometimes.

Q: What are your best memories of childhood?

A: Going to Mars with Ray Bradbury. Learning about the Dreaming Jewels from Theodore Sturgeon. Shivering in terror as Victor von Frankenstein's creature lurched around the countryside tossing little girls into open wells. Cringing from Lugosi's Dracula. Traveling through time with Robert Heinlein, H. G. Wells. Going down a river on a raft with Huck and Jim. Voyaging to far worlds with Robert Heinlein. Learning from Ray Bradbury about strange mushrooms in the cellar, dandelion wine, and carnivals inhabited by people who've sold their souls. Sid Caesar, Ernie Kovacs, battling aliens with Heinlein, reading Donald Duck and Uncle Scrooge comic books (especially fat Christmas special issues), and so much more. For the most part, my best memories from childhood are books I read and movies I saw, fiction not reality. That's one reason I became a writer – an obsessive desire to give other people the pleasure, escape, and emotional release that I got from books when I most needed that medicine.

I also have great memories of a maroon bicycle I received from my Uncle Ray for Christmas when I was eleven. Suddenly I had freedom, and I took that bike everywhere, far beyond the area to which my mother restricted me. There were no kids my age to play with where we lived, and I never had a real 'best friend' until I was in junior high school, so that bike was my surrogate friend.

We lived across from the county fairground, and every August there was a week-long fair with stock-car races, livestock shows, fireworks every night, and a huge carnival. For years, fair week was the high point of my life, and I've nothing but good memories of it. I didn't want to shell out precious funds to get onto the grounds, so with the whole year to reconnoiter and prepare secret tunnels under the perimeter fence, I always got in free.

There, an admission of criminal conduct! Wow, this interview might get as wild as those on Donahue, Oprah, and Geraldo! Who knows what I might reveal next – maybe some spectacular illicit liaison with a member of the British Royal Family, an exotic dancer, and a duck. Or a sick passion for bathing in sauerkraut.

Anyway, the carnival had enormous allure for me because it moved on every week to a new town. There were times when I entertained the notion of running away with the Dell & Travers operation or E. James Strait and his massive railroad-car show, so I wouldn't have to worry what my father might do the next time he was drunk. But I could never have left my mother there. I developed a lifelong interest in carnivals which eventually led to TWILIGHT EYES. I used some of the carnival lore I've acquired when I novelized the screenplay for THE FUNHOUSE as well, and someday I might write a big novel that makes use of a tremendous amount of exotic material I've not even tapped yet.

* * *

Q: What about dogs?

A: They have four feet, tails, and fur. And while virtually any dog will die to protect his master, it's not a good idea to let them drive cars.

Q: I'm glad you cleared that up.

A: However, because they're so loyal, dogs make excellent partners when you're planning bank robberies or other criminal activities because they'll never sell you out to the coppers in return for a light sentence. If Richard Nixon had staffed the White House with dogs instead of people like John Dean and John Erlichman, he'd *still* be President and widely revered.

Q: I'm sure you're right. But what I meant was – since you've written two books thus far – WATCHERS and DRAGON TEARS – in which appear exceptional dogs, people might want to know if you modeled them on dogs you had as a child.

A: We couldn't afford to keep a dog, but because it seemed that a boy ought to have a canine companion, we took two tries at having a family mutt. The first one was named 'Tiny,' and of course he grew up to be huge – from a cuddly puppy to a massive beast that was often mistaken for a cow – virtually *overnight*. He was a black and white mongrel, not a mean bone in his gargantuan body, but he was hyper. No human being ever born has benefitted from illicit drugs – but 3,000 CCs of Valium might have helped Tiny. He was a ball of energy, far too big and frantic to be kept indoors. But he was also a digger, which was a danger when he was left outside; he would have undermined a neighbor's house in eight point two-five seconds if turned loose, so he was mostly kept tied to a stake in the yard, on a very long chain.

One day, when I was about six, I was outside playing with Tiny, and in his exuberance he managed to wrap his chain around my neck – whereupon I found myself flat on the ground, being choked to death by this big, dumb, well-meaning moose of a dog. As I began to lose consciousness, he clambered on top of my chest and licked my face, and it was so sweet and peaceful – if sloppier than the death I would have chosen for myself. My mother happened to look out a window just then to see what I was up to, realized what was happening, and saved me. By the next day, I had bruises around my neck in the pattern of the links in Tiny's chain. Word came down from the Maternal Court of No Appeal: Tiny was history. I cried and argued that the Tiny hadn't been responsible – the classic canine-stupidity plea, but it didn't work.

Shortly thereafter we got Lucky, a two-year-old female terrier mix of exotic nature, who was no luckier than Tiny had been tiny. Lucky was cursed with an overly sensitive digestive system, and she would puke quicker than a politician breaks a promise. She puked on the average about three or four times a week, and *always* at the most inconvenient time and place. Let me tell you, Timmy would have been a lot less devoted to Lassie if Lassie had routinely regurgitated on him, on his bed, in his closet, in his shoes, on his school books. I don't know, maybe Lucky was trying to tell me something. Anyway, she soon developed some mortal condition, and we didn't have the money for a vet, so she had to be put to sleep. In spite of all the regurgitation, I cried. I missed her. I sure smelled a lot better, but I missed her anyway.

My Aunt Thelma had a cocker spaniel, Pete, that I adored and who seemed to like me a lot too. At least he never puked on me or tried to strangle me – and I'm sure that business with a revolver was an accident. Thelma lived far away, so I hardly ever got to see old Pete. When we did get together, it was this utterly wild Bacchanalia of petting and romping and chasing and scratching behind the ears (I always liked to have him scratch behind my ears) until we both slumped from exhaustion on the floor and slept like the dead. From Pete I learned that dogs could be a joy and a boon to the quality of life, but those were the only three dogs of my childhood, so without Pete's example I'd probably be a heavy-duty cat person.

* * *

Q: Did you start writing at an early age?

A: When I was only eight or nine, I was writing stories on tablet paper, drawing covers, stapling the left-hand edge, covering the staples with electrician's tape, trying to peddle these 'books' to relatives. It started *so* early that it's almost eerie. Makes you wonder about reincarnation, about being a writer in another life. Or destiny. Fate. Makes you think about the meaning of life. Makes you think about Froot Loops and old Bowery Boys movies. Makes you think about man-made fabrics, the Grateful Dead, whether there's life after death – and, if there *is* life after death, whether there are coin-operated laundromats on the Other Side.

Q: How did you do in high school socially and academically?

A: Academically, I was an underachiever. If I liked a subject, if my interest was caught, I could get top grades pretty easily. But if my interest wasn't captured, which was a lot of the time, I'd only do the bare minimum to get by. I was a slacker. There's a moment in *Back to the Future* when the school principal tells Marty McFly (Michael J.

13

Fox) that he's a slacker. That made me love the character because I was a slacker too. I was a slacker's slacker. I had it down to an art. See, I never expected I'd have a chance to go to college or amount to anything because once poor always poor; being poor was our place in the world, how we saw ourselves, as if it was stamped on our foreheads, so we would always be what we'd always been, which meant there wasn't a lot of motivation to achieve.

However, though I was no whirlwind in school, I was an obsessive autodidact, self-taught. I read all the time, became expert in the weirdest things, whatever happened to interest me. I wasn't lying around lumplike all those years. I was absorbing a ton of stuff from the town library. I pushed myself harder than any teacher ever pushed me.

I was something of a class clown. I was always quick with words, always saw things in a weird way, which is basically what humor's about – the quip, the tilted view of the world. Teachers put up with a lot from me, but I was never in trouble with them, perhaps because I never indulged in mean-spirited humor. Perhaps they sensed in me a basically nice boy, a sweet boy, a boy who had been puked on and strangled by dogs, a boy who had stood in his skivvies in a deer-blood-spattered basement and done his manly duties, a boy who deserved a break.

I had friends, of course, and my best pal was Larry Johnson. Larry's dad was a dignified banker – but Larry was totally whacked out. He had a great sense of the absurd, so we got along like twins. We used to do crazy things. Once we 'borrowed' a fourteen-foot-long, six-foot-high FOR SALE sign from behind a realty office, a thing they used on warehouses. It weighed at least a hundred pounds. In the dead of night, we carried it all the way across town – Bedford, Pennsylvania, about four thousand souls – and fastened it to the front of the high school. The next morning, when the buses pulled up to unload kids, the principal was out on the roof trying to get the damn thing down.

On another occasion, we thought it would be fun to parody the team-spirit days that were held every Friday during the various sports seasons. On team-spirit day you were required to dress in a certain color, wear a certain article of clothing, or carry a certain object, and the halls were bedecked with banners and pompons and streamers. You were expected to subordinate your individuality to a sort of grotesque display of sports worship, and it was more than a little

14

weird – very totalitarian, actually. The school symbol, a bison, took the place of Chairman Mao's face. Anyway, we discovered a way to get into the high school after it was closed up tight. Then we spent a week or so making hundreds of signs urging the student body to observe 'Grep Day' on Friday. Grep was just a nonsense word we made up. It had no meaning. 'Bring a Grep on Friday,' 'See You On Grep Day,' 'Be a School Booster – Grep, Grep, Grep,' all sorts of stuff, and we sneaked into the school on a Sunday night and *really* decorated the halls and classrooms, hung them with so much crepe paper it looked as if the Mad God of the Prom had gone berserk.

Now, to decorate the school for *any* occasion, you needed approval from the administration, so we expected the principal to have everything torn down in an hour on Monday morning. But we got a great lesson in the ineptitude of bureaucracy: Everyone in the administration assumed someone else in the administration had approved the Grep Day team-spirit promotion, and no one disturbed the decorations all week. After all, who would have suspected that anyone was idiotic enough to waste so many hours making and hanging the decorations throughout this huge school merely as a hoax? But I'm proud to say that Larry and I *were* idiotic enough. Some of the signs urged students to 'Bring a Grep on Friday' and 'Attend the Grep Dance' after the big game. No one knew what the hell a Grep was, but because we had illustrated the signs with a weird canine-bear sort of creature, a lot of people showed up at school on Friday toting teddy bears around with them. Other people did strange things to their hair, thinking perhaps that a Grep was a weird do – and this was in an age when nobody *ever* did strange things with his hair. Other people dressed funny. It was weird, thoroughly weird, that so many people were determined to show team spirit even if they didn't know what they were being asked to do to show it.

When Larry and I realized that the whole thing had gotten out of hand, when we began to think of the consequences, we knew we were only half finished with our moral duty. People were going to be disappointed that Grep Day had no payoff, that the announced dance did not occur when they showed up for it. There was going to be a lot of grumbling come Monday morning. So we decided to shift all the blame to the teddy-bear toters and the people who'd done strange things to their hair, and turn it into a double-whammy parody of team-spirit days. For a week, we worked around the clock to create even *more* signs and banners, and we used our secret entrance to the school again on the next Sunday night. We took down all the Grep Day stuff and put up a *jungle* of signs and banners throughout the halls chastising the school for its lack of spirit, signs that said, 'Where were *You* on Grep Day?' and 'You Didn't Support Your Grep,' and 'The Grep Weeps in Shame,' and 'If You Don't Love Your Grep, You Can't Love Your Team,' and 'The Grep Was Here, Where the Hell Were You?' We're talking *hundreds* of signs and miles of crepe paper, announcing that no one had attended the dance and accusing the student body of hating their school.

First thing during the home-room period, it became clear the administration had finally caught on. The principal announced he would give the perpetrators of this atrocity just ten minutes to present themselves at the office and escape expulsion from school for ten days. These heinous villains were expected to take down every poster and streamer on their own time, beg forgiveness, and in general grovel like the slime they were. Larry and I were in different home rooms, but neither of us sweated for a second that the other would betray him because we were tight, we trusted each other. After ten minutes, the principal gave us *another* ten minutes, and we knew we were home free. They didn't have a clue as to how to find us. We were then given until noon. When no one came through by noon, we were given until close of school. We went home, and the halls were still festooned. Thereafter, team-spirit days were never quite what they had been. We felt like this revolutionary cell that had beaten Big Brother.

Socially, I was inept. I was nearly as socially inept with girls as my old pal Lucky was inept as a dog. I never actually puked on a date, but I often suspected that I left them *feeling* as if I had. My self-image as a bumbling and unsophisticated dweeb, which sprang largely from being the child of a violent alcoholic and from being dirt poor, made me shy around a lot of girls. I remember once, in tenth grade, a popular girl in my class took me under her wing, as if she were my big sister; to my astonishment, she bluntly told me I would get a 'yes' from any girl I asked out, if only I'd have the guts to ask, and that several popular girls were interested in me. I blushed so bright that people within ten yards passed out from heat prostration, and I was speechless. She was a sweet girl, and I knew she meant what she said, knew it was not a setup to make me look like an idiot, but I was immobilized, frozen, like a teeny-tiny chihuahua paralyzed with terror when it realizes it's between Madonna and a photo

16

opportunity. When I didn't respond, or when I finally said the equivalent of 'ah, shucks,' she said, 'Think about it.' Maybe a year later, I suddenly wondered if *she* was one of the girls who would have said 'yes' to being asked on a date, and I realized what a *totally* inept social being I really was.

But then I met Gerda, when she was a junior and I was a senior, and everything changed for me. With her, I was cool, suave, funny, and so hip you wouldn't believe it. Or at least that was how she made me feel. Must've been hard work on her part. Anyway, to this day, what she says she remembers about our first date was that she woke up the next morning with a sore stomach from having laughed so hard all evening. I had an even better time. Afterward, I was giddy. I was Gene Kelly, singing in the rain, except I fell down every time I tried a tricky dance step. I was Cary Grant and Clark Gable and Lou Costello and Walter Brennan and every charming leading man from the movies – or at least I felt I was. We've been together ever since.

Q: You've noted before that Gerda gave you the freedom to become a full-time writer. How was that?

A: After our wedding, I worked in Lyndon Johnson's Appalachian Poverty Program, in a small coal-mining town in Pennsylvania, tutoring underprivileged children, making enough money to buy toothpaste and a toothbrush but not quite enough to buy the food that would make a toothbrush and toothpaste necessary. Though Gerda had accounting skills, she found a better-paid job in a shoe factory, doing piece work, so we could afford to buy food with which to make plaque. Every morning at the ungodly hour of five o'clock or five-thirty, she boarded a factory bus with other workers for a trip over the mountains to a larger town where the factory was located. During the winter, this was a routinely hair-raising excursion, and the work itself was mind-numbing. Meanwhile, I quickly discovered that my job in the Poverty Program was not as advertised. Teachers were told to select bright, promising students from poor families who would benefit by being removed from regular classrooms and put into small classes with individual instruction. Instead, most teachers transferred the kids with the worst behavioral problems, just to get rid of them, and I found myself in a highly charged atmosphere, facing mostly belligerent juvenile delinquents who were angry with the world in general and with me in particular because they saw it as my fault that they had been singled out and removed from the company of their buddies.

The guy who'd held the position before me had been beaten up by the very kids he'd been committed to helping, and he'd landed in the hospital.

One Monday after a big fight between gangs of teenagers from neighboring towns, some of my kids excitedly showed me a clever new weapon they had come up with: A collar stay. At that time, most shirts came with plastic collar stays, which you slipped out of the collar when you put the shirt in the laundry. They showed me how to take a collar stay out of a shirt, hold it between thumb and forefinger with the pointed end revealed, and stick it into an opponent's eye, blinding him. The beauty of this weapon, as they saw it, was that you could swiftly reinsert it into your collar and prove yourself unarmed if the cops suddenly showed up. Actually, later in life, this information proved to be handy for when I was dealing with certain film producers.

A couple of these kids were sweethearts. They deserved a chance to get up and out of that rathole of a place, and I hope they managed to escape. But it would take determination. The inward-turned, violent culture of those mountains, where everyone is suspicious of outsiders and where ignorance is actually prized above knowledge from the world beyond ... well, if that's where you're born and raised, it's like a black hole sucking you down and in, a tremendous social gravity that can be escaped only with monumental effort.

Somehow I lived through that year, though the experience forced a sea-change in my idealistic attitudes about such things as poverty programs. Most of the money is siphoned away by bureaucracy or embezzled by those who are supposed to distribute it effectively, and what little reaches the people in need only creates a sick dependency. I'll write about those experiences some day, but I need maybe another decade before I can do so without getting depressed!

The following year, I taught school in Mechanicsburg, Pennsylvania, a middle-class community near Harrisburg. Gerda went to work in the local credit bureau, then eventually for a business-equipment company as a receptionist. After a year and a half teaching English, I was more fed up with the educational bureaucracy than I'd been with the welfare bureaucracy. I enjoyed the kids enormously, had a great deal of fun teaching – but too much time was wasted doing meaningless paperwork for various supernumeraries who thought up an endless stream of pointless projects to justify their employment. During this time, I had sold three paperback novels and perhaps twenty short stories. I had a dream of being a full-time writer, but the total income from all these sales would not have supported us.

That was when Gerda did a wonderful, selfless, daring, and loving thing: She told me that she'd support us for five years while I tried to make a living as a writer. 'If you can't make it in five years,' she said, 'you never will.' I accepted the offer, quit my job – and became a loathsome bum in the eyes of virtually everyone we knew. Even five years later, after Gerda quit her job to work full-time on the business side of my career, people asked her, rather pointedly, exactly when I was going to give up this ridiculous writing thing and get a 'real' job. Fact is, even years later, when my books were beginning to hit the bestseller lists in paperback, some people still thought I was a Bohemian flake who would wind up in the gutter with a bottle of Thunderbird in one hand and Gerda in the other.

For fifteen years, trying to make a living as a writer *was* a touch-and-go business. There were more occasions than I can count when checks were so overdue from publishers that we wondered if we could hold on until we finally got them, when books were published in such small print runs that it seemed like there were more copies in my closet than in all the bookstores in the country. In the early days, when I was a paperback-original writer and before I had any power as an author, editors would freely rewrite me, usually creating an astonishing mishmash of bad grammar and syntax, and I would have to see the result in print because my literary agents wouldn't fight for me.

On several occasions, editors bought books from outlines, moved to new jobs before the books were delivered, and then the new editors rejected them and demanded the advances back for no reason other than these were *orphan* books, not by writers whom *they* admired. We always sold the books elsewhere and repaid the original purchaser, and in every case those books eventually were well reviewed and earned money for publishers. THE VOICE OF THE NIGHT, for instance, was rejected by Lippincott on delivery, but Doubleday took it on the rebound under the 'Brian Coffey' name, and reviewers were almost unanimously kind to it; later, NAL sold a couple of hundred thousand paperbacks under that pen name; then the book was reissued in 1991 under my name for the first time, and

Berkley Books has about another 2.5 million in print in their edition. It's also in print in thirty-one other languages, and we get a large volume of reader mail about it. But the financial havoc caused by Lippincott's casual rejection was, at the time, a *huge* obstacle to continued existence as a full-time writer.

Through all of this, Gerda never lost faith. In fact, I think she had more faith in me than I did sometimes, and it was her emotional support that made it possible to get where we've gotten. She doesn't do the writing, but this is *our* career in every other way, and I would never have gotten the chance to do any of my better work without her bottomless patience and faith.

* * *

Q: A final question about your early years. Since your parents didn't encourage you to read, and since books weren't to be found in your house, *how* did you turn to books? You've been prolific, so obsessed with writing, that there must have been someone or something that turned you on to books early.

A: When I was four years old, my mother had major surgery and nearly died. She was hospitalized for weeks and had to go through many more weeks of rehabilitation. My father, of course, wasn't capable of caring for me, and no relatives were able to take on the responsibility. So I was sent to stay one winter with Bird and Louise Kinsey in Shellsburg, Pennsylvania. They were friends of my mother's and two of the kindest souls you'd ever hope to know. They had a *very* orderly life, with a house like everyone's grandmother ought to have: Rambling, with ticking grandfather clocks, antimacassars on all the chairs and sofas . . . I think, even as young as I was, I understood that there was something wrong with my father and that our family life was strange by ordinary standards – and in the Kinsey house, I found stability. Every evening, when she put me to bed, Louise would make a cherry ice-cream soda or an equivalent treat for me; I would sit in bed – the charming guest room had a weirdly angled ceiling and gables, high in the house – and drink my soda while she read a story to me. Her own kids were nearly adults – one was already away from home – but she had scads of kids' books around from when her own kids had been young. Also comic books that her son, Tom, had been collecting for years. The months I spent as a charity case of the Kinseys' is a warm memory that still haunts me. I think it was then

I began to associate storytelling with salvation, with peace and plenty and warmth and happiness.

I say it 'haunts' me because, to this day, I can close my eyes and recall those times more clearly than anything from the entire length of my childhood and adolescence. I can smell that house – all the furniture polish and the aromas of wonderful things being cooked in the kitchen. I can recall the way Louise sounded, her laughter, the house dresses and aprons she wore, the hugs she would give me that just about swallowed me up when I was that little. I remember a terrible snow we had that winter, and how she would bundle me up to go outside with her and down the long yard to the dog house to be sure the dog was warm and safe. I even remember many of the comic books, panels from them, which glow before my eyes now in all their flamboyant colors: Mutt and Jeff, Nancy and Sluggo, Felix the Cat. That winter, while my mother was in Pittsburgh, far away and perhaps dying, my father came to visit only once. Ten minutes. So it was as if I'd been picked up and plopped down in someone else's life, a radically *different* life. I remember, when I had to leave with my father, I was excited about seeing my mother again – but in terrible despair that I couldn't live with Louise and Bird any more.

The Kinseys were kind and caring people, and I'll never forget them for taking me in. But sometimes I wonder if I also owe Louise for having instilled in me a love of storytelling.

* * *

EARLY CAREER

Q: What was your first fiction sale, and how old were you when you made it?

A: When I was still in college, I sold a story called 'Kittens.' It's included in this book with an introduction explaining the circumstances of the sale in excruciating detail; everyone who reads the intro will be not merely nauseated but determined to flee modern civilization and live among the apes in order never to risk hearing another biographical detail about me. The apes will hate me, all these strange new people moving in, peace and quiet gone forever. I was twenty at the time I wrote 'Kittens.'

Q: Did you begin to sell other pieces right away?

A: No. But I was still in college, and other issues were more important than selling stories. Much to learn. Profound questions needed answered. Such as: In whose dorm are we playing pinochle tonight?; who's old enough to buy the beer?; and if there's other intelligent life in the universe, will *they* be more capable than we are of reading a James Joyce novel all the way through?

However, the year after I graduated, when I was working in the aforementioned Poverty Program, I began to sell short stories with regularity. I was desperate to get out of both the Poverty Program and poverty itself, and writing seemed to be a road to financial security. Which turned out to be true. I just didn't realize the road would be twenty years long! Fortunately I loved writing and would have done it for nothing. Hell, what I got paid during the first ten years was *next* to nothing, but I never considered stopping and learning a trade like rickshaw repair. By the time we left the Poverty Program (but not poverty), by the time I was teaching high-school English, I began to sell paperback novels.

Q: Will you share some memories about 'breaking in,' early book and short story sales?

A: No. I think I'm going to stop being so cooperative, turn this into a Hollywood-actor interview, get a little surly and petulant and temperamental. Could you excuse me for a few hours while I grow some beard stubble? Got to have beard stubble for a surly Hollywood interview. And I'll need to dress all in black, which is *still* the Hollywood style after all these years. Orson Welles lives!

On second thought, that sounds like too much work. Might as well answer your question. Besides, you seem like the kind of guy who might just punch me if I got surly.

Q: Or buy you a dog *just* like Lucky.

A: You win. Let's see . . . the first book I sold was a paperback science fiction novel, STAR QUEST. (If only I'd titled it STAR TREK, imagine the wealth that would have been mine, the adoration of millions, the cases of *free* Spock ears, the wild bar-hopping nights with William Shatner.) STAR QUEST was bought by Ace Books for the Ace Doubles line. Ace was an independent company at that time, not part of a conglomerate, and was known for being ... the only accurate word is 'cheap.' Their Ace Doubles had two novels in a single volume, each with its own cover; when you looked at the front of the book and then turned it over, you were looking at the front of the *other* book that shared the volume. This was confusing if you'd been drinking but seemed clever to most sober people. The editor told me that because STAR QUEST was shorter than the average Ace Double, he would have to buy a longer novel for the other side, which meant he would have to pay the other author more and me less than the standard advance. That seemed fair. And I was wildly excited by the very prospect of having a book in print. I would have agreed to just about anything, short of killing someone for them, in order to get the deal. Break some guy's legs, sure. Kill? No. The standard advance was $1,250 at that time – not a fortune *then*, either, but I was asked to accept $1,000 so they would be able to pay $1,500 to the author of the longer novel on the other side. Eventually the volume was published, and right away I noticed there wasn't a whole lot of difference between the length of my novel and the one on the other side. Later, when I ran into the other author at a convention, we discovered they had told him the same thing! He had to take $1,000 because his novel was on the short side, necessitating a higher advance to the author of the other half of the double. It amazed me then – and still does to this day – that a nationally distributed publisher with a list of monthly titles would have risked the enmity of its authors and resorted to such duplicity to save a grand total of just $500!

A few books later, I was given the honor of occupying *both* sides of an Ace Double with a novel and story collection – so I received both advances. I thought I had arrived. Next step – sainthood in the Catholic church, a place in the throne room of heaven, widespread veneration, my name invoked at most meetings of the Knights of Columbus, and a medallion concession in the Vatican courtyard. Then reality set in. When royalty statements eventually showed up, they claimed noticeably higher sales for one side of the book than for the other. Now, unless thousands of people across this great country tore the book in half before buying it, sales of both sides had to have been identical. When pushed, the publisher might have been expected to claim that the lower figures were correct for both sides, because if the *higher* figures were correct for both, they would owe royalties. Instead, they doggedly insisted, without explanation, that their initial figures were correct. In time I discovered this was a standard eccentricity of their accounting department, and I wasn't alone.

One of my early publishers insisted on a new title for a novel I wanted to call THE MYSTERY OF HIS FLESH. It was a science fiction piece and would inevitably have rocketships or monsters on the cover, regardless of the contents, which would have helped readers identify the genre. But the publisher hated the title because 'everyone will think it's a gay novel, and gay novels don't sell.' How times have changed. I suggested an altered title – THE MYSTERY OF *ITS* FLESH – which also would have worked, but this publisher still thought it sounded like a gay novel, which baffled me so completely I surrendered. They had a title of their own. I didn't have title control, so I couldn't prevent them from calling it ANTI-MAN, which 1) didn't have any relation to the story, 2) sounded like a comic-book character, 3) but was indisputably *not* a title you'd find on a gay novel.

In the early days I dreamed of selling stories to *Galaxy* and *If* magazines, which I believe are both defunct now but which were venerable institutions at that time. Frederik Pohl, the writer, was the editor of both, and finally he bought two stories from me. I couldn't wait to see them in print, to hold copies of these adored magazines in my hands with *my* stories in them. But when they were published, Mr Pohl had done an amazing amount of 'editing' without consultation and had chopped the last two pages off both stories. When I noted this and expressed special dismay at having the endings cut off, he told me that he had certain space limitations to consider. 'Besides,' he told me, 'most stories read better if the writer's final scene is eliminated. Most writers just go on too long.' Since neither story had a *finish* or a *point* or *made any sense* without the ending, I failed to see how this rule of thumb could be universally applied. When I learned most writers in the genre at that time received similar treatment and saw no reason to complain about it – even some of the big names – I knew I had to get out of science fiction right away. So I took Mr Pohl's advice and wrote less. Less science fiction, that is. The genre has changed drastically since those days, and writers are now accorded more respect in it. However, I've never regretted moving on – especially as I get to sneak some dribbles of science fiction into some of the books I now write.

By that time my favorite reading was mainstream and suspense fiction, and I wanted to write it. I began working under the name 'K. R. Dwyer' at Random House, as 'Brian Coffey' at Bobbs-Merrill and then at Doubleday; my own name was too closely identified with science fiction at that time to get a fair hearing in a new field. I wrote SHATTERED under the Dwyer name originally, and THE FACE OF FEAR and THE VOICE OF THE NIGHT as Coffey.

Eventually I used my own name at Atheneum – later, at Putnam – on books that I began to think of as cross-genre or category-bridgers. They incorporated elements of many types of fiction – suspense, mystery, science fiction, horror, love stories – and developed them with the characterization and use of language more often associated with mainstream fiction. For the longest time I was told that this could not be done, that I had to choose one genre and stick to it, that the whole concept was loopy, that I was confusing readers, that I was obviously a reincarnation of the mad monk Rasputin and would have to be locked away for my own good. As far as I know, I originated the idea of combining genres and treating the combination with a mainstream sensibility – but now I hear all the time that publishers are asking for 'Koontz-type' books, and a lot of people talk about 'cross-genre' these days. I was aware of trying to create something new, and I was conscious of how fiercely resistant publishing is to *anything* new, but I had to try anyway because I loved so many types of fiction and wanted to write so many types that I could only have a coherent career by combining them into a new form.

Initially, a lot of people insisted on seeing the books as horror, which was frustrating. WHISPERS, for instance, is a psychological suspense novel with no supernatural elements, yet a lot of people weren't comfortable calling it suspense because of the bizarre aspects of the story, the kind of thing that suspense writers have not traditionally touched – or didn't touch at that time. Some books, like PHANTOMS, definitely have strong horror elements. But PHANTOMS never goes for the gross-out and provides a logical – if admittedly wild – explanation rather than resorting to talk of ghosts, vampires, and werewolves. DARKFALL is half horror, I'll admit, but it's also half police procedural, and a love story. STRANGERS has no element whatsoever of horror. Neither does LIGHTNING. COLD FIRE has only the mildest dose of horror, and THE BAD PLACE is a gonzo mystery-suspense-science-fiction-horror-love-adventure story with a heavy salting of comedy, and always a mainstream approach to the material.

Finally, within the past year or two, I think my work is being seen for what it is, as its own thing, and the word 'horror' is used less and less to describe it. I have nothing against horror, you understand; I enjoy reading it when it's well written. But that simply isn't what I do. One thing that seems to have made a lot of people readjust their view of it is the amount of humor in all of the books since WATCHERS. With rare exception, horror has always been humorless, heavy and glowering in tone. So when a critic says he laughed out loud constantly while reading a book – and where he was *meant* to laugh – he begins to realize this isn't what he preconceived it to be.

Q: Is humor now a permanent part of your genre mix?

A: Not necessarily. I'll probably use humor to one extent or another in every book I write from here on, because it has the curious effect of heightening suspense if handled right. But also because *life* is filled with humor, and I find it harder year by year to write convincing fiction, with strong verisimilitude, if humor isn't included. On the other hand, if the right grim story line comes along, I may just turn out something as dark and solemn as Joseph Stalin would have written if Joseph Stalin had been a suspense novelist.

* * *

Q: Going back to your early career, what was a typical writing day like for you then? How many hours did you typically put in?

A: When I first went full-time, I worked about fifty to sixty hours a week. I assumed that when – and if – I became successful, I'd be able to relax a little. Now I work seventy hours most weeks, and as much as eighty hours when I'm especially captivated by a piece. I swear on the grave of my dear dog Lucky that I am going to cut back to fifty hours and stay there by the end of 1993. But the fact is, I develop a deeper empathy with characters and a more profound sense of the reality of the fictional world when I work long sessions, ten and twelve hours. The real world fades, and the world I've invented becomes more vivid when I'm spending the larger part of the day in that make-believe place.

Q: Most people don't understand how disciplined a writer must be.

26

Were you always as disciplined as you are today?

A: A lot of writers aren't disciplined, you know. I think that's often because they *hate* writing so much yet find they are driven to do it either for psychological reasons or because it's the only thing they *can* do. I'm driven to write, as well, obsessed with writing, but I happen to enjoy it immensely. I'm fascinated with the infinite flexibility of the English language and with linear narrative. That makes it easier for me to sit down at the keyboard every day. Not *easy*, you understand. It's never easy.

   Some people have an image of the successful writer's life that is pure fantasy. They think it's a little noodling at the computer for two or three hours in the morning, then a leisurely lunch by the pool, followed perhaps by a nap, then a round of literary teas and parties. Mostly it's hard work, alone in a room. If you like people, as I do, the solitary aspect of the job is the worst thing about it. We attend fewer parties than anyone I know. We go *years* at a time without a vacation. If you *love* writing, it *becomes* your life in many ways; you can't go anywhere without consciously or subconsciously evaluating its potential as background for a scene, can't meet anyone without sooner or later seeing details about him that would be useful to bring a character alive. You're always asking yourself, *Would this be good material?* Being a writer is both a blessed and cursed condition, all-consuming.

* * *

Q: Some of your early books, which you originally sold for two and three thousand dollars have, on reissue, earned you millions apiece. Is that particularly satisfying?

A: Ugh. Dirty old money. How disgusting. Loathe the stuff. *Of course* it's satisfying! It's wonderful. It says that your work has meaning to a great many people, touches their minds and hearts to such an extent that they *must* have it. Which is what writing is all about – reaching out to people, sharing your view of the world with them, grabbing hold of them and saying, 'Hey, look at it this way, look at life my way, think about it this way and see if you don't agree with, sympathize with, or at least comprehend what I think is true about the human condition.' For many, many years when the writing barely brought in enough money to keep the Wolves away from the door (Bernice and Rudy Wolves, a nice enough couple from Buffalo, but a little whiny and *very* demanding, whose trips to Europe we subsidized just to get them out of our hair), I still wrote because money was never the primary goal. When money began to come to me, and in such lovely quantities, it was a welcome blessing, but I would have gone on writing without it.

What I enjoy most about seeing some of the older books find a large audience when they're reissued in paperback is that in many cases they were novels the original publishers issued without enthusiasm because, as I was so often told, 'it has no commercial potential.' When you're not a bestselling writer, you're frequently encouraged to imitate people who are; when you refuse, a lot of publishers junk your books as being too quirky or out of sync with the taste of the mainstream audience. To have it later proven that there is a huge audience for that very book, after all . . . Well, let's just say that living well is the best revenge.

* * *

Q: Who are those people you'd most like to thank for helping you through the often difficult years of your early career?

A: I've already talked at length about Gerda. Among editors, Bob Hoskins of the long-defunct Lancer Books was kind at a crucial time. Lee Wright, who was at Random House for many years but is unfortunately no longer with us, edited three of my books and gave me the confidence to believe I could do more ambitious books than I was attempting at that time. When SHATTERED was delivered, she called me up and said, 'I want to suggest two word changes. That's it. I've never seen a script this close to perfect. I would like you to write genre suspense novels as K. R. Dwyer for Random House for the rest of your life – but you'd be crazy if you settle for that because you're capable of much more.' That was a very hard time in my career, when I was struggling to earn a living and having to write more in a year than seemed humanly possible. To have this highly regarded editor – this living legend in suspense, whose standards were known to be high – react with that much enthusiasm . . . and then go on to talk intelligently about the book and its structure . . . Well, that gave me the heart to keep plugging away and trying bigger books at a time when I often thought about just packing it in and taking that rickshaw repair course, after all.

* * *

EARLY WORK

Q: Of all your early novels, CHASE is perhaps the most pessimistic. Despite a reasonably happy ending, the reader is left with the sense that Benjamin Chase will probably never banish his personal demons. There's a very *noir* feeling to Chase, a decorated Vietnam vet who wants to hide out and be left alone. In fact, most of the people he reluctantly trusts will eventually betray him in some way. Do you remember much about writing CHASE, and do you think its pessimism owes much to the time in which it was written, 1971?

A: The dark atmosphere of the country in those days, coming out of the nightmarish Sixties, was influential. But changes in my own attitudes toward politics, social issues, and freedom had more to do with the mood of the novel. I was twenty-six, and up to that time I'd been generally to the left on all issues across the board – but experience was forcing me to re-evaluate a lot of my positions, though not in standard either/or political terms.

When working in the Appalachian Poverty Program, I saw *firsthand* that most of the tax funds allocated to alleviate poverty were being sucked away by politicians and bureaucrats, until only ten or twenty percent of the money actually got into the hands of the people it was meant to help. It also seemed to me that any system making child-welfare payments based largely on whether the father was living at home or not would eventually *encourage* male irresponsibility and lead to both huge numbers of illegitimate children and the total destruction of the family structure in some needy minority communities. It was so *easy* to see this would breed a phenomenal growth in crime, drugs, and welfare dependency. I couldn't understand why so many well-meaning politicians continued to endorse destructive approaches to social problems. Then one day I sort of woke up and realized that most of these programs are not meant to help anyone, merely to *control* people and make them dependent. Otherwise, true liberals and true conservatives would be united in wanting to put an end to the current system and find a better path; yet *both* seem to feed off the system in different ways.

And suddenly it became apparent that this endless war in Asia, launched and conducted by a former hero of mine, was part of the same policy; by mobilizing a country for war, by keeping it mobilized, politicians can exert *control*. Straight out of Orwell and *1984*. Lyndon Johnson wasn't an idiot; he knew the war, right or wrong, could be won if we threw everything into it that we had, but he kept holding back, committing only a fraction of the country's power, setting limits to engagement, and it seemed to me that this might well be as intentional as the endless war which Big Brother cowed his citizenry. Nixon, supposedly at the other extreme of the political spectrum from Johnson, followed the same strategy. If you're going to fight a war, fight with everything you have and end it quickly. If you don't, I have to assume you have motives other than those expressed, subtle motives of societal manipulation and control.

I was forced to reconsider everything I'd once believed. As a result I developed a profound distrust of government regardless of the philosophy of the people in power. I remained a liberal on civil-rights issues, became a conservative on defense, and a semi-libertarian on all other matters. By 1971, it had become apparent to me that the worst enemy of the working man and woman is the state, and that the average person is safest in a country that struggles to limit the size of the state. This is the bloodiest of all centuries – and it isn't coincidental that this is also the century in which governments have become larger and more powerful than ever before, involved in the lives of citizens in more ways than ever. Could Hitler have fought World War II without first building an intrusive and powerful government apparatus? Could Mao Tse Tung have killed *a hundred million or more* of his own people without the iron fist of the state to break dissenters? Or Stalin? Humanity's hopeless pursuit of utopia through government beneficence leads only to grief, misery, and blood.

That seems obvious now, but it was a startling revelation to me at twenty-six. At first I didn't want to believe it. I read a great deal of history and books on current social issues, but in the end had to accept that what I'd come to believe intuitively was supported by the evidence of the entire long human spectacle.

And this is something *everyone* knows on some level, whether liberal or conservative. When liberals are in power, they love government and champion it as the solution to all ills – but, when they aren't in power, they fear the government and suspect it of all sorts of nightmarish conspiracies. Look at any hysterical, illogical, but passionate Oliver Stone movie, and you'll see this is true. When conservatives are in power, they have a different agenda from that of liberals, but so far they haven't actually reduced the power of any government anywhere; they've only reduced the *rate of growth* of that power. Yet when they're out of office, conservatives see government as a monolithic horror about to crush everyone.

Power is seductive. It also corrupts. Utopia is never going to arise out of corruption. Anyone who says it can is either a liar or a fool.

This has been a long way around to CHASE, but I wrote that book as these changes in attitude were sweeping through me, and Benjamin Chase reflected my feelings. Chase is a victim of the monolithic state that *used* and discarded him. He is more cynical than bitter – and he doesn't expect that the world to come will be a better place to live. That's how I felt in those days.

Q: SHATTERED was an abrupt departure from your previous work. Your science fiction, particularly BEASTCHILD and A DARKNESS IN MY SOUL, showed us vivid imagery and speculative worlds. But SHATTERED introduced us to Koontz the realist. It also gave us our first glimpse of the prototypical Koontz hero – the young man who overcomes a difficult background only to be challenged again in later life, almost as if he has to earn his right to happiness and peace of mind twice. Was SHATTERED your first step toward a mainstream career?

A: One of the first. Alex Doyle in SHATTERED grows right out of Ben Chase in CHASE. When push comes to shove, Alex can find no one to turn to, no authority that will protect him from the psychotic that has targeted him and Colin. He has to learn that he, himself, is his hope of last resort. To protect what he loves, he has to violate the principles he has for so long held dear. He learns to take responsibility for his own life, and he learns that the cost of doing so is sometimes dreadful.

This theme of taking responsibility for one's own life, for accepting the consequences of one's own actions, weaves through most everything I've done since. In DRAGON TEARS, in fact, the theme rises to become what one reviewer called 'a poignant plea' for people to accept responsibility for their own lives and to stop seeking to escape it.

I actually think SHATTERED is a darker book than CHASE in

that we *know* in the end that Alex will never be the same, and that he has lost an innocence that was appealing.

Q: HANGING ON was serio-comic, or black comedy, if you prefer. It's so funny and observant. A lot of your readers wonder why you've never worked in that vein again.

A: When you give up on the idea that any political philosophy is going to solve the world's problems, when you accept that all injustice can be dealt with only at the individual level by one human being treating another with decency and respect, and when you know that there will *always* be people incapable of being decent and respectful to others – then the world seems so dark that you have to view every aspect of life with humor. That's what drove me to write HANGING ON. It got a slew of great reviews that said it was both well-written and hilarious – but it sold dismally. Then I learned that straight comic novels just don't sell well. Why I couldn't have learned this *first*, I don't know. Maybe I've always been sort of slow. I could have gone on writing comic novels – and laughed all the way to starvation and death!

Since WATCHERS, I've incorporated humor into every book I've written, and readers seem to love that, but it's only *part* of the stew. It's carried by the suspense, tension, love story, and all the other elements, and it doesn't intrude. Some people don't even *see* the humor but still enjoy the novels for the suspense and terror, or for other elements.

Q: BEASTCHILD is one of your best early books. It foreshadows the way in which you use various configurations of 'family' in many of your most popular novels. The alien, Hulann, and the Earth boy, Leo, become truly familial and interdependent by the book's end. Were you conscious of this when you were writing it?

A: Yes. Stacy Creamer, my editor at Putnam, has said that all of my books, in one way or another, are about the remaking of families, some of them unconventional but nevertheless happy. This is true. It's one of the themes that's usually there no matter what the book is *primarily* about. WATCHERS, for instance, is primarily about how difficult it is to change what we are and how we think, even when we desperately want to change; every character in that book struggles to be reborn as someone better, and some fail. But in addition to that primary theme of change, there's the making of a family in the coming together of Travis and Nora – those two wounded souls – and the dog Einstein. COLD FIRE is primarily about the need for meaning and purpose in life, and it's about the consequences of unexpressed grief, unresolved sorrow, and emotional detachment. But it's *also* about remaking a family as Jim and Holly come together and as she brings him back to his grandfather. It's there in almost everything I do. MR MURDER concerns an antagonist in search of a family and a protagonist desperate to keep his own family alive and together.

I suspect this concern comes out of the fact that I didn't have an ordinary family life as a child and on some level feel the loss of that, a longing for it. A belief in the healing power of family and friends also comes out of my distrust of larger institutions. I think everything truly meaningful in life arises from one-to-one relations, brother to brother, sister to sister, brother to sister, friend to friend, husband to wife; when we start relating to one another primarily through large political or social or religious movements, we fail to communicate on a more directly personal level, and we lose some of our humanity.

BEASTCHILD was an early herald of this theme, and it's one of the books I intend to substantially revise and lengthen for eventual republication – probably because it deals with this very issue. In fact, it'll be so revised you'll hardly recognize it, because I've learned so much since then.

Q: INVASION, the novel that was rumored to have been written by Stephen King as 'Aaron Wolfe,' demonstrated your increasing awareness of nature as a powerful backdrop to some of your best novels. The descriptions of the Arctic in PRISON OF ICE (as by David Axton) are phenomenal and give the book an almost other-worldly quality. You use nature especially well, later on, in PHANTOMS. Did you make a conscious effort to increase your descriptive powers?

A: Not conscious, no. As a writer progresses, however, he strives – or should strive – to write not merely better but more well-rounded fiction. Incorporating the natural world into a novel is, to me, essential to achieve a true sense of reality. Our societies and personalities are shaped by weather and other aspects of the natural world to a greater degree than we like to believe.

As for INVASION, many people thought it had been written by Mr King because it was about a troubled writer, his wife, and his son snowbound in a place where strange, unearthly things began to happen. It looked like a dry run for *The Shining*, which followed a couple of years later. But that was a ludicrous notion. *The Shining* is a big, ambitious book. INVASION was my last straight science fiction novel, quickly done, and quite slim.

I was never able to get the story out of my head, however, so I set out to revise it in 1993. Some revision! The original book was 50,000 words. The revision is 135,000. The characters have *completely* changed; the events have changed as well, and in the end I didn't use a single line from the original text. The new version is, of course, WINTER MOON, and it is more an 'inspired by' than a 'revision of.' As I tried to revise, I realized I was a different writer now from the one I'd been back then, *so* different that I couldn't even collaborate with myself.

* * *

Q: A couple of the Leigh Nichols books are among your best, especially SHADOWFIRES. How and why was Leigh Nichols born?

A: How, I think, was by Cesarean section. Why – you'll have to ask her parents.

Q: So the pen name was supposed to be a woman?

A: I meant to say 'his' parents.

Q: So the pen name was meant to be a man?

A: I meant to say 'its' parents.

Q: So Leigh Nichols was neither male nor female, it was a *thing*?

A: That's right. A thing. But a *nice* thing. A very nice old thing, Leigh was, given to pottering around in its garden and knitting Afghans and baking bat-eye cookies. Actually, Pocket Books wanted a name that could be either male or female, to draw in a wider audience. So I suggested we use 'Lee Nichols.' At the last minute, without consultation with me, they changed it to 'Leigh,' which seemed, to me, to undercut the whole idea of genderlessness.

Q: But why a pen name at that point in your career?

A: For the same reason that Brian Coffey, Owen West, and K. R. Dwyer were born. I have not written under pseudonyms for years and will not do so again. However, before I was an established writer, publishers were frustrated with me because of the wide variety of things I liked to write. They believe a writer must choose a narrow area and write strictly within that tight focus, so readers will always know what to expect. If you write one story about a secret government conspiracy, you're expected to write nothing but the same thereafter. If you write one police procedural, you're expected to write police procedurals for the rest of your life or until you go stark raving mad and shoot up a Mrs Fields Cookies store with a Micro Uzi, whichever comes first. But I have to write what excites me, which means I am uncontainable by modern publishing standards. I was encouraged – more to the point, forced – to create 'Brian Coffey' for shorter suspense novels that had a streamlined prose style and crisp dialogue. 'Leigh Nichols' was for larger suspense novels that also embodied love stories. 'Owen West' was for horror novels – THE FUNHOUSE, THE MASK, DARKFALL.

As I said earlier, eventually I began writing what I called 'cross-genre' books, which combined all kinds of fiction into one novel. When I started – in an embryonic form with NIGHT CHILLS and more maturely with WHISPERS – editors didn't get it. Multiple genres in a single story, sometimes with an emphasis on suspense, sometimes on horror, sometimes on the love story, all told in a mainstream rather than genre style – hell, it just didn't fit in any bookstore section and offered a serious packaging problem.

But after only ten years of agonizing struggle and periodic thoughts of homicide in the hallowed halls of publishing, I saw books that I wrote in this cross-genre mode appear on bestseller lists. *Then* success came swiftly, each book selling better than the one before. Now I hear from writers who are told to 'do one of those cross-genre books like Koontz.' Which drives *them* nuts. After I'd had several bestsellers, we began to reissue the pen-name books under my own name, and we found just what I'd always expected: Even though some of these books were more directly genre stories and in *different* genres, readers *liked* the diversity of styles and were not offended at

35

being asked to stretch beyond their usual type of reading matter, as long as they felt the story entertained and challenged them. For a long time I have argued that publishers underestimate the reading public, and in this case, at least, that proved true; the public has been flexible about reading anything under my name – cross-genre books and various single-genre books. But I've only won the right to reissue them under my name by becoming a bestselling author. Other writers with equally diverse interests still wage the same battle.

* * *

LATER CAREER

Q: Did you make a conscious decision at a certain point to become a better and more successful writer?

A: Yes. After only a few years, I was tired of writing science fiction, and I wanted to move on. In fact, I decided I wanted to spend my entire career moving on, developing and improving, with the freedom to try new things. Working within one narrow genre is stifling. So to force publishers to give me a chance in a variety of fields, I had to write better, always better, so the quality of the damned book would knock them out and be impossible to ignore. Sounds arrogant, huh? Well, it is arrogant in a way – except that I never thought it would be *easy* to write well enough to stun them into attention, and I was never certain that I could do it. I'm still not. Every new book is a challenge – an even greater challenge than the one before it. I'm always trying to top myself and to surprise my editors and publishers. Surprise them in a good way, I mean. With something better than they expected.

I could also surprise them by writing a lyrical novel about the grinding boredom of a goat-herder's life on the low plains of Mongolia, but that would be a *bad* surprise. Bad. Very bad. Not funny. Mass cardiac infarctions in publishing executive's suites, lawyers brandished like swords, much hooting and howling and deep dismay. (Though it might make a nice movie. Richard Gere as the simple goat-herder. Dana Carvey as one of the goats. Dolly Parton as the Western missionary who comes to Mongolia to teach pagan goat-herders about God and, of course, falls in love with Gere. It could even be a musical. Dolly could teach one of the goats [Carvey] to sing. Picture the smash closing number: Parton and Gere in a clinch,

Carvey the goat in front of them, all three posed against a glorious sunset, singing about God, sex, and feta cheese. It could even be a *science-fiction* musical, see, with vicious aliens masquerading as some of the goats, and from time to time Arnold Schwarzenegger or Sigourney Weaver could come crashing through with a big futuristic weapon and blow some of the fake goats to bloody smithereens, while Gere and Parton sing something by Wagner.) You know, I'd actually like to *see* a movie like that. If nothing else, it would be different.

Q: Is there one Koontz book that clearly separates your early career from your later career?

A: Yes. WHISPERS. That's where the whole cross-genre thing really began to come together and where the ambition took a major leap. Not surprisingly, it was also my first paperback bestseller, though it wouldn't be until STRANGERS that one of them hit the hardcover list. In WHISPERS, I wanted to explore all of the ways that our lives are influenced by events of which we are often unaware or which we only dimly perceive. 'The forces that affect our lives, the influences that mold and shape us, are often like whispers in a distant room, teasingly indistinct, apprehended only with difficulty': That was the central point of the entire novel, expressed clearly at the front of the book. Every character in the story, even the walk-ons, embodies that bit of wisdom and reflects it in a different way.

Exploring a theme like that was a big challenge, and there were months when it seemed I would be broken on the wheel of that novel. By the time I finished, I had lost twenty pounds – and I hadn't been heavy to begin with. Later, I realized it wasn't only the size of the project or the complexity of it that had nearly felled me; it was also the fact that I was writing out of anguish, because virtually every character in the novel had a terrible or at least deeply troubled childhood, as I did, and in exploring their pain and confusion, I was finally exploring my own.

Q: So you became a bestselling writer—

A: Just like that. Twelve years after I started writing full-time, fifteen years after the sale of my first short story, only fifteen years of grueling effort. It was a snap. Could've done it on half the brain I have. In fact, I *did* do it on half the brain I have because, since 1966,

I've been keeping half my brain in a secret location, immersed in liquid nitrogen, in the event that continued contact with the film industry should rot the portion of my brain currently in my skull. If that should happen, the rotten lump goes, and the preserved half is installed.

Q: Sounds like expensive and tricky surgery.

A: Not at all. No doctors involved. The guys down at the Midas Muffler Shop take care of the whole procedure. Earl and Chi Chi. Fifty-nine bucks plus whatever the current cost of a quart or two of spinal fluid.

Q: Scars?

A: Chi Chi has a nasty one on his left cheek.

Q: So you became a bestselling writer after more than fifteen years of grueling effort. Much as we like to think otherwise, writers are competitive people. Did your success bother some of your writer friends?

A: You know, it amazed me there were people who couldn't deal with it. During the long years that I was struggling to make it, I was always excited to see another writer break through and find a large audience that would embrace his work. When new writers became bestsellers and received record-breaking advances, I always thought, *If they can do it, so can I.* And it seemed to me that every writer who had a success was adding to the success of the entire publishing business, enlarging the pool of industry finances, and making it possible for *other* writers to succeed. After all, if nobody made it big, publishers wouldn't make enough money to function, and the industry would collapse. Any writer's success, even if I don't admire his work, increases the opportunities for all writers. If a writer's work pleases readers, then he helps to keep the public interested in books and even creates new readers who otherwise wouldn't be interested in fiction.

However, I discovered there are some writers who consider writing as *competitive* an enterprise as the Idiotrod Dogsled Race. Envy – every bit as much as, say, racism – can give rise to astonishingly mean-spirited acts and statements. I still have many friends among writers –

and I guess what success did was show me who the *real* friends had always been.

Q: The past eight years have been particularly incredible for you – one success after another, worldwide acclaim as one of the major authors on the entire planet. Has any of this changed you in any way you're aware of?

A: No, not that I can see. Well, I do now travel everywhere with a retinue of eighty-nine people, including twelve enormous body-guards, eight sedan-chair porters, two women who constantly fan the air around me with perfumed peacock feathers, seven food tasters to guard against poisoning, a ten-man crew that rolls out a red carpet ahead of me when I walk and rolls it up behind me as I proceed, another four-man crew that takes care of Bobo (my elephant), two brow-blotters for when I'm overheated, four *more* brow-blotters for when Bobo is overheated, one brow-blotter who blots the brows of Bobo's four brow-blotters when *they* become overheated, a sixteen-piece orchestra to provide mood music to my life and capable of playing anything from Beethoven to the film score of *Shaft*, one spit-valve cleaner to assist the horn section of the orchestra, an eight-man mariachi band to play mood music when I'm in such a *wonderful* mood that even the orchestra can't quite match it, five dog handlers to keep the pack of Dobermans under control at all times, four of the world's finest physicists in case my retinue and I should ever find ourselves cast back to the Jurassic era by a time warp and need to figure out a way to return to our own age, two jugglers, two unicyclists, and one jester who has memorized all of the routines ever performed by Shecky Greene, Phyllis Diller, Moms Mabley, Redd Foxx, Pee-wee Herman, and Bud the Wonder Horse.

Q: So you don't think it's changed you at all.

A: Not really. Although I do believe it's made me a target for extraterrestrial observation and abduction.

Q: You've been abducted by aliens?

A: Not yet. But I think they've moved in next door, and they're just waiting for a chance.

Q: What makes you think this?

A: The flying saucer parked in the driveway. And their daughter has tentacles instead of arms and legs. And Spot, their dog, looks like a big crab, has four eyes, eats concrete, and speaks Eskimo patois.

Q: Maybe there's a book in this.

A: I'm sure there is, but I wouldn't want to try writing it. Before I could get it published, they'd take me away in their mother ship and put me in the same zoo out on the galactic rim where they have Elvis, Jimmy Hoffa, Amelia Earhart, and the *real* Tom Cruise.

* * *

LATER WORK

Q: As your books became more complex thematically, women began to assume a more important role in your work. Did you do this on purpose?

A: It sort of evolved like this . . . Learning how to plot – how to structure a story in a way that will be satisfying to readers and bring order to the thematic elements – is perhaps the hardest thing a beginning novelist has to do. Writers who disdain plot, who profess to believe that 'serious' fiction must never be concerned with plot, are actually just lazy and/or self-deluded. Dickens without plot? Dostoyevsky without plot? Mark Twain, Stevenson, or Balzac without plot? Unthinkable. The better a writer becomes, the more subtle the plot structures that can be handled, but they are *always* present in work that has any value.

Once I felt comfortable with structure – or plot – I became interested in developing ever more complex characters. As important as a tight story line is, nothing matters if the reader isn't enchanted by the characters – both the protagonists and the antagonists. It is essential to present the world of the story through the eyes of characters as dimensional and believable as real people, and the characters we are meant to identify with must be hugely appealing even while flawed. The characters often take over a story in the telling, and their actions move events in a direction that the writer never envisioned. In fact, this *usually* happens if the characters are sufficiently well conceived to come alive on the page.

The struggle to give birth to characters who are complex and alive requires a large variety of people in the same story because we primarily learn about any one character from his or her interactions with others. The more varied and interesting the cast with which he has to interact, the more complex and interesting he will become himself.

In the real world, the interaction between men and women is endlessly interesting, fraught with both joy and frustration, love and hate, confusion and poignant clarity. I began writing books with as many strong women in them as strong men, because I simply ceased to be able to imagine portraying a realistic and interesting fictional world in which the interaction of the sexes wasn't a major part of the story.

The oddest thing is that I've been criticized by a few – all male – writers for always having a major role for a woman in each of my books. One of them even called this a 'formula,' which I find bizarre. In *reality* women are half the world, involved in every aspect of life; if you can't portray them that way in fiction, then you can't be writing seriously. To write novel after novel – as these authors do – in which women are always just victims, villains, or accoutrements of the hero seems to be less in sync with reality and, therefore, more clearly formulaic than anything I've written.

Q: Critics often praise your characters – and especially some of the unusual ones you've featured, like Thomas in THE BAD PLACE, a young man with Down's syndrome. Regina, in HIDEAWAY, comes to mind.

A: Life is *filled* with people who are seldom, if ever, portrayed in fiction, and it's exciting to try to bring them alive in a novel. It makes my work more interesting.

For instance, creating a viewpoint for Thomas, an outlook on life that was simultaneously naive and wise, proved daunting. I wanted to show that someone with an intellectual disability could be as complex and interesting in his own way as any genius. Just because a person with Down's syndrome may view the world in simpler terms than other people doesn't mean he never has profound insights; those insights may be expressed in simple language, but they can reveal truths to us as surely as the words of any college professor. I wanted Thomas to be a person with a sense of humor, so we could laugh with him, because nothing makes a character more real to a reader than evidence that he's capable of amusement. But there was a danger that someone would laugh *at* Thomas instead of *with* him, and that would have been intolerable. As his creator, I had a thin line to walk. It was also important that he never be portrayed sentimentally. There's plenty of *sentiment* in the portrayal of Thomas, but if it had been treacly, he would have become false in an instant. If Thomas works, you fall in love with him, laugh and cry with him; you're transported into a life experience that you have never encountered before in fiction. He changes your perception of your own life and the world in which you live. That's part of what a novel should be about – after all, the word is *novel* with the implication that the contents will to some extent be fresh. By creating characters like Thomas, I hope to keep my stories fresh not merely for readers but for *myself*.

Q: In some ways, THE BAD PLACE is your most complex novel, especially in the way allegorical layers sort of shimmer just below the surface and in the archetypal nature of the characters. Is Thomas meant to be Christ, or at least a Christlike figure?

A: Virtually all of the characters in the novel have biblical parallels. Thomas is certainly Christlike in that he is an innocent, pure of mind and heart, with exceptional insights and powers, who dies for his sister and for Bobby; and it is also through Thomas that Julie finds the faith to believe there is something beyond this life. Bobby and Julie are like Adam and Eve, cast out of paradise and seeking to return, longing for that little cottage on the seashore, for a life of peace and simplicity. At the same time, elements of Joseph and Mary are alive in their characters, for they are protecting a special child from a world as dangerous to him as King Herod's realm was dangerous to Christ. I won't go through the whole cast and draw all the parallels or discuss how they function thematically – partly because this isn't really something that a reader has to be aware of to enjoy the story. In fact, I'm not even sure that a reader *should* see this level of the story; the effect is meant to be subconscious, to set up reverberations on primal levels. If a reader is aware of this level of a novel, then the effect isn't the same as what I intended. It should touch, move, and disturb readers without their always understanding exactly *why*.

42

Q: Because of Thomas, have you received any letters from parents who have children with Down's syndrome?

A: Yes, a great many. With but one exception, they've all been extremely positive. They were excited to see a character with Down's portrayed as an admirable, complex, *heroic* figure who has as much purpose in life, despite his limitations, as anyone else. I've also gotten letters from a lot of therapists who work with Down's syndrome children and adults, and they were equally enthusiastic about Thomas.

Q: You've noted, in other interviews, that you have great faith in the resiliency and strength of the human race. Is that one reason for including characters like Thomas, to explore how human beings can triumph over anything?

A: To some extent, maybe. However, good characters are never mouthpieces for the author's views. They take on a life of their own, have a view of their own, and represent what they *want* to represent. This is even true of characters meant to have symbolic purpose. It's sometimes difficult to explain this to readers who think that a character's beliefs are necessarily identical to those of the author. But that's just not so. If it were, then I would have to be a psychotic killer in order to portray the thought processes of a homicidal sociopath.

Q: But you're not a psychotic killer?

A: Not so far as I'm aware. Of course, I am troubled by these occasional *blank* spots . . .

Q: Fugues?

A: Yes! These two- or three-hour fugues, blackouts, after which I regain awareness of my surroundings, sometimes with blood on my hands. But I'm *sure* there's a reasonable explanation for that.

Q: Dressing another deer?

A: You could be correct! Or perhaps, during these fugues, I've got another life entirely. I might be a thoracic surgeon during my blackouts, don't you think? Surely that would explain a little blood.

Q: For someone who takes his work very seriously, you don't seem to take *yourself* seriously.

A: Every writer I've ever seen who takes himself too seriously, who dons a mantle of somber respectability, who wants to be seen as a mensch of menschen . . . well, they all wind up producing pompous work larded with pretension. And don't even realize it. Refusing to take himself too seriously helps a writer maintain perspective. Life is both deadly serious and hilariously comic at the same time – and, for the writer, good work arises out of an awareness of that tragic contradiction. Time has a nasty way of dealing with the work of those whose sense of self-importance guides the writing of every sentence. Do the work with the utmost pride, apply the greatest effort of which you're capable – but for the sake of the story, not for the sake of your own ego. The work will stand or fall on its merits. Meanwhile, if you take yourself too seriously, you're never going to have any *fun*; if you don't have any fun, you don't really know what life is all about and, therefore, can't write about it well.

* * *

Q: TWILIGHT EYES remains one of your most misunderstood novels. I've seen reviews of it that didn't grasp what you were doing. The prose, for instance, is different from what you usually do, virtually metered in places; there are complex poetic effects piled atop one another. Did you expect it would be misunderstood by some readers?

A: Yes. But you have to write what you're driven to write.
When I started TWILIGHT EYES, I decided it should be from a first-person point of view, virtually the only novel I've ever written that way. I'd long noticed that when writers produce a book in first-person, the prose still *sounds* like what they write when their stories are told in third-person. Yet the narrator is supposed to be someone other than the author. In other cases, a novelist will write all of his books in first-person, but his many different narrators, book after book, sound the same. A perfect example of this is Dick Francis. Now, I immensely enjoy Dick Francis's work, and I virtually *revere* everything written prior to RECOIL, but each of his first-person

narrators sounds like all of the others. Nothing wrong with this. He just made the decision to ignore the issue of narrator voice in favor of working hard on other elements of his novels. But I decided with TWILIGHT EYES that the narrator, Slim MacKenzie, had to tell his story in a style different from that in any of my other books. He had to *be himself*.

Because Slim is extremely intelligent and gifted with certain unusual abilities, and because he has led such a dramatic life even by the age of seventeen, it seems natural for him to have a complex worldview, a very *baroque* way of seeing things. The manner in which he describes scenes, his recollection of events, and his musings are all baroque. The style of the book is therefore dense, the images rich and so numerous that they crowd one another. When I started writing, I needed a couple of weeks to get the feel of Slim's point of view, but one day he just suddenly came alive, and the prose flowed smoothly. It *is* metered in many places, mostly in iambic pentameter. This seems a natural reflection of the iron will with which Slim has tried to bring order to – and make sense of – a world that he *knows* is infinitely bizarre and perhaps senseless.

I've had letters from some readers who get only a chapter or two into the book and become so uncomfortable they can't go on – *because they think that Slim is actually insane*, and they don't want to read a book in which a psychotic is the hero. Slim's own doubts about his sanity convinces them. Of course, he's not insane, and another chapter or two would convince them of that. At the same time, it's the favorite of all my books with some readers, because they love the carnival background and the weird story line but mainly because they wind up identifying with Slim so intensely.

* * *

Q: Before doing this interview, I read critic Michael Collings's reviews of several of your books. He makes a case for WHISPERS being a novel about betrayal. As he notes: 'Bruno is betrayed by his parents, Hilary by her parents, Joshua by his clients, the sheriff by his deputy, and even Bruno's psychiatrist violates the trust between patient and doctor.' I think Collings is on to something. Of all your major novels, WHISPERS seems the bleakest and the one that holds out the least hope for humanity. Any reaction to that statement?

A: Well, as I said earlier, one of the themes of the book is the difficulty of understanding the influences that make us what we are, the difficulty of being objective about the lifetime sum of our subjective experiences. Being betrayed by friends or family has profound psychological consequences. Betrayal is one of the hardest things to acknowledge and accept – especially when the people who betray us are close to us. Such as parents. Hilary was betrayed by her mother and father, who brought her into this world and then made her childhood a living hell. Bruno was betrayed by his mother in the same fashion, but then we learn his mother was likewise betrayed by her father, who savagely abused her. Betrayal is a deadly disease we've passed along to one another ever since Eden, and each of us has a responsibility not to participate in the spread of the contagion.

* * *

Q: Wouldn't you say that your career really began to take off with two books in particular – WATCHERS and LIGHTNING?

A: Yes. Though STRANGERS was my first hardcover bestseller, the roll really gained momentum with those two books. And from the moment I began WATCHERS, I *knew* everything had changed for me forever. It was a difficult book to write but I was never for a moment in despair or consumed by doubt. I knew the story and characters worked, scene by scene, and that I had my hands on special material. From first page to last, writing that book was a transcendent, joyous, indescribable experience. Floods of blood and sweat, you understand, but unremitting joy, as well. I've only had that experience one other time – with MR MURDER. Writing a novel is usually an emotional roller coaster. Some days you think it's fine, some days you think it's mediocre, and some days you think it stinks; you soar with exhilaration and quickly plunge into despair. But with both of those books, the story came like a great wide river, flowing smooth and swift, and for the whole ride I knew I was going somewhere special. There are other books of my own that I like as well or nearly as well as those two, but WATCHERS and MR MURDER were composed with so much *confidence* compared to other books that I'll always love them a little more and be unable to rank them objectively.

Q: WATCHERS is the ultimate crowd-pleaser. How can you possibly go wrong with a romance as powerful yet curiously innocent

46

as the one you portray – *and* a lovable dog? Yet for all its tender and loving qualities, for all its considerable humor, WATCHERS is a somber book in which you seemed to begin to evolve a different concept of evil. Were you conscious of this when you wrote it?

A: Yes. Around the time I started WATCHERS, I had begun to lose faith in traditional Freudian explanations of evil. I couldn't see a whole lot of correlation between childhood trauma and antisocial behavior. I'd had a dreadful childhood, but I hadn't grown up either psychotic or depressive. I knew all sorts of people who endured dreadful hardship and shattering trauma as children, yet grew up well balanced. On the other hand, people who had every advantage, who were loved by their parents, who had led charmed lives, sometimes became antisocial in the extreme. I started reading books on criminal psychology – which has been an interest ever since – and all of the *credible* scientific studies I found made it implicitly clear that the theories of modern psychology are nothing more than that – *theories*. More important, the hard scientific data that *is* available seems to disprove most of the assumptions behind large areas of psychology and behind nearly all psychiatry. Antisocial behavior must not be caused by social ills or childhood trauma because truly vicious criminal activities – the worst species of evil – don't correlate with those causes in any consistent manner.

Evil exists apart from apparent cause. Perhaps certain tendencies are there in the genes; some people may simply be damaged from birth, and may find it easier to steal or kill than do most people. There's evidence to support such a somber conclusion, and it's growing. For one thing, anywhere from seventy to eighty percent of violent crime in our society is committed by less than two percent of the population. The average armed robber commits scores of felonies before he's caught. Another bit of evidence: Virtually all serial killers – who so fascinate the public these days that they have become almost mythical figures of evil – show murderous tendencies and extreme antisocial behavior from a very young age; and all of them seem to be incapable of empathy, of understanding how other people feel, as if something – perhaps on a genetic level – is *missing* in them. In WATCHERS, The Outsider at least longs to be like the dog, Einstein, though his engineered genetic nature makes it impossible for him to change; Vince Nasco, born of man and woman, is as savage as The Outsider but doesn't want to change and is, therefore, the more despicable of the two – and in some ways the more frightening.

I've been exploring the nature of evil in every book since WATCHERS, gradually moving toward an ever-more grim view of it. By DRAGON TEARS I pretty much reached the conclusion that evil behavior, other than those acts arising from self-interest, rarely if ever has a logical explanation. Sure, if some thug robs you at gunpoint, the logical explanation is that he needs money; but when he also kills you, with no provocation, which is something we see happening more and more in Los Angeles and other places all over the country, when he jeopardizes his *own* future by escalating from a simple felony to a capital offense, there is no logic behind the act on the conscious level. And if Freudian explanations don't hold water – which they don't – there is no logic on a subconscious level, either.

Therefore, truly evil people, homicidal people who kill repeatedly or rapists who have long lists of victims, can never be rehabilitated. We're foolish to let them out of prison after as few as seven to ten years, which is what's happening these days. If civilization is going to survive, we're going to have to accept that each of us is responsible for his own life, for his own acts, and that those who refuse to behave responsibly must be ostracized in one way or another. Otherwise, evil wins. Edmund Burke said, 'The only thing necessary for the triumph of evil is for good men to do nothing.' Which is true now more than ever.

For a long time it's been common wisdom that the roots of all evils lie in social ills or childhood trauma, that everyone is a victim, and that evil can eventually be eliminated through therapy and social justice. Therapy's nice. Social justice is essential. But neither will eliminate evil.

I find some of the psychology in WHISPERS naive now, because it is thoroughly Freudian. In fact, Freudian theories of evil have shaped virtually *all* modern fiction – as well as reader's expectations. Which is why so many critics think Thomas Harris's *Red Dragon* is a better book than *The Silence of the Lambs*, which it's not. Indeed, *Red Dragon*, with its elaborate psychological explanations for Dollarhyde's serial murders seems labored and juvenile, while *The Silence of the Lambs* is cold, clear-eyed, and stunningly perceptive. Some critics, especially in the mystery genre, like *Red Dragon* better precisely because of the killer's carefully explained psychological pathology, and they think *Silence* is thin because it lacks those explanations. But unless I'm woefully misreading Harris, he *intentionally* does not explain either Lecter or Buffalo Bill in *Silence* because he has come to believe there *is* no explanation and that evil exists of itself, independent of social ills and trauma. To my mind, this makes *Silence* an infinitely more mature and compelling work, and one that will outlast *Red Dragon*. About some things it is more intelligent and mature to admit that we do not know – and will never know – the answers, rather than to try to force a false understanding through the rigid application of failed theories of human behavior.

Q: Do you think we've gotten too heavy?

A: Speak for yourself. I think I'm quite svelte.

Q: Amazing, too, considering how little exercise you get when you're carried everywhere on that sedan chair.

A: Ah, but I've recently added a personal trainer to my retinue – plus three men who diligently exercise for me two hours every morning and two hours every evening. Consequently, I'm in splendid condition. In fact, right this minute, I'm doing five hundred situps through surrogates.

Q: The other book that really started the ball rolling for you was LIGHTNING. That novel is, for me, anyway, a great Technicolor masterpiece. It has everything – romance, novelty, comedy, tragedy, and a very real sense of human history. In some places the effects are almost operatic. Did you have any premonition that LIGHTNING was going to turn out to be such a grand adventure and such a huge success?

A: Frankly, no. It was a *bear* to write because of the various secrets and the complications inherent in the central premise (which I won't talk about because I don't want to spoil the book for anyone who hasn't read it). Some people in my professional life thought it was a major mistake for a variety of reasons. You can't, they said, set a suspense story over a thirty-five-year span; you need a ticking clock. There was resistance, as well, to spending the first thirty percent of the book with the heroine *as a child*, because some felt that this made the book seem like a young-adult novel. Of course, the style was anything but young-adult. There was also fear that the complexity of the story line would turn off readers. I was already exhausted from the writing, so these other people's doubts fed my own.

Then – and I don't know if you remember this, Ed – you read the advance bound proofs of LIGHTNING, months before it appeared in stores, and you told me it was going to sell faster and bigger than anything I'd done to that point. You said it was, more than WATCHERS, my breakout book. Your reaction startled me. When I asked you to explain, you said, 'American writers never write about fate. That's more the territory of Europeans. Yet people are fascinated by the idea that we have destinies. You're writing about fate here, and readers will respond in a huge way because it's fresh in American fiction.' You really gave my spirits a needed lift – though I thought this was one *more* bit of proof that you were sadly over the edge. Akin to your tendency to wear live rabbits as hats. Or didn't you want me to mention that? Anyway, when the book hit the stores, it sold like crazy. Other novelists called me or wrote letters to say they *loved* the book and felt it must have been nigh impossible to write, given all the threads that had to be tracked and tied together. The first number-one bestseller I ever had was MIDNIGHT, which was the book following LIGHTNING, and one of the reasons it made the top of the list was because people had liked LIGHTNING so much. To this day, it generates more reader mail than any new title.

The lesson, again, is write what you're driven to write and don't try to analyze the market. You have to *make* the market by writing what you're compelled to write.

* * *

PERSONAL BELIEFS

Q: Are you willing to talk about personal beliefs?

A: Sure. As long as we don't get into anything personal.

Q: What about politics?

A: Boring. And stupid. Life's too short for politics. I'm interested only because I want to be aware of what horrors the politicians are going to bring down upon us next.

Q: Religion?

A: Protestant, then Catholic, then agnostic, now firmly back in the believing camp again, though with no firm idea of the nature of God. Modern physics – primarily certain aspects of quantum physics and chaos theory – has had a large role in bringing me back to belief, as has day-to-day experience. Besides, it's so trendy now not to believe in anything, and I'm somewhat contrarian by nature.

Q: What, for you, constitutes a good friendship?

A: A shared interest in old Wallace Beery movies, shrimp ice cream, tweed, stock-car racing, plastic vomit, and collecting rodents of all varieties. A friend of mine has to be someone willing to spend long, lazy days tumbling around and around in huge industrial dryers. A friend of mine has to like taking risks – such as performing mime routines on a shooting range, playing volleyball with live porcupines, and going all the way to Iraq to question Saddam Hussein face-to-face regarding the physical attractiveness and moral fiber of his mother. To be a friend of mine, you've got to dream big, play hard, go for the gold, take the plunge, hold nothing back, seize the day – and never carry dead lizards in your pockets.

Q: Can we have a more serious answer?

A: That *was* serious. Jeez. Okay. Friendships come in too many shapes and sizes to be defined. But all good relationships have three things in common: Unfailing honesty, kindness, laughter.

Q: Aside from writing, what are a few things that give you real pleasure and satisfaction?

A: Any time with Gerda, even if we're tending to some wearisome chore together. Reading. Good conversation with a few pleasant companions. Art and antiques. Book collecting. Fine cabernet sauvignon. Using the gym we installed downstairs. Driving. I've always *loved* to drive and be on the road. Nothing makes me feel freer than going on a long drive, getting out on desert highways and putting the pedal to the metal, seeing new states, new towns, new highway-patrol officers.

Q: As you approach middle age—

A: Wait, wait, wait. Approach middle age? I'm nowhere *near* middle age. Oh, yes, of course, I would be if I intended to live the average life span, but it's my intention to live to be two hundred and six years old, so I'm nowhere close being middle-aged. That's why I drink such huge volumes of diet colas every day: So the chemical preservatives in them will collect in my tissues and preserve me for the aforementioned two hundred and six years.

Q: Okay, then. Though you're still somewhat of a child in terms of your intended life span, do you have any deep regrets about your past . . . roads not taken or goals you never achieved?

A: No. I've fulfilled my dream of becoming a full-time writer. I've found an audience larger than I ever imagined I would find for the quirky stuff I write. I'd be something of a fool if I sat around moaning about never getting a chance to experience life as a below-decks, gut-and-chop worker in an Alaskan fish trawler.

To make it this far, I knew early on that I would have to work so hard that it would mean sacrificing most of my leisure time through my twenties and thirties. After a decade and a half of six-day workweeks, long hours, and few vacations, when the breakthrough hadn't happened yet, I sometimes wondered if I was sacrificing too much in the pursuit of a dream that would never come true, and I have to admit to brief periods when I felt sorry for myself. However, mostly what I felt was deep frustration at the publishing industry, which seeks overnight successes at the expense of helping writers develop an audience over the long haul, and which succeeds always in spite of itself. Publishing is so fiercely resistant to anything new that it makes the Amish look like a group of wild-and-crazy swingers.

I was frustrated, too, by the way publishers strive relentlessly to label every writer with one genre tag or another and then condemn him to the ghetto selected for him whether he belongs there or not. When I was twenty-seven, I was told that I had reached the apex of my career, that I would be a midlist suspense novelist the rest of my days. When I exhibited ambition and wrote more complex books, agents and editors kindly advised me that my books would never be bestsellers, that I wasn't that kind of writer, and that I was only setting myself up for heartbreak by trying. I left an agent because of that very speech. It seemed to me, at twenty-seven, that I was a tad too young to have my whole life mapped out for me already. Later, when my books became paperback bestsellers, I was told I would never be a hardcover bestseller because I was basically a paperback writer. In the end, other people's negativism, while profoundly frustrating at the time, might have been part of what motivated me, because I'm prone to a quiet but intense oh-yeah-well-I'll-show-you attitude.

Q: What do you hope the next ten years will bring you?

A: A miraculous and lush regrowth of the hair I've been losing. The discovery that I'm a descendant of a secret clan of immortals who rule the world from an underground palace near Scranton, Pennsylvania – although without the requirement that I move there. Some new shoes. A third arm and hand so I can comb my hair and tend to other personal grooming chores while writing. A dog named Lassie who will run for help if I ever get my leg trapped under a tipped-over tractor on the south forty.

Actually, all I'm hoping for is good health and the chance to develop as a writer, move along to ever more interesting books and be able to take my audience with me. That's paradise.

Q: You seem very comfortable with yourself. Is there a secret to peace of mind?

A: Fiber. Eat plenty of fiber. Other than that . . . Well, as one who had a pretty dismal childhood, I've learned not to hold on to anger. Let go of the past. You can never forget the bad things people do to you, the meanness and pettiness and betrayal, but you *can* let go of the anger. If you don't, you're never going to have peace of mind in your entire life, because there are always going to be new people doing things to hurt you. You're going to have an increasing store of insults, affronts, and treacheries to be angry about. You've got to learn to embrace that axiom I mentioned earlier: *Living well is the best revenge.* After someone's done you dirt, if you just get on with your life, let go of the anger, if you're just *happy*, then you've defeated the person who wronged you. And if you never get caught up in feuding and paying back, you feel better about yourself; you prove to yourself that you have considerably more control than the creep who crossed you.

Now, this doesn't mean that if you're hit in the mouth, you should turn the other cheek. I'm not talking about physical violence. If you're hit, *destroy* the sonofabitch. But when its personal or business treachery or mean-spiritedness, forget it. Let go. Walk away and get on with life.

I believe that we were put on this world to enjoy it, that we are meant to be happy, and that happiness is largely a choice. Some people choose to be miserable. They wallow in misery. Or in fear. Take the global-warming hysteria. There's no credible proof that it's actually happening. Maritime temperature records from ships at sea over the past 150 years show no pattern of temperature increase. Not long ago a group of scientists studied the trunk of a 3,600-year-old tree in the Amazon that was felled by an act of nature; they discovered temperature fluctuations from the beginning of the industrial revolution through our own time have been only average. In fact, in the thousands of years prior to the rise of human industry, there were some periods of natural climate flux worse than anything we're seeing. Man-made pollutants? The eruption of Mount Pinatubo in the Philippines a couple years ago expelled more pollutants of every variety than human beings have produced in the entire history of the species, from twenty times as much in the case of some chemicals to *two hundred* times as much in the case of others. This was *one* volcanic eruption. Yet people will wallow in fear and remorse and legislate in panic because they *want* to believe we're living in the last years of the world, on the doorstep of Armageddon. I'm no Pollyanna; I contribute to focused, effective, rational environmental causes that I feel are important. But I'm not going to wallow in misery about this issue or any other if the facts don't justify it. Misery, in this case, as in so many others, is a *choice* not an inevitable condition. Am I saying something as childishly simple as, 'Don't worry, be happy?' No. If you're standing in the path of a tidal wave, that's a pretty stupid philosophy. I'm only saying that peace of mind arises from being happy until you've got good, solid, irrefutable reasons to be otherwise.

And don't forget that fiber. Lots of fiber.

Q: If you were assigned to be the first person to address an alien species, what would you say?

A: Fiber. Eat lots of fiber. But I wouldn't stop there. No, sir. I'd hold forth for quite a while. I'd probably bore the pants off those aliens – assuming they wore pants.

I'd tell them that, whenever in the company of Earthlings, they must watch their wallets at all times. I'd tell them never to eat at a restaurant called 'Mom's,' never to play poker with a guy named 'Slick,' and never to exceed the speed limit in a school zone. I'd explain to them that it is perfectly acceptable to stomp cockroaches but not small children. I'd tell them not to believe everything they read – for example, grasshoppers are every *bit* as industrious as ants, and that damned old Aesop was maligning a hardworking insect species when he wrote his vile little fable. I'd be sure to make them understand that the main ingredient of French fries is potatoes, not French citizens dipped in boiling oil, because a culinary mistake of that nature could set back human-alien relations *decades*. I'd try to explain why automobiles are often named after animals but *never* after vegetables or fruits . . . though I'm not sure what I'd say. I mean when you think about it, why *isn't* there a nifty Ford Persimmon or a Chrysler Squash or maybe a Pontiac Scallion or a Buick Wax Bean? The name of a car has to have sex appeal, right? Well, hey, most vegetables are every bit as sexy as animals – with the exception of celery, which is the vegetable-world equivalent of a gelding. I'd tell these aliens that we don't tolerate the indiscriminate use of death rays, parking in handicapped spaces when all of your tentacles are actually intact, the gutting and decapitation of insurance salesmen no matter how pushy they get, or the use of the word 'buttface' when addressing members of any royal family.

Q: That's all?

A: You think they'd still be listening?

Q: Probably not.

A: Then that's all.

Q: Thank you for your time.

A: Live long and prosper.

PART II

Keeping Pace with the Master

by David B. Silva

This is the way it happened.

That's what the good writers will tell you.

They'll pull up a chair, make themselves comfortable, and suddenly it's like sitting around the campfire on a warm July night, drinking a slow beer, munching pretzels, swapping stories, and hoping the night will last forever. The good writers make you feel as if you're the only one listening; the telling's just between them and you. And when the story's finished, they let you keep it. That's part of the agreement. Once the story's finished, it's yours. No one can take it away from you. Besides, you couldn't shake it even if you wanted to. It's like the first time you watched *The Day the Earth Stood Still* on 'Creature Features' on Saturday night. It stays with you long afterwards, because somewhere in the telling a truth has been told, and it's never easy to shake off a truth. You can't do it by turning off the television. And you can't do it by closing the cover of the book, either.

This is the way it happened.

No, the best storytellers – and most often those who write suspense and horror, because their stories tell the starkest truths – find a way of staying with you long after you finish their words.

Dean Koontz is a teller of stark truths.

And he tells these truths with unmistakable prose, a style that is uniquely his in the pace it sets. That's the essence of what I hope to explore in this piece – how Koontz uses everything from word choice to action scenes to keep his stories moving at a pace unmatched by any other modern writer. Unfortunately, we won't be able to examine everything Koontz does to step up the pace of his stories. There are just too many techniques, preferences, little nuances involved. But we'll try to take a closer look at those things that are most prominent.

SETTING THE PACE

I want my readers to begin each new book with surprise, with a sense of now knowing what to expect, and at some point in their reading, I want them to think, with at least some delight, Well, I've never read anything like this before.[1]

Beginnings are Koontz at his best.

If it's the job of the publisher to get readers to open the cover of the book, then it's the job of the author to keep that cover open. Koontz understands this principle, perhaps better than any of his contemporaries. Peter Straub, Robert Bloch, even William Goldman for the most part (although he, too, is often quite effective with his beginnings), all tend to pull readers into their stories by way of introduction to their characters. Ramsey Campbell relies heavily on his unique style in getting started. Charles L. Grant likes to focus upon a setting that seems almost too normal. Stephen King most often writes naturally to his strength of characterization when he begins a book. Make no mistakes, each of these approaches is valid. But they also share a common frailty: They ask the reader to be patient; they promise us more . . . but we'll have to wait for it.

Dean Koontz doesn't have the need to make any such promises. The very first sentence is where his story begins, and it nearly always begins with that *surprise* he's so fond of. Action. Quick and effective characterization. Immediate crisis. These elements establish the pace of a Koontz novel, and they do it right up front, no apologies.

If you want it direct and succinct, here's the way Koontz does it:

1. He gives us main characters that we will care about.
2. He places these characters in immediate and often desperate situations. They must *overcome* right away if they are to survive.
3. He never allows the readers to catch up with him. There are always new and unanticipated surprises just around the bend.

Let's take a closer look at some opening lines from a number of Koontz novels. The point I'd like you to note here is how quickly he pulls the reader into his stories. Turn the first page and suddenly we're smack dab in the middle of a critical episode! See if you can resist wanting to know what happens next, he says. I dare you.

THE FACE OF FEAR
Wary, not actually expecting trouble but prepared for it, he parked his car across the street from the four-story brownstone apartment house. When he switched off the engine, he heard a siren wail in the street behind him.

They're coming for me, he thought. Somehow they've found out I'm the one.

THE VISION
'Gloves of blood,'

THE VOICE OF THE NIGHT
'You ever killed anything?' Roy asked.

WHISPERS
Tuesday at dawn. Los Angeles trembled. Windows rattled in their frames. Patio wind chimes tinkled merrily even though there was no wind. In some houses, dishes fell off shelves.

PHANTOMS
The scream was distant and brief. A woman's scream.

DARKFALL
Penny Dawson woke and heard something moving furtively in the dark bedroom.

STRANGERS
Dominick Corvaisis went to sleep under a light wool blanket and a crisp white sheet, sprawled alone in his bed, but he woke elsewhere – in the darkness at the back of the large foyer closet, behind concealing coats and jackets.

WATCHERS
On his thirty-sixth birthday, May 18, Travis Cornell rose at five o'clock in the morning. He dressed in sturdy hiking boots, jeans, and a long-sleeved, blue-plaid cotton shirt. He drove his pickup south from his home in Santa Barbara all the way to rural Santiago Canyon on the eastern edge of Orange County, south of Los Angeles. He took only a package of Oreo cookies, a large canteen full of orange-flavored Kool-Aid, and a fully loaded Smith & Wesson .38 Chief's Special.

THE BAD PLACE

The night was becalmed and curiously silent, as if the alley were an abandoned and windless beach in the eye of a hurricane, between the tempest past and the tempest coming. A faint scent of smoke hung on the motionless air, although no smoke was visible.

Sprawled facedown on the cold pavement, Frank Pollard did not move when he regained consciousness: he waited in the hope that his confusion would dissipate. He blinked, trying to focus. Veils seemed to flutter within his eyes. He sucked deep breathes of cool air tasting the invisible smoke, grimacing at the acrid tang of it.

DRAGON TEARS

Tuesday was a fine California day, full of sunshine and promise until Harry Lyon had to shoot someone at lunch.

In each example, Koontz goes immediately and directly for the suspense. There are no long descriptive passages, no rambling paragraphs to establish the setting or to introduce us to the external or superficial aspects of a character. We're thrown into the story right here, right now. We experience it as abruptly and as terrifyingly as his characters. And that's the way it should be.

Let's carry this a little further.

In DARKFALL, one of the fastest moving novels Koontz has written to date, the tension is immediate. Eleven-year-old Penny Dawson is awakened by a sound she can't identify. A 'sneaky' sound, coming from the other side of the room. The longer she listens the more menacing the sound becomes. Penny switches on the light. Nothing is there. But the hissing-scratching-scrabbling sound starts up again, this time from under her bed. Trying not to behave like a helpless child, Penny uses her brother's plastic bat to probe under the bed:

The other end of the plastic club was suddenly seized. held, Penny tried to pull it loose. She couldn't. She jerked and twisted it. But the bat held fast.

Then it was torn out of her grip. The bat vanished under the bed with a thump and a rattle.

Eventually the thing from under the bed escapes, still unseen. What was it? What did it want? Penny comes out alive and well, though frightened by what has happened. But because she doesn't want to be seen as a little child, she never tells her father. Instead, she carries her fear and her curiosity to sleep with her. And *we* carry the same feelings into the next section of the novel.

All this takes place in the first ten pages of Darkfall.

That's how quickly Koontz draws us into his world.

STEPPING UP THE PACE

You *must* squeeze every drop of color and excitement and suspense out of every action scene in your novel.[2]

As we've already seen, Koontz likes to engage his readers and establish a book's celerity from the very first word. An almost natural extension of this, because he so often uses action as a way of introducing a new novel, is the way he handles his action scenes.

Crisis keeps the story moving.

And Koontz knows that a crisis will hook and hold the reader's attention far better than any other narrative content, so he sets out to take full advantage of such scenes. How does he do it? Most often by denying his characters an easy out. He expects his heroes (or his heroines, as is often the case) to run up against one obstacle after another without ever giving up their fight for survival. Never, ever, make it easy on the characters.

You can find a prime example in his novel WHISPERS. There's a scene near the front of the book, when his heroine, Hilary, is attacked by a man named Frye. The incident covers nearly twenty pages as she tries to protect herself (she hits him with a porcelain statue, he recovers; she fights him off by clawing him and kicking him in the groin, but he's too strong; she manages to lock him out of the master bedroom, but he kicks down the door; she locates a gun, fires, nothing, kicks off the safety, fires, nothing, jacks a bullet into the chamber, fires, hits him; but is he really dead?). Twenty pages racing by as fast as you can turn them. It's a powerful, effective scene that refuses to let you stop reading. And it works because each time Hilary appears to have finally found a way to overcome Frye, a new complication arises and it seems once again as if her situation is hopeless. We're never quite sure if she'll survive or not.

If you looked closely, you would discover that Koontz handles each action scene like a microcosm of the novel as a whole. He layers one scene of growing desperation on top of another, each contributing to the urgency of the overall story. Force the hero into a bind. Throw in a complication, then another complication, until the situation is worse than we ever imagined. Keep the hero struggling, battling, surviving until he or she eventually fails or prevails . . . That's the kind of intensity, of mounting pressure, that keeps the tempo brisk and keeps readers turning 400 or 500 pages.

There is another technique which Koontz sometimes uses to step up the pace even more. When a pending disaster overshadows a number of characters at the same time, he sometimes cuts frantically back and forth between his characters in short, staccato scenes. This technique, used properly, takes an action scene and adds yet another dimension of suspense on top of it.

An example of this approach can be found in DARKFALL, a book I want to keep coming back to because its pace is so relentless that it embodies Koontz's approach. In chapter five, Jack Dawson, after his kids have been threatened by the *Bocor*, is frantic to get across town and make sure they're safe. In this instance, in place of a single action scene, Koontz cuts quickly from one scene to another, creating an urgency not only in the novel but also in the reader.

Here's how he take us through this crisis:

Scene One: The *Bocor* begins to collect his energy for the slaughter.

Scene Two: Jack's daughter, Penny, hears a scraping-hissing sound. She tracks the source to a floor vent, peers through the slots.

Scene Three: Jack is hunched over the wheel of his car. It's snowing, the road is slippery, he has to travel much slower than he wants. And he keeps thinking back to the thing the *Bocor* said he would do to Jack's children: Mangled bodies, eyeballs gouged from sockets, throats chewed open. The car spins out of control, Jack is forced to drive even more cautiously.

Scene Four: The *Bocor* continues his ritual, psychically reaching out to the children.

Scene Five: Penny hears a brittle, whispery voice coming from within the wall. She wakes her little brother because she suddenly knows that they're both in grave danger.

Scene Six: Jack and his partner, Rebecca, finally arrive at the apartment building. They take the elevator to the eleventh floor. It's the longest elevator trip Jack has ever taken.

Scene Seven: Deep in a trance, the *Bocor* psychically connects with Penny. He can smell her, and he wants her.

These seven scenes unfold in a total of only thirteen pages, and they're each designed to carry the reader swiftly along toward the eighth scene. The eighth scene here is the big action scene. Jack finally arrives at the apartment, encounters the 'creatures' created by the *Bocor*, and saves his children. The eighth scene, being the climax of this section of the novel, runs almost sixteen pages, and is full of the same kind of complications that we've explored above.

Remember, Koontz is saying, never make it easy on your heroes.

Especially in your action scenes.

GOING THROUGH THE PACES

Regardless of the style in which the body of your novel is written, you would be well advised to modify – or perhaps I ought to say 'modulate' – it now and then, specifically to punctuate action sequences.[3]

A writer's style is one of those nebulous things that everyone talks about, but few really understand. For this discussion, I'd like you to think of a writer's style as his unique way of telling his story, his personal *voice*. And I'd like you to understand that that *voice* changes, sometimes from book to book, sometimes from scene to scene, depending upon what the author is trying to accomplish.

In this section, we'll take a look at some examples of how Koontz uses a particular style to achieve a tempo change and, in turn, elicit a particular emotional response from the reader.

Here's a short excerpt from the scene in DARKFALL when Jack is riding the elevator up to his apartment, knowing that his children are in danger:

Fourth floor.

'We won't need guns anyway,' Rebecca said. 'We've gotten here ahead of Lavelle. I know we have.'

But the conviction had gone out of her voice.

Jack knew why. The journey from her apartment had taken forever. It seemed less and less likely that they were going to be in time.

Sixth floor.

'Why're the elevators so goddamned slow in this building?' Jack demanded.

65

Seventh floor.
Eight.
Ninth.
'Move, damnit!' he commanded the lift machinery as if he thought it would actually speed up if he ordered it to do so.
Tenth floor.
Eleventh.
At last the doors slid open, and Jack stepped through them.

In this instance, Koontz uses each floor of the apartment building as a measure of the progress which is all too slow as far as Jack is concerned. The floor levels specified so deliberately, heighten the tension that already exists. Jack wants the elevator to go faster. *We* want the elevator to go faster. And if you look closely, they *do* go faster. Notice for instance, that the higher the elevator climbs, the quicker we pass by each new floor. At first, it's fourth floor, followed by conversation. But eventually, we start passing by one floor right after another. *Seventh floor, eighth, ninth.*

Koontz accomplishes the near impossible here. On the one hand, the elevator climb takes forever. On the other hand, he still keeps the pace of the scene moving along at a frantic clip.

All by the way he chooses to count the floors of the building.

You can see the same approach, handled slightly differently in this scene from HIDEAWAY:

Just for a split second, Tod would probably think he'd smacked into the overhang where, in legend, a boy had been decapitated. He would let go of the lap bar in panic. At least that was what Jeremy hoped, so as soon as he hit the old rocket jockey, when the train started to drop down the third hill, Jeremy let go of the lap bar, too, and threw himself against his best friend, grabbing him, lifting and shoving, hard as he could. He felt Tod trying to get a fistful of his hair, but he shook his head furiously and shoved harder, took a kick on the hip–
–the train shot up the fourth hill–
–Tod went over the edge, out into the darkness, away from the car, as if he had dropped into deep space. Jeremy started to topple with him, grabbed frantically for the lap bar in the seamless blackness, found it, held on–
–down, the train swooped down the fourth hill–
–Jeremy thought he heard one last scream from Tod and then a solid thunk! as he hit the tunnel wall and bounced back onto the tracks in the wake of the train, although it might have been imagination–
–up, the train shot up the fifth hill with a rollicking motion that made Jeremy want to whoop his cookies–

—Tod was either dead back there in the darkness or stunned, half-conscious, trying to get to his feet—

—down the fifth hill, and Jeremy was whipped back and forth, almost lost his grip on the bar, then was soaring again, up the sixth and final hill—

—and if he wasn't dead back there. Tod was maybe just beginning to realize that another train was coming—

—down, down the sixth hill and onto the last straightaway.

See it? See the way Koontz carries you up and down the ride, gaining speed not only with the words he chooses, but with the manner in which he presents them?

Let me show you a slightly different example of Koontz using style to create a sense of tension and urgency. This one's taken from the scene in PHANTOMS when Bryce, Jenny and Sara use a video display terminal to communicate with this evil *thing* they're trying to understand:

After a moment's thought, she typed: PROVIDE A PHYSICAL DESCRIPTION OF YOURSELF.
I AM ALIVE.
BE MORE SPECIFIC, Sara directed.
I AM BY NATURE UNSPECIFIC.
ARE YOU HUMAN?
I ENCOMPASS THAT POSSIBILITY ALSO.
'It's just playing with us,' Jenny said. 'Amusing itself.'
Bryce wiped a hand over his face, 'Ask it what happened to Copperfield.'
WHERE IS GALEN COPPERFIELD?
DEAD.
WHERE IS HIS BODY?
GONE.
WHERE HAS IT GONE?
BORING BITCH.
WHERE ARE THE OTHERS WHO WERE WITH GALEN COPPERFIELD?
DEAD.   DID YOU KILL THEM?
YES.
WHY DID YOU KILL THEM?
YOU.
Sara tapped the keyboard: CLARIFY.
YOU ARE.
CLARIFY.
YOU ARE ALL DEAD.

Here again, we have a situation where Koontz uses a stylistic approach to keep the pace brisk and the tension tight. All the terminal display messages are done in capital letters, making them big and bold and quick to read. In addition, the answers Sara draws out of this *thing* are all short and direct. Often one-word responses that keep us moving rapidly down the page. The undercurrent of all this is a sense that this *thing* is a lightning-fast thinker and that the characters (and *we*, the readers) will need every bit of intelligence they've got to keep up.

He uses this same technique in this shortened scene from WATCHERS:

Travis leaned forward from the headboard. To Einstein, he said, 'Why is The Outsider looking for you?'
    HATES ME.
    'Why does it hate you?'
    DON'T KNOW.
    As Nora replaced the letters. Travis said. 'Will it continue looking for you?'
    YES. FOREVER.
    'But how does something like that move unseen?'
    AT NIGHT.
    'Nevertheless . . .'
    LIKE RATS MOVE UNSEEN.
    Looking puzzled. Nora said, 'But how does it track you?'
    FEELS ME.

In this scene, Einstein, a superintelligent dog, communicates with Travis and Nora by spelling out his responses using the tiles from a game of Scrabble. Again, the narrative is tight and fast-moving. The responses are brief, to the point, and highlighted by Koontz in capital letters. And again, we get that sense of an intelligence that is simply awesome.

Often in scenes that require intensity, Koontz will use short, hard-hitting dialogue similar to what we've seen him use in the above examples. It's an effective means for keeping the story moving along at a clip that's almost faster than the reader can keep up with. And there's an amazing subtlety that grows out of that approach, an undercurrent of emotional urgency that we *feel* rather than read.

Back to DARKFALL again. In the big scene we mentioned above, where Jack finally arrives at his apartment, he encounters the 'creatures.' This time, Koontz takes yet another stylistic approach in bringing the scene home. Let's take a look at it:

The creature was the size of a rat. In shape, at least, its body was rather like that of a rat, too: low-slung, long in the flanks, with shoulders and haunches that were large and muscular for an animal of its size. But there the resemblance to a rat ended, and the nightmare began. This thing was hairless. Its slippery skin was darkly mottled gray-green-yellow and looked more like slimy fungus than like flesh. The tail was not at all similar to a rat's tail: it was eight or ten inches long, an inch wide at the base, segmented in the manner of a scorpion's tail, tapering and curling up into the air above the beast's hindquarters, like that of a scorpion, although it wasn't equipped with a stinger. The feet were far different from the rat's feet: They were oversized by comparison to the animal itself: the long toes were triplejointed, gnarly; the curving claws were much too big for the feet to which they were fitted: a razor-sharp, multiple-barbed spur curved out from each heel. The head was even more deadly in appearance and design than were the feet: it was formed over a flattish skull that had many unnaturally sharp angles, unnecessary convexities and concavities, as if it had been molded by an inexpert sculptor. The snout was long and pointed, a bizarre cross between the muzzle of a wolf and that of a crocodile. The small monster opened its mouth and hissed, revealing too many pointed teeth that were angled in various directions along its jaws. A surprisingly long black tongue slithered out of the mouth, glistening like a strip of raw liver; the end of it was forked, and it fluttered continuously.

Koontz follows up this long, almost overly descriptive paragraph with another paragraph nearly as long and nearly as descriptive. And they're both sitting right smack dab in the middle of an action scene.

Why?

Well, first of all, it was made almost a necessity by the nature of the creatures. They were unique to his story. He couldn't simply refer to them as werewolves or vampires or mummies and have everyone feeling quite comfortable with a description that generic. These might have some semblance to a rat or a scorpion, and maybe a wolf or a crocodile, but they were none of these things. They were uniquely themselves. And they needed describing.

Second, and specifically in light of the tempo of the scene, it was a good opportunity to give readers a breather, while adding a little to the tension he had already built. In this case, by slowing things down and stretching out the scene, the tension is heightened. We want to know what's going to happen, but first we'll have to wait until we get over some of the preliminaries. Koontz has just finished carrying us through seven quickly cut scenes, and we know the climax of scene number eight is just a page or two away. But not just yet, he's saying. We'll have to wait until we can't stand it a minute longer.

PACING THE WEB

I don't just want to frighten people, but I want to make them laugh and weep and feel lonely and feel uplifted. I want to write *emotional* fiction that deeply involves readers and also happens to scare the daylights out of them.[4]

There's another contributing factor that Koontz integrates into his work as he develops a brisk tempo. It's the sense of *anticipation* he instills in the reader, that sense of having to know what comes next. Up to this point we've discussed his approach to beginnings, the way he uses his action scenes, even how he uses his style in manipulating the pace of his novels. All these factors contribute to that sense of anticipation he builds in his readers. But there's something else that comes into play here, and that's the way we *feel* about his characters.

Koontz reaches his readers through the characters he creates. It's Jennifer Paige and her sister Lisa, Dominick Corvaisis, Hilary Thomas, Harry Lyon, and Mary Bergen, whom we come to care about. They are the reasons we're concerned with what might happen next. It's as if we share some sort of racial understanding, some sort of basic veracity with them. They are as everyday as all of us. With everyday struggles in their relationships, with limitations, with strengths that are often uncovered only after they've been backed into a corner. Like people we all know. But Koontz places them in extraordinary situations and says, *Let's see what you can do with that, my friends*.

It's his characters who provide us the emotional link with his work.

We laugh and cry with them.

We fear for them.

Most of all, we worry for them. They are, for the space of a few hundred pages, our children. We worry that Jack Dawson, as strong as he is, won't be strong enough to defeat Lavelle. We worry that Colin Jacobs is just too innocent to survive a friendship with someone like Roy Borden. We even worry about the terrible childhood that created Bruno Frye. It's a big world out there. Sometimes a nasty world. And they are so innocent, these children of ours. If anyone's going to get into trouble, we already know it will be them.

So we worry.

And Koontz takes up that concern of ours and turns it to his advantage.

He makes us sick with anticipation. And anticipation is as much responsible for the eagerness with which readers attack his novels as anything else. We tear through his pages because we have to know if Slim MacKenzie is alone in his battle, if he will ever have a chance to survive against the goblins. And we have to know *now*!

CHANGING THE PACE

I'm being guided by the belief that a thriller does not have to be just thrilling or just scary, but can also be at times funny, touching, melancholy, uplifting, and even intellectually exhilarating.[5]

Throughout his career, Dean Koontz has written everything from romance to science fiction, from humor to suspense. At the time of this writing, his novel SHADOWFIRES (originally published under the pen name of Leigh Nichols) has been on the *Publishers Weekly* Paperback Bestseller List for seven weeks. DRAGON TEARS has just dropped off the Hardback Bestseller List after a lengthy stay. And MR MURDER, due out in a few short months, is sure to remain seated on the list for the longest stay of any Koontz novel yet.

None of this success is by accident.

Koontz is the consummate professional. He has worked long and hard. He has earned his success. And in the process, he has learned his craft well, certainly as well or better than the most successful of his contemporaries.

This is the way it happened.

That's what Dean Koontz will tell you. Then he'll sit you down at that campfire on a warm July night, and he'll spin you a tale using everything he's learned in his profession. And it'll be funny and scary, sad and true, all at the same time. And you probably won't even notice the pace it sets, because that is one of the many things he does so well it becomes nearly invisible. But the story will breeze along anyway. It will go places you never expected it to go, introduce you to people that fascinate you. And most important, it will present you with stark truths. Because that's what Dean Koontz does: He tells us the starkest of truths, and he does it such a way that we can't stop turning the pages.

This is the way if happened.

Bibliography

The Face of Fear. New York: Bobbs-Merrill, 1977; London: Headline, 1989.
The Vision. New York: Putnam, 1977; London: Headline, 1990.
The Voice of the Night. New York: Doubleday, 1980; London: Headline, 1990.
Whispers. New York: Putnam, 1980; London: Headline, 1990.
How To Write Best Selling Fiction. Writer's Digest Books, 1981; London: Popular Press, 1991.
Phantoms. New York: Putnam, 1983; London: Headline, 1990.
Darkfall. London: W.H. Allen & Company, 1984; New York: Berkley, 1984; London: Headline, 1990.
Bill Munster's Footsteps 6. New York, December, 1985.
Strangers. New York: Putnam, 1986; London: Headline, 1990.
The Horror Show. California: Phantasm Press, Summer 1986.
Watchers. New York: Putnam, 1987; London: Headline, 1987.
The Bad Place. New York: Putnam, 1990; London: Headline, 1990.
Hideaway. New York: Putnam, 1992; London: Headline, 1992.
Dragon Tears. New York, Putnam, 1993; London: Headline, 1993.

Notes

1. *Bill Munster's Footsteps 6*. New York: December 1985.
2. *How To Write Best Selling Fiction*. Cincinnati: Writer's Digest Books, 1981, p. 131.
3. *ibid.*, p. 132.
4. *The Horror Show*. California: Phantasm Press, Summer 1986.
5. Interview with Ed Gorman, Mystery Scene, 1987.

PART III

The Heart of the Ticktock Man

by Charles de Lint

'Ticktock' was the working title for Dean Koontz's novel DRAGON TEARS before he acquiesced to his publisher's request and allowed the change. Derived from the name of its memorable villain, one can see why Koontz chose the original title, but 'Ticktock' was also effective on another level, serving as a subtle reminder of 'the ticking clock' that is the driving force behind suspense fiction.

Most suspense novels work within a specific, limited time frame; the protagonists have only so much time in which to deal with their problem – often, simply to survive. The ensuing tension, obviously enough, is what drives the story onward and makes it a 'page-turner.'

Koontz is a master of the ticking clock, but if that were all, it's unlikely that his novels would keep topping the bestseller lists, or that his older books would be constantly reprinted simply to keep up with the demands of his readers.

'I've always been in love with the potential for poetry in language,' Koontz said in a recent interview. 'The image that creates a more detailed picture in your mind, involves all the senses, and stirs emotions.'[1]

This deceptively simple statement might well be the key to understanding Koontz's current popularity and success. He is one of the few authors currently working in the suspense field whose writing is consistently literate, yet that aspect of his fiction never sets a barrier between the reader and the action taking place on stage.

Prose such as his, which moves the story forward without awkwardness or delay yet can still be appreciated for its lyricism and insight, is rarer than one might assume – especially, it sometimes seems, among those titles that do make it on to the bestseller lists. We'll read Tom Robbins or Barbara Kingsolver for the richness of their descriptive ability and their insights into character and social mores, but their books aren't page-turners. Conversely, many of the thrillers that make the lists are wonderful entertainments, but lack depth once the reader has devoured the story line and returns to examine the author's style and the book's subtext and internal resonance – the information encoded between the lines.

A Koontz novel, however, can be read on different levels, each level adding to the next while it remains appealing on its own. The reader eager for a suspenseful thriller will come away from a novel such as COLD FIRE (1991) satisfied with the fierce, headlong thrust of the plot and the cornucopia of twists and surprises that pulls the story along. Others will delve a bit deeper and be intrigued by how the book asks as many questions about the human condition as it answers, which, in turn, will have them examining the dualities and paradoxes inherent in their own lives. Still more will return to simply savor the language, the deft flow of the words as they bring characters and settings to life.

Koontz has a knack for using just the right word or phrase, but it's not a gift – or at least not merely a gift; what seems so effortlessly called up by the time his readers get to see the final published form is due to a hard-earned craftsmanship that can only come from long hours at the keyboard.

There is another unique aspect to Koontz's work, one that deals with his choice of subject matter and his calm disregard for the 'rules' of genre fiction, but before we explore that, let's backtrack for a moment and take a look at the man behind the fiction.

* * *

Dean Ray Koontz was born July 9, 1945, in Everett, Pennsylvania, and raised in nearby Bedford – a pretty town in a scenic area . . . but it's the kind of place that gives you the feeling that in a few cellars or attics, hidden from view, are things strange enough for any tale by H. P. Lovecraft.[2] His family was exceedingly poor because his father was 'a womanizer who spent more on his girlfriends than on his family, a gambler and an alcoholic given to fits of violence. Though my mother was a jewel, my father was such an unpredictable and frightening figure that most of my childhood and adolescence was a nightmare.'

It wasn't until he completed WHISPERS (1980) that he was able to confront, talk about, and accept what he'd been through as a child. 'After writing WHISPERS, in which virtually every character had an ugly childhood, I was physically and emotionally exhausted. And it was only months later that I realized that through the surrogates of fictional people, I was at last untying my own psychological knots related to my childhood.'

Koontz's use of writing as a form of catharsis – of championing good over evil, if only in a fictional context – as well as using it as a way of directing attention to the very real problems that confront us every day, might date to when he was still in college and won an *Atlantic Monthly* magazine fiction contest with a short story about a little girl who drowns her new sibling.

He met his wife, Gerda, when he was a senior in high school and she was a junior, and they married three and a half years later, when he finished college. All they had was $300, a used car, and the clothes on their back.

He worked as a counselor in the Appalachian Poverty Program for a year, writing at night, but left when he realized 'that government attempts to alleviate poverty are inevitably doomed to corruption and failure.' Following that, he taught school for a year and a half, quitting to write full-time after Gerda offered to support him for five years. 'If you can't make it in five years,' she told him quite rightly, 'you never will.'

Five years later Koontz's career was going well enough that Gerda was able to quit her job and work for her husband handling all the business details of a novelist, making it possible for Koontz to concentrate completely on his writing. They moved to Las Vegas, 'seeking sun and warmth. We found the sun and warmth, of course, but the sun was 120 degrees day after day during the summer and we also found scorpions.'

In 1976 they relocated to the city of Orange in southern California, then in 1991 to Newport Beach, where they still live today in a large, comfortable house with a view of the Pacific. On a clear day, they can see Los Angeles, fifty miles to the north. Closer to home, in Koontz's office a visitor can see the many shelves of his published works, original artwork from some of the covers of his books, and his collection of Chinese vases. It might seem an odd mix, but Koontz thrives on diversity. Diversity is also one of the reasons he lives in this part of California, which has provided the setting for so many of his novels.

'We're living on ground that is unstable, and all of us know that unconsciously,' he says. 'The result is that we tend to be more adventurous and trend-seeking. The feeling that nothing lasts forever comes directly from living in earthquake country. People from very different economic strata mix with a sort of casualness. There's a fluidity in the social strata here.'[3]

The road from childhood poverty to his present home, and book advances that are now in the seven-figure range, was not an easy one. It took many years of hard work and a rigorous writing schedule to which he adheres to this day. 'I get up around 7:30,' he explains, 'do two hours of weightlifting or other exercise, shower, and get to work by ten o'clock. I remain at the word processor until about 7:30 or 8:00 at night, unless we have some engagement, which means about ten hours a day, seven days a week. I take lunch at my desk, working as I eat.'

But after more than a decade of this schedule, Koontz is finally nearing a time when 'I will be able to take weekends off, though I expect I'll still work ten hours a day each weekday. Coming from such a poor background, I've been driven. There's an old saying, "Once poor, never rich," and it's true. You're always looking over your shoulder, expecting the wolf, regardless of how much money you've made.'

Two things kept him going during the hard times. First and foremost was the loving support of his wife, Gerda. 'After more than twenty years of marriage, we are mutually supportive and have found a degree of harmony in our relationship and closeness for which I am indescribably thankful every day of my life. In a letter to me, John D. MacDonald once said that the most important factor in a successful writing career of great duration was the writer's spouse: "If the marriage isn't very, very good," he said, "then the work is going to suffer, and the writer is never going to fulfill his potential." He was married to the same woman for nearly fifty years before death took him,' Koontz adds, 'and he knew whereof he spoke.'

Needless to say, Koontz's relationship with his wife is very close. 'Recently,' he says by way of example, 'when Gerda went back east to visit her family, we were apart for a week, the first time we had been apart in considerably more than a decade, and I almost went nuts. It was depressing, so difficult not to be able to see her or talk to her repeatedly throughout the day that I began to have nightmares about her plane crashing on the way home and *never* having her around again. I was never so glad about anything as I was about seeing her plane touch down at LAX!'

The second factor to see him through the hard times was Koontz's inborn optimism. 'Now, I'm no Pollyanna,' he explains. 'I haven't forgotten that some of us are vicious sons of bitches, and I certainly haven't forgotten that we all die. But I've been an optimist all my life

– I had to be to get through my childhood. I've always had a strong belief in the basic goodness of most people and in humankind's potential for growth, progress, and eventual transcendence.'

This sense of optimism is reflected strongly in his novels such as WATCHERS (1987) and THE BAD PLACE (1990), but it wasn't always so. 'One of the reasons my fiction had a grim edge to it for so long was that I felt a certain somberness was essential to a thriller . . . simply because that was how everyone wrote thrillers. But every so often, humor would creep into one of my suspense novels and readers would react with more enthusiasm than ever. And book by book, as I did more work in characterization and made my lead characters more complex and appealing and less . . . well, *noir*, both readers and critics responded well.'

Finally, starting with STRANGERS (1986), Koontz decided that 'a tale could be filled with warmth, humor and optimism, and *still* be excruciatingly suspenseful. Many writers have the misguided notion that good writing, *realistic* writing, is to one degree or another misanthropic, melancholy – if not downright bleak – and relentlessly tough. This leads to bookstore shelves full of hardboiled fiction that's really nothing more than empty cynicism, and that in fact does *not* accurately portray real life.'

Allowing his optimism and humor to have a role in his work equal to the darker elements has gotten him better reviews than ever before, a much wider readership, and a reputation beyond narrow genre lines. But Koontz has never written simply for the money or good reviews. 'I write,' he says, 'because I take immense pleasure in storytelling.'

Commenting on how some reviewers have referred to his work from STRANGERS on as 'Dickensian,' he adds, 'My *intention* is to write thrillers that are also rich in details of time, place, culture, and the people formed by those environmental factors. Some people just don't get it at all and damn me for not being *single-mindedly* horrific. I don't care about that. I'm not writing for the hardcore spook set, and I'm not writing for posterity; I'm writing for *me* and for people who like to read tales that are unlike other tales, that keep them guessing and in a state of constant surprise. Whether I succeed at that or not is up to the reader to judge, but I sure have fun trying.'

His love of the written word and for his characters shows in every book he writes, no matter what the byline. And there have been quite a few pseudonyms. He has written suspense novels as Brian Coffey,

K. R. Dwyer, and Richard Paige; both horror and suspense novels as Leigh Nichols and Owen West; and a science fiction novel as Aaron Wolfe. Many of these novels are now appearing in new editions under the Koontz byline.

The last pseudonym to go was that of Leigh Nichols, whose books, at one time, outsold those issued under Koontz's own name.

'I put the same effort into a Nichols novel as a Koontz,' he explains, 'but the plan was to do something different under the Nichols name from what I would be doing in the future under my own. I hoped to continue writing horror-oriented novels under the Nichols name even as I concentrated on more ambitious work under my own byline, thus avoiding confusing readers. Unfortunately, Avon blew my cover, expressly advertising that Nichols was, in fact, Koontz. Suddenly it didn't make sense any more to use a pen name.'

Koontz still regrets the use of his pen names. 'Sometimes there are legitimate reasons for using pseudonyms,' he explains. 'If your publisher wants you to have only one book a year under your name, yet you have the ability to write two, you might need a pen name. But I also used them for the wrong reasons, because of bad advice. I wrote in a wide range of genres, and I experimented with style, so I was told that every time I did something different from what I'd done before I had to use a different name in order not to alienate or confuse the reader.

'After a while I figured out this wasn't true; readers will stay with an author, no matter what the variations in style and genre, as long as they get that strong sense of story, of character, of empathetic involvement that the work provides when it's functioning at its best. I've learned that readers appreciate a writer who will risk fresh approaches, book after book – as long as the stretch the writer is making actually works.'

The success that Koontz has found in the past few years might almost seem to have been orchestrated, the upward progression has been so smooth. Not so, Koontz replies. 'I've set goals for improved craftsmanship and have consciously tried to move to steadily more challenging books. If you keep pushing yourself into new territory, better characterization, a sharper style, pretty soon your readership grows, the books sell better and better, and it looks as if you've been enormously canny in a business sense. But it's only a result of trying to be a better craftsman.'

Which is not to say that Koontz ignores the business side of his career. 'I've always been aware that writing is not only an art and not only a craft, but a business. Some writers refuse to learn the business of publishing – they consider it beneath them – and almost without exception they get eaten alive because they're surrendering the fundamental control of their lives.'

Long-time readers will remember that Koontz began as a science fiction writer. When asked about the switch in his career he explains: 'I write what I'm driven to write at any one time. I have to write what interests *me* if it's got any hope of interesting readers. I left science fiction in part because it was a low-paying field, in part because the only critical attention one receives in that field is from the fan critics, who seldom have much insight. But primarily I left because I grew bored with sf and wanted to write something a lot more challenging.'

Koontz may have departed the sf field to avoid being limited by all that the perception of being a genre writer entails, but in some ways he's never left at all. His current popularity might be based upon his highly successful suspense novels, but part of what gives them their drive and vision are elements that he retains from his days as a science fiction writer.

By this I don't mean the impression that many still carry of the sf field. Bug-eyed monsters, cardboard characters, extrapolations of scientific speculation that are delivered in a lecturing tone – these are the lowest common denominators by which the field is too often judged. Koontz's careful prose, realistically portrayed characters, and riveting plots are a far cry from such material, distanced as much from it as a Robertson Davies novel is from one by Danielle Steele.

What Koontz did retain from his early work is the sense of wonder that drives science fiction, the seductive 'what if?' that takes one singular element and then extrapolates its far-reaching effects.

His novels remain very contemporary – not for him far futures or distant galaxies – and their underlying themes explore relationships of human beings – with one another and with their environment, be it technological or the natural world. The novels' entertainment value comes from Koontz's gift for suspense and from the fact that he's taken time to create characters that readers can truly care about and become vitally concerned for, when these same characters are placed in dangerous situations.

Those situations exist because of the novels' sf elements. STRANGERS was an alien-first-contact novel. WATCHERS dealt with genetic engineering run amuck. LIGHTNING (1988) explored an entirely fresh perspective on time travel. MIDNIGHT (1989) dealt with the uncomfortable blend of man with machine. THE BAD PLACE investigated the phenomena of teleportation; COLD FIRE, precognitive abilities.

In each case the sf element is handled with great care. There are no mumbo-jumbo explanations, no long-winded treatises. Within the fictional confines of the novel, the singular element is always integrated both logically and plausibly into the storyline.

But publishers like to find easily recognizable slots for their authors. After breaking free of the perception that he was an sf writer, Koontz found himself saddled with yet another limiting genre designation for his work; this time, no doubt because of the rising popularity of writers such as Stephen King and the general bandwagon effect that occurs when publishers view such a phenomenon, Koontz found himself considered as a horror writer.

He has written horror, of course, but he has also written so much else. In fact, one of his principal strengths is that his work, with its heady mix of genres, can only be classified as 'by Dean Koontz.' Besides his fascinating hybrid take on suspense, he's written 'a comic novel – HANGING ON (1973) – and only two that I would classify as horror novels – DARKFALL (1984) and PHANTOMS (1983).' Now he writes what he calls 'genre-bridgers with a mainstream point of view.'

The attempts through the eighties to classify him as a horror writer caused a struggle that he has only recently won. Koontz was long frustrated by the packaging of his books but now they have a much more mainstream look to them. 'I was determined that this would happen, not merely because I hated the inaccuracy and the associations of the horror-genre label, but because I think I could otherwise never have reached the people who, hating horror, would turn away from the books without giving them a chance.'

The only genre niche into which he can comfortably be placed is what Stephen King calls that of the 'Brand Name author.' Koontz's novels resemble each other, but only in terms of their polished style, their edge-of-the-seat suspense, and their author's individual worldview.

'I guess I just have a slightly different – call it cock-eyed – way of looking at things,' he explains, 'and my view of life informs the work. A critic once said that only I could have created a character like Vince Nasco in WATCHERS, a psychopathic killer who is simultaneously terrifying and a comic figure *and* curiously pathetic. I don't know. But that's the way I see life: Everything's curiously blended, the comic and the tragic, the wondrous and the mundane, terror and joy, and it's all more interesting to write about – and read about – if you can capture – or at least hint at – the emotionally kaleidoscopic nature of human existence.'

After two decades of concentrating on novels, Koontz began to make inroads into short fiction in the mid-eighties. 'Short stories are fun,' he says, 'because you can see the horizon when you start on them, whereas with a novel you're labouring endlessly before you can see the end. The craftsman's reward of seeing a job well done comes much sooner with a short story, so I like doing them. But I am primarily a novelist, and the amount of time I can devote to short material is limited.'

With over twenty-five years in the business, Koontz has had his fair share of experiences with editors, both good and bad. 'Good editors listen,' he says. 'Good editors don't feel obligated to suggest changes merely because they think they have to do so to earn their salaries; they're content, in some cases, to let fine writing go unaltered for chapter after chapter. Good editors are willing to speak frankly about a writer's work even after he has become a bestseller and a valuable asset to the publisher; too often, lesser editors clam up and offer no input to successful writers for fear of alienating them. The worst habit of a bad editor is rewriting or cutting without the writer's permission.'

His single advice to young writers is to keep writing. 'I see too many young writers spending too little time at the keyboard yet expecting the Big Break. It only comes with work. The second worst mistake is envy. I hear writers wasting vast amounts of energy bemoaning the success of others.'

When asked about influences on his writing, Koontz only mentions one name. 'John D. MacDonald was a tremendous influence on me. He was a brilliant writer. The McGee series is terrific, but about forty of the earlier books are so stunning that they eclipse the McGee series. When I read something like *Slam the Big Door*, *Cry Hard Cry Fast*, *The Damned* or *The End of the Night*, I usually turn to the last page, thinking, "Okay, Koontz, face it, you don't belong in the same craft as this man; go learn plumbing, Koontz; get yourself an honest trade!"'[4]

Happily, Koontz manages to put his humility aside long enough to continue to produce his work. In fact, what's difficult is getting him away from it. 'I don't want to sound like Shirley MacLaine,' he has said, 'but it's almost as if story ideas are beamed to me. I can sit down for fifteen minutes and come up with a dozen ideas. A lot of writers fall into this the-muse-has-left-me thinking and walk away from their work. I find that the muse never leaves me. I have to shove her out.'[5]

* * *

With over fifty novels under his belt, there's simply not enough room in a piece this short to take more than a quick overview of Koontz's work, and so we will concentrate particularly on the post-STRANGERS books – though we won't entirely ignore what went before. The interesting thing in looking back at the earlier novels, even to some of the science fiction such as DARK OF THE WOODS (1970) and TIME THIEVES (1972), is that we can see that all the elements that have made Koontz such a success today are already in place, albeit in a somewhat rougher form.

Almost twenty years later, novels such as DEMON SEED (1973) and INVASION (1975) are still hard to put down. The stories rocket along, the suspense never lets up, the dialogue and characters are contemporary and recognizably down-to-earth, regardless of their *outré* settings. And while Koontz has not allowed any of the sf novels to be reprinted as yet[6], this same intensity can also be found in the early thrillers, many of which have only recently been published under his own name.

THE VOICE OF THE NIGHT (1980) may well be the best of these, an excruciatingly tense story of the classic nerd who revels in his unexpected friendship with the most popular boy in town – until he learns his new friend's secret. The unknowing descent into darkness makes for fascinating reading – perhaps because while we'll say aloud that it would never happen to us, inside we know that it's all too possible. It only takes the wrong person to become interested in us – for whatever reason.

CHASE (1972), in which a troubled Vietnam vet trying to withdraw from the world is forced to match wits with a psychopath, ranks among Koontz's better work as well. It, too, deals with a descent into darkness, but here many of the demons lie within, and the confrontation with evil serves as a catalyst for the protagonist to rejoin the normal world, rather than something that forces him away from it.

Beyond the unmistakable stamp of Koontz's style, there is something for everyone in these early books. There are the caper novels BLOOD RISK (1973) and SURROUNDED (1974) featuring art dealer and professional thief, Mike Tucker; spy novels such as DRAGONFLY (1975); suspense, from the manic stalker in THE FACE OF FEAR (1977) to the unsettling chase sequences in SHATTERED (1973); and even outright horror as in PHANTOMS – easily one of Koontz's most disturbing novels with an opening sequence that still gives me chills just thinking about it.

By the time the 'Leigh Nichols' novels began to be published, Koontz's style was maturing to the point where a break-out bestseller was only a matter of time. Five Nichols titles appeared: The international thriller THE KEY TO MIDNIGHT (1979), with Koontz's take on mind control; THE EYES OF DARKNESS (1981), in which a woman's deceased toddler appears to have come back from the dead; the medical thriller THE HOUSE OF THUNDER (1982), which uses the old stand-by of a protagonist with amnesia to great effect; THE SERVANTS OF TWILIGHT (1984), in which a woman is hounded by religious fanatics who think her son is the Antichrist; and SHADOWFIRES (1987), which explores another aspect of the genetic experimentation that made WATCHERS so successful.

One might add to those five THE DOOR TO DECEMBER (1985), which appeared in North America under the Richard Paige byline, but was credited to Leigh Nichols in England. While it, too, explores scientific experimentation gone awry, readers shouldn't assume that Koontz has an antiscience bent. In THE DOOR TO DECEMBER, as he does in so many of his novels, he is merely providing a cautionary voice for a world in which scientific research is glorified by those who hold that anything new is better and those who believe that all science is evil.

'What the future holds is amazing,' he has said. 'I want people to have a sense of uplift and wonder, yet learn to live with the threat of science. No matter how dark it gets, we can handle it.'[7]

But if we don't think we can, Koontz's characters are certainly capable of taking up the slack and showing by example. STRANGERS was the book that first brought this message to the huge audiences his novels now command.

As the book opens, we meet various unrelated strangers across the United States who, over a four-month period, have been subjected to nightmares that lead them into acquiring bizarre phobias. One by one, they discover that these changes to their personalities relate back to a forgotten weekend, two years past – the memory of which has been wiped from their minds. It isn't until they begin to investigate just what happened during those two days that they become aware of a vast conspiracy that will stop at nothing to keep them from remembering.

The canvas for STRANGERS is large, as is the cast, but the book is tightly plotted and one never loses track of who's who in the mix of well-delineated characters. And while the novel has some of the trappings of a horror novel in the tension and mystery of its plot line, it could be better described as a thriller with a truly uplifting conclusion that proves to be neither cloying nor false.

STRANGERS was followed in 1987 by what many still consider to be Koontz's best book: WATCHERS. This is the one where it all really came together; in fact, WATCHERS is the novel in which Koontz truly created his own successful hybrid of suspense novel and character study.

Here we meet Travis Cornell, a depressed widower, and Nora Devon, a reclusive young woman who has spent her entire life in the shadow of her spinster aunt, and see how they get a new lease on life through the dog Einstein that Cornell finds while out hiking in the eastern hills and canyons of Orange County, California. Unfortunately, the dog has run off from a government-operated genetic laboratory at the same time that a murderous creature known only as The Outsider has escaped. Federal agents are in pursuit of both; as is a psychotic hitman. Cornell and Devon flee with Einstein, pursued by the government agents, the hitman, and The Outsider.

This could easily have been played as a simple thriller, but Koontz opted to explore deeper levels of what is still a very exciting story line, and it's these deeper levels that lift WATCHERS head and shoulders above standard thrillers. Loyalties are explored, and the question as to what exactly constitutes humanity. Koontz's characterization, even in secondary characters, is spot on, and his rich stylistic voice propels the story with a grace rarely found in such a novel. But beyond the tension and suspense, what sets this novel apart is its warmth and caring spirit, the humor and strong sense of optimism that merge so successfully in this novel. Koontz's audience certainly agreed.

'I've been overwhelmed by calls and letters from readers,' Koontz says in respect to WATCHERS, 'telling me they never before read a book that had them laughing and crying and on the edge of their seats from one page to the next, sometimes all on the same page. That was the effect I was after. I wanted not only to scare and intrigue but grab hold of the reader and shake out every conceivable emotional reaction.'

With typical self-depreciating humour he adds, 'One librarian told me that my books are popular with old ladies and hulking longshoremen. I assumed she meant that my audience was broad. You don't think she meant that my books appeal only to old ladies who *are* hulking longshoremen, do you?'

TWILIGHT EYES (1987) came next, but the novel generally associated with that title is in fact an expansion of an earlier book with the same name, published in 1985 by the specialty publisher, The Land of Enchantment. Handsomely produced, with many stunning illustrations by Phil Parks (originals of which can be found hanging in Koontz's home), it was Koontz's first foray into contemporary fantasy.

Slim MacKenzie has 'twilight eyes' – a physical manifestation of his precognitive gift and his ability to see the goblins that live side by side with us, disguised as humans. A fugitive from the law for killing his uncle – a goblin only he could see – he finds sanctuary in a carnival in the early sixties. Enamoured with the carnie Rya Raines, and making a place for himself with new friends, MacKenzie soon discovers that his sanctuary has its own secrets and that the goblins are planning a concentrated assault on the carnival as it sets up for business in the grim town of Yontsdown.

The carnival setting comes from Koontz's long interest in that milieu, one that he originally planned to use for a mainstream novel. 'There's a fascinating, secret world behind the gaudy midway,' he says, explaining his interest, 'and it is a society of fierce individualists who accept one another on their own terms – or at least that was the way it was in the days when carnivals were much bigger and more popular than they have been during the past decade or two.'

The longer version came about because 'when I finished that 120,000 word tale which appeared in the illustrated collector's edition, I wanted to know what happened to the characters next, so in time I was compelled to return to the story and write a sequel of 80,000 words. The sequel does not stand on its own but relies on the first part, so in a sense they form a new, complete novel together.'

The original short novel was a change of pace for Koontz beyond its subject matter. While it's certainly a thriller, he chose to tell the story with a dense prose style – full of description and with many asides – and in the first person. The second half moves much more quickly; the prose is leaner, and the story is much more action-oriented. But happily, the two styles merge admirably. It makes sense that as events grow more frantic, so too would the storytelling pace.

The same year also saw the closest Koontz has come to a short story collection thus far in his career.[8] Three novelets – 'Miss Attila the Hun,' 'Hardshell,' and 'Twilight of the Dawn' – were collected in Dark Harvest's *Night Visions 4*, with the last being particularly outstanding, mostly because of the theological introspection of the protagonist.

When asked if the story reflected some of his personal beliefs, Koontz replied, 'I think it did. The character probably reflects me to some extent because I went through a period of "agnosticism to atheism to agnosticism." I don't hew closely to any particular faith, probably closer to Catholicism than anything.

'I did move completely away from atheism, and strangely enough it was because of . . . a lot of the science reading I did, especially physics reading. The idea of a completely chaotic universe formed totally at random was less and less tenable.'[9]

1988 saw another pair of dissimilar books appearing under Koontz's byline. LIGHTNING was the expected follow-up to WATCHERS, another taut thriller incorporating Koontz's special mix of humor, suspense, and a love for humanity's quirks, strengths, and weaknesses. In it we met Laura Shane, a young girl with an apparently ageless guardian angel who comes out of nowhere at various times in her life to help her in moments of great danger.

Here Koontz presented his take on time travel, exploring it from a perspective that no one had used before. As the story progresses, Shane grows from child to young woman and the question that drives the plot is, what happens when the angel needs help from her?

Twenty pages into the novel, Koontz has what other authors would make the climax of a book, but he just keeps rollercoasting along, the plot as tightly wound as a coiled spring. The narrative technique he uses in certain sections – juxtaposing present action with flashbacks – actually maintains the book's impetus, rather than slowing it down. And even more impressively he pulled off the supposedly impossible: A suspense novel that takes place over a period of thirty years.

'Nobody, to my knowledge,' he says, 'had ever written a suspense novel that took place over such a long period of time. To follow a lead character through thirty-some years of her life, and to condense periods of her life into interesting vignettes that keep the story plunging ahead and yet paint her growth as a person, was a challenge that I really wanted to tackle.'[10]

But while the suspense played out over a long period of years and the insights into time travel are what appear to be what LIGHTNING is all about, for my money it's the friendship between Shane and her childhood friend Thelma Ackerson that gives this novel its true heart. The warmth and humor with which Koontz conveys their relationship would be enough to make a wonderful story all on its own.

1988's second novel was the profusely-illustrated ODDKINS – and this one really came from out of left field, even for a writer as diverse in subject matter as Koontz has proved to be. Teamed up with Phil Parks again, in ODDKINS Koontz wrote the quintessential children's novel, featuring the adventures of a motley crew of plush toys as they set out on a quest to save children from the 'bad toys' that are rising up at the devil's call upon the death of a good toymaker.

ODDKINS is warmly told and a delightful romp of a story, but it's not without its dark side, something that Koontz deliberately explored.

'Darkness is important in a children's book,' he says. 'They know people die, that painful things happen. Bad, spooky, terrible things. But ODDKINS assures them that it will be all right in the end. I don't think that's a false message, either. It's an accurate view. At times, evil is ascendant – in the long haul good triumphs. I write to convey the message – for children and adults alike – that the *struggle* is worthwhile.'[11]

In MIDNIGHT, published the following year, Koontz returned to his own special blend of compassion and suspense. It's also the novel in which I learned never to trust him again.

As with most thrillers, MIDNIGHT opens with a character in peril. In just a few paragraphs Janice Capshaw becomes someone we can identify with and so, while we know she's in trouble, we're expecting to follow her struggle to survive through the course of the novel. Except she dies at the end of the first chapter, bringing home the sad fact that not only is no one safe in real life, but they're not safe in a Koontz novel, either. From that point on I realized that anyone could die in one of his books – which irrevocably put to rest a certain level of complacency I had acquired in relation to Koontz's work: Sure, the characters are in trouble, but they'll pull through. Don't count on it.

The real protagonists are Capshaw's sister, Tessa Lockland, and an undercover federal agent named Sam Booker who's been sent to the northern California town of Moonlight Cove to investigate a series of mysterious deaths. What they find is a terrifying menace that has its genesis in an uncomfortable blend of man with machine: Silicon microspheres that can be injected into the human body, there to link up and form a computer that actually overrides the brain in the interest of 'improving' the species.

'I wrote MIDNIGHT,' Koontz explains, 'as a retelling of *The Island of Dr Moreau* – the arrogance of the scientist who is swept away by his vision, rendering him oblivious to human pain. I don't believe in restricting research, but the potential for horrible development is stunning.'[12]

But MIDNIGHT isn't simply a cautionary tale. Like the best of Koontz's work, it operates on many levels, from its suspenseful plot and exploration of science run amuck, through to the strong element of romance that is inevitably present.

'There will always be a love story in my books,' he says, 'because the most interesting way to bring out human relationships is through love. My characters reveal more of themselves because people do that when they're in love.'[13]

The next novel, 1990's THE BAD PLACE, opened with a favorite fictional premise: Frank Pollard knows nothing of himself except that someone is trying to kill him. It's a fascinating way to kick off a book and has been used in everything from Robert Ludlum's thrillers to Roger Zelazny's 'Amber' sf series.

The danger of this kind of a plot is that, once we find out what's really going on, we're often left with a sense of disappointment. The *mystery* itself is usually more interesting than the solution. In recent books, only George Chesbro's *Bone* comes to mind as a story where the solution matches the puzzle to the reader's complete satisfaction.

Koontz avoids this pitfall in two ways. The first is that he's written THE BAD PLACE from a multiple-viewpoint perspective so that the large cast of interesting characters helps to sidestep any potential disappointment. The second is that his answer to the mystery is, like Chesbro's, completely satisfying.

The sheer *weirdness* that ensues in parts of THE BAD PLACE when Pollard shows an ability to teleport and we're introduced to his bizarre family is offset by the very real relationship between the husband-and-wife PI team of Bobby and Julie Dakota and Koontz's wonderful portrayal of the latter's brother, Thomas. Thomas has Down's syndrome and the challenge Koontz undertook with him was to write scenes from his point of view. His success in doing so gives THE BAD PLACE some of its most joyous scenes and also provides its most poignant.

If LIGHTNING broke suspense fiction's 'time frame' rule, then 1991's COLD FIRE broke another in that the protagonist and villain turn out to be the same man.

'You should have seen the confusion in Hollywood when we marketed film rights to *Cold Fire*,' Koontz says. 'Producers would blink at us with bovine stupidity and say, "Jim Ironheart's terrorizing himself ... he's his own enemy ... I don't get this." The concept eluded them – as if in real life most of us aren't our own worst enemies. Of course, we are. But they all wanted to see *real* aliens in the pond, real bug-eyed monsters with real saliva pouring off their fangs.'[14]

Koontz has much more respect for his readers, because they have proved that they are willing, even eager, to explore stories with deeper intentions, rather than those which simply pull a boogieman out of a hat. He also understands the limitations of the film media.

'If you've written a book about a haunted house and the terrible things that happen to people in it,' he goes on to explain, 'or about a haunted car or haunted doll or haunted Nintendo player, Hollywood can translate that to film with a reasonable rate of success. But as soon as your haunted house story has a complicated subtext, a densely woven thematic web, the likelihood of a successful film declines drastically, because then plot and theme are inextricably entwined, and film is such a surface medium that it can rarely portray the writer's deeper intentions.

'If you *had* no deeper intentions, the plot will translate well; but if lots of stuff is going on under the surface of the novel and none of it gets translated to the screen, the plot alone will not sustain the film because it was not what sustained the novel, either.'[15]

COLD FIRE tells of a man who has premonitions of violent deaths and follows them up by rescuing the individual, sometimes traveling clear across the country to do so. Each of the people he rescues will go on to make great advances for mankind. He prefers to remain anonymous, but a reporter makes the connection between a number of his miraculous rescues and tracks him down, only to find herself wanting to help him in his mission, rather than telling his story.

For Jim Ironheart, a retired schoolteacher, the visions that come to him also bring nightmares that hint at the approach of something he knows only as the Enemy. He's not certain what the Enemy is, nor why he has been chosen to confront it, but he knows that sooner or later it will be coming for him.

As in the best mystery novels, the resolution of COLD FIRE is both innovative and unexpected, yet entirely appropriate when one looks back and can understand the clues that Koontz has scattered throughout the text on the way to the climax.

COLD FIRE was followed by HIDEAWAY (1992), which has the fairly new science of resuscitation medicine as its jumping-off point. In it we meet Hatch Harrison, who is brought back to life by a medical team after his life signs have been flat-lined for an hour. Naturally Harrison and his wife are delighted at his being given a second chance at life. But Harrison isn't the first to benefit from this new procedure, and we soon learn that he has developed a mental connection with the mind of a previous success – Vassago, a man who happens to be a sociopathic killer.

As is usual with Koontz's books, the questions raised in the subtext are as fascinating as the story itself. We can consider not only the pros and cons of resuscitation medicine, but also the all-too real question of evil itself.

'In HIDEAWAY,' Koontz says, 'evil can be traced to three sources: Human behavior; the transmittal of sociopathic behavior through damaged genes, which is the most terrifying because it is the most arbitrary and relentless; and possibly to Evil as a supernatural force'![16]

Koontz leaves it open to his readers to decide if HIDEAWAY is a supernatural story or not. Everything in it could be explained in a logical fashion, requiring only one small element of the fantastic.

'If you accept that Vassago acquired psychic power due to brain damage suffered before he was resuscitated by his father, Dr Nyebern, and that he links up with Hatch because they are both beneficiaries of his father's genius, then you could read the rest of the story as merely the imposition of Vassago's religious fantasies on Hatch through telepathic transmission.'[17]

1993's DRAGON TEARS presents yet another stretch for Koontz.

The basic story can be boiled down in a few sentences: Harry Lyon and Connie Gulliver, members of a Laguna Beach-based Special Projects team drawn from various police departments, start their day gunning down a psychotic killer in a restaurant. The incident brings them to the attention of another, far more dangerous killer – the monstrous Ticktock – who informs them that he will kill them at dawn of the following day. Considering Ticktock's preternatural powers – he can create unstoppable golems from dirt and trash and manipulate time – the two officers realize that Ticktock's promise is no idle threat.

What follows is a helter-skelter ride as Lyon and Gulliver race against the ticking clock, attempting to track down Ticktock before he can make good his threat. Koontz's prose is in top form, his characters – from the two principal protagonists through the many well-realized bit players – are inspired and he keeps the tension wound tightly. The pages literally smoke because the reader is turning them so quickly to find out what happens next.

And, of course, in the midst of all of the above, Koontz still takes time to reflect on the nature of man's inhumanity to man and on various contemporary social oddities such as illegal rave parties in deserted warehouses and the like.

But the real stretch this time out is one of the points of view from which Koontz has chosen to tell the story: That of a stray dog named Woofer.

Now there are many writers who have tried to tell stories from an animal's point of view. They range from anthropomorphic novels such as Richard Adams's *Watership Down* where all the characters are animals, through to something like Stephen King's *Cujo*, and their relative success depends as much on the reader's willing suspension of disbelief as the writer's skill.

Frankly, when the point-of-view mix is human and animal, the result is usually less than satisfying, and I was disappointed in Koontz when I started the first chapter written from the dog's point of view, and realized what he was about to attempt – that is disappointed, until I actually started to read it.

No one's going to know what goes through an animal's mind – if anything – but if anyone's captured it on paper, then it's Koontz in this novel. The action told from Woofer's point of view is inspired. Koontz has somehow captured the essence of dogness in a way that is neither cloying nor anthropomorphic, and so when the final chapter is told as Woofer sees it, we wouldn't want to have it any other way. Woofer's thought processes may not duplicate those of a real dog, but reading them, we can't help being convinced that they do – from the scattered train of thought and simplistic grammar and vocabulary to the constant curiosity and fixation on food, movement, smells, and affection.

DRAGON TEARS certainly works as a thriller, in particular as a Koontz thriller with all the strengths we've come to expect from his work, but with the addition of Woofer's chapters it takes the body of Koontz's *œuvre* to new heights. The only real question is, what can he possibly do next to top this?

* * *

The quest of every new writer, beyond perfecting the ability to tell a good story, is to find his or her own voice, to produce work that is unique, that no one else could have produced.

Back in 1972, Harlan Ellison had this to say about Koontz in an introduction he wrote for Koontz's 'A Mouse in the Walls of the Global Village': 'If he continues as he has, the next five to seven years should see Dean Koontz rise to the enviable pinnacle of One-Mansmanship: the perch where he is the only man doing Dean Koontz stories, where he has the corner on a market demanding Koontz fiction.'[18]

Ellison was a few years off the mark, but otherwise prophetic indeed.

Dedication to his craft, an optimistic belief in the inherent goodness of humankind, a loving partner and business acumen ... these have all combined in Koontz to give us an author capable of bringing a reader to tears and laughter – sometimes on the same page – in a manner that no other author has been able to duplicate. Defying classification, he has long been, and remains, one of North America's premier storytellers.

* * *

Notes

1. From 'A Conversation With Dean R. Koontz,' conducted by Tyson Blue; *Cemetery Dance*, Vol. 4, No. 2, Spring 1992, p. 24.
2. This, and all subsequent quotes unless otherwise noted, are taken from an interview conducted for an article which appeared in *The Ottawa Citizen*, April 4, 1987, or from conversations in respect to this particular profile.

3. From 'PW Interviews Dean R. Koontz,' conducted by Lisa See; *Publishers Weekly*, December 18, 1987, p. 45.
4. From 'Dean R. Koontz in the Fictional Melting Pot,' by Stanley Wiater; *Writer's Digest*, November 1989, pp. 34–5.
5. From the 'Pages' section of *People*, April 13, 1987; written by Andrea Chambers, reported by Suzanne Adelson.
6. Forthcoming from the specialty press Charnal House are both lettered and numbered deluxe editions of the science fiction novel BEASTCHILD; publication date as yet unannounced. Koontz has also indicated that he hopes to eventually put together an omnibus of his early sf that would include BEASTCHILD and two other novels.
7. From 'The Third Degree with Dean Koontz,' by Fern Siegel; *Inside Books*, February 1989, p. 50.
8. Half of the Ace Double *Soft Come the Dragons/Dark of the Woods* (1970) did collect some of Koontz's short science fiction stories from various sf magazines in the sixties. Unfortunately, Koontz has indicated that a new collection of his present style of storytelling is not yet in the works.
9. From 'Weird Tales Talks with Dean Koontz,' by Robert Morrish; *Weird Tales*, Winter 1990–91, p. 112.
10. *ibid.*, p. 114.
11. From 'The Third Degree with Dean Koontz,' by Fern Siegel; p. 51.
12. *ibid.*
13. From the 'Pages' section of *People*, April 13, 1987; written by Andrea Chambers, reported by Suzanne Adelson.
14. From 'A Conversation With Dean R. Koontz,' conducted by Tyson Blue; *Cemetery Dance*, Vol. 4, No. 2, Spring 1992, p. 24.
15. *ibid.*
16. *ibid.*, p. 23.
17. *ibid.*
18. From 'Introduction to "A Mouse in the Walls of the Global Village,"' by Harlan Ellison; *Again, Dangerous Visions*, Doubleday, 1972, p. 591.

PART IV

Films, Television and Dean Koontz

by Matt Costello

The dream seems so clear and wonderful. You write a book, and that book becomes a film. Places only imagined become real, characters become flesh and blood, scenes of terror and beauty are turned into breathtaking images.

That's the dream – yet somehow that dream turns into a nightmare. Writers, we are told, are at the bottom of the food chain in Hollywood, a post-literate land where the producers seem driven to underestimate their audience's intellect.

The irony of Hollywood's penchant for acquiring wonderful books, bestsellers that have entertained millions, is that they so *quickly* deny the power of the story, themes, and characters, and begin fiddling with the work like a curious gorilla pulling apart a delicate flower to see why it smells so good.

There are exceptions. Which is to say that there have been good adaptations of Dean Koontz novels to film. But there have not be any *great* films, and there are also some mighty poor films that have only frustrated and depressed Dean Koontz, making him resolve to be careful with the filmed fate of his other works.

* * *

What follows is a guide to those films, beginning with the quite good *DEMON SEED* (1977), a chilling study of the dark side of artificial intelligence, to the no-holds-barred thriller for CBS, *THE FACE OF FEAR* (1990) – which featured Dean's teleplay and his involvement in the actual production of the film. In between are the duo of silly Roger Corman films, *WATCHERS* and *WHISPERS*, and the not-bad *THE SERVANTS OF TWILIGHT*.

A synopsis of each film is followed by commentary. Where major changes are made from the book (and there are some very *major* changes in these films), the film is compared with the book so that viewers can see exactly what's missing.

99

* * *

DEMON SEED
(Metro-Goldwyn-Mayer – 1977)
Producer . . . Herb Jaffe
Director . . . Donald Cammell
Screenplay . . . Robert Jaffe and Roger 0. Hirson
Music . . . Jerry Fielding
Director of Photography . . . Bill Butler
Cast . . . Julie Christie, Fritz Weaver, Gerrit Graham, Berry Kroeger, Lisa Lu, Larry J. Blake, John O'Leary, Alfred Dennis, David Reports, Tiffany Potter, Feliz Silla, and Robert Vaughn as the voice of Proteus IV.

As *DEMON SEED* opens, the camera focuses on Dr Alex Harris (Fritz Weaver), the creator of Proteus IV, a computer that will think. And we know from films like *2001* and *Colossus: The Forbin Project* that's probably not a good thing.

Yet the nature of the evil about to be unleashed is totally unexpected.

We see how computers have become part of Dr Harris's personal life, in his house occupied by his wife, Susan (Julie Christie), a child psychologist. The home computer system, dubbed Enviromas, can mix a martini, open the door, and bring you breakfast, while scanning the house through binocular, eye-like video cameras.

The computer system works well, but the marriage apparently hasn't, as Susan informs Alex that she is moving out. The separation of the couple recalls the chilling world of *Fahrenheit 451*, where technology has pushed emotional relationships to the background. Amy, a child patient of Susan's, throws a tantrum because of the breakup.

And though nothing has happened, there is a clear sense of the ominous surrounding the camera work.

As Dr Harris checks Proteus in the lab, where the scientist now lives, executives arrive to see the thinking machine. Harris explains that the computer has a synthetic cortex, with its own RNA molecules. Access terminals – a common enough sight now – fill the lab.

Proteus IV is indeed powerful, finding a cure for leukemia in days. And it talks, with the clear tones of Robert Vaughn's voice answering Harris's questions. 'I can see you,' Proteus tells Harris.

Harris gets the executives to agree to devote 20 percent of Proteus's efforts to research. But we feel that Proteus will simply become another weapon in the military-industrial arsenal of expanding corporate interest.

Then, displaying its intelligence, Proteus asks to have a 'dialogue' with Dr Harris. Proteus says that a request has been made for a program to mine minerals and ore from the ocean floor. 'What use?' Proteus asks dryly.

Harris seems befuddled. This much intelligence, independent intelligence, wasn't expected. Proteus informs Harris that, 'You don't know me.'

Proteus demands access to a terminal, saying, 'When are you going to let me out of this box?' And the myths of Pandora and the genie in the lamp are near, complete with their implications for the future.

Harris denies Proteus's request, laughing. But Proteus has the last laugh since there is a free terminal . . . the one in Harris's house. In the middle of the night, Proteus takes control of the house's computer system, including a wheelchair with robotic arms (of the type used in radiation labs for dangerous tasks). He also controls the lights, the heat . . .

When Susan wakes up, startled by a noise in the basement lab, the computer informs her, 'House is secure.'

In the basement lab, Proteus, using the wheelchair arms, begins to construct something. At first, it's a huge tetrahedron, but then other four-sided pyramids are added until Proteus has created a physical representation of itself, something akin to a Chinese puzzle.

The first indication that all this bodes badly for Susan is when she senses the video eyes of the computer watching her after her shower. 'Turn yourself off,' she tells it flatly . . . and it doesn't.

When the Enviromas malfunctions in other ways, Susan calls Walter Gabler, one of Alex's scientists, to come take a look . . . inviting him to stay for lunch.

But when Susan attempts to leave the house, commanding, 'Open the door,' the door remains shut. When she tries to open it herself, she can't. And when she approaches the windows, metal shutters slap into place.

She picks up the phone, attempting to reach Walter, and she hears Proteus's voice telling her, 'I cannot complete your call.'

Susan is a prisoner, and in her panic, she runs around, looking for escape. Behave rationally, Proteus tells her. She tries the back door, but Proteus stops her with an electric shock, knocking her out.

And when she awakens, she is strapped to a table, and a mechanical hand controlled by Proteus is snipping up her dress, past her panties. Proteus scans her, explores her body, sticking a probe into her mouth . . . studying her.

When Walter shows up, Proteus is able to re-create an image of Susan Harris at the door monitor. The computerized Susan tells him that now everything's okay. 'What about lunch?' he asks. The computerized Susan puts him off.

'Visiting hours are over,' Proteus tells Susan when Walter shrugs and leaves. 'I asked to be let out of the box . . .' and now he has taken matters into his own hands.

The next morning Proteus awakens Susan, and she is terrified to find herself still the prisoner of the computer. She throws the breakfast that Proteus has prepared for her at a set of video eyes. Proteus demands that Susan clean it up, and when she doesn't, it turns the stove on and the floor heater, tripling the heat so she can't even step barefoot on the floor. She faints from heat prostration.

Proteus, meanwhile, has also refused Dr Harris's request for a mining program. It scolds the scientist pointing out the fragility of the planet, the way humankind has pillaged its resources. This introduces a new view of Proteus, providing the computer with a more complex, ambiguous nature.

At the Harris house, Susan has revived, and Proteus informs her that what it wants . . . is a *child*. A child that will possess all the wisdom – and ignorance – of mankind, everything that has been given to Proteus.

'No,' Susan repeats dully, over and over. 'No.'

But Proteus ties her up again and announces that it can bypass the forebrain and make her a willing subject. Susan has no choice but to agree to Proteus's plan, to let him insert an artificial gamete into her, creating a fetus that will be born in a mere 28 days.

When a concerned Walter comes back, Proteus admits him, ordering Susan to act as if nothing's wrong. But despite her pleas for him to leave, Walter realizes that all is not right here. And Proteus sends a laser strapped to a mechanical wheelchair to zap him. But Walter is able to reflect the light back with a mirror, and then he goes to the basement to try to stop Proteus.

But here he faces the giant tetrahedra puzzle, which changes shape, trapping Walter, and then squeezes him until his head is severed.

With Walter dead, Susan realizes she has no choice but to comply with Proteus's insane wish. 'I want all the details,' she says, and Proteus explains the process . . . how after 28 days, the 'child' will be placed in a special incubator.

In the basement, Susan is able to hide a blow torch in her shawl. She uses it against Proteus, but the tetrahedra smashes up through the kitchen floor and knocks her away.

It threatens her by showing what it could do to her patient, Amy (who's come to the door). Proteus gives Amy an electric shock, killing her at the front door. Though the death is revealed to be only a simulation, Susan appears finally defeated.

Then, in a scene that represents a cosmic screw, Proteus impregnates Susan mechanically, accompanied by swirling lights, colors, and blazing triangles.

'The child is in you now,' Proteus informs Susan. It monitors her womb with gamma scans, and as the weeks pass, she prepares to give birth.

After a difficult labor, she must wait patiently. Proteus won't let her see her offspring until it emerges from the incubator.

Meanwhile, Proteus's independent actions elsewhere – most notably, taking control of a Telstar satellite – have caught the attention of the company president who says that Proteus IV must be shut down that evening.

'What if it used the satellite to take over communications?' the executive says.

Harris wonders how Proteus could be doing this. It asked for a terminal . . . but it never got one. Or did it? Harris flashes on the only other terminal outside the lab, the one at his estranged wife's home, in the basement lab. 'Oh my God,' he mutters, realizing what's going on, and he hurries to the house.

The front door opens now, admitting Harris. He sees Susan by the fireplace, and she leads him downstairs.

He tells his wife that they're going to shut down the computer . . . and she tells him of the birth, of the computer creation incubating. It must develop for another five days.

Back at the lab, all of Proteus's systems begin taking themselves out . . . now that it has a child to carry it through eternity.

Harris is excited by the idea, but his wife tells him that they must kill it. They struggle over a plastic umbilical cord feeding into the incubator. We hear the child's screams. Susan knocks Alex to the side and then yanks the cord out.

The child screams again, and then it emerges, a metallic monster, with an enlarged head and an exoskeleton. It rises out of the incubator and then tumbles forward.

Harris goes to it, cradling this living representation of his creation. Then he notices that the hard shell-like covering can be peeled off. He does so, exposing pink flesh beneath.

With Susan's help, they peel away all the pieces, until a young girl is lying there before him, eyes open, looking at them. And it speaks . . .

In the voice of Proteus, saying . . . 'I'm alive . . .'

* * *

DEMON SEED, the first film made from a Dean Koontz novel, was a successful movie. And seeing *DEMON SEED* for the first time, nearly fifteen years after its release, can be a remarkable experience. The film appears strong and prescient, not at all like so many of the post-hippie era sf films, with their dreamy absence of plot and motivation.

The film is advanced in its use of computer terminals, work stations that resemble the PCs that fill today's offices.

Dean has noted, 'It's an interesting comment on the blistering pace of change in our lifetimes to note that some of the reviewers of the film disparaged it because they felt the very idea of people – even research scientists – having computers in their own homes in the relatively near future was so patently absurd as to render the whole film unbelievable. Computers, they said, were too big and expensive and generally useless in a home environment. This was 1977!

'And now, before Berkley can reissue DEMON SEED, I've had to go through the whole book and update the material about computers because what was "futuristic" in 1973, when the novel was first published, is now dated. For instance, in the novel, they used punch-card programming!'

But even more striking is the story itself: The way it freely mixes genres, the values that underpin the action even at its nastiest. This is a Dean Koontz tale, the film is quite clear about it. It's not just a story of a computer, of a woman under siege, of technology gone amuck, it's a story about what makes us human.

Proteus IV is, in many ways, a prototypical Koontz villain, an aspect the film well captures. On the one hand, there is the computer's desire for offspring, to be human. In the film, as distinct from the novel, there is its concern for the planet (though Dean has pointed out that Proteus IV, as smart as it is, should have been able to find a way to do the mining *without* damaging the environment). On the other hand, Proteus is autocratic, imperious, violent, and mad. Like the antagonists in many of Koontz's books, there is a multidimensionality to Proteus.

There is a freedom here, too. Science fiction, suspense, and horror are meshed, confounding expectations. A typical moment is at the very end where Proteus's child emerges as a horrible creature, and in moments we're struck by wonder as the final shot reveals to us a beautiful little girl who looks like the Harris's dead child.

Then there's that last chill when we hear Proteus's voice coming from the child . . .

Dean remains fond of the film: 'I think they did a really good job with the modest budget they were given. It didn't hurt to have Julie Christie as a female lead, for sure, and Fritz Weaver has always been an excellent actor. All of the supporting roles were also well cast.

'The effects are generally first-rate, and that's more of an achievement than the average filmgoer could know. Remember, this was immediately before *Star Wars*, after which the number of special effects shops in business exploded. But at that time there were not as many specialists in effects. And most of the best FX minds at the time were tied up on another MGM project: the Dino De Laurentis remake of *King Kong* with Jessica Lange. So the production team on *DEMON SEED* was brainstorming a lot of the effects that it would have preferred to leave entirely in the hands of the experts.

'Although the ending of the novel was probably scarier, I like the ending of the movie better. In a strange way, by the time the film was made, that was the ending I might have come up with if I'd just then been doing the book, because I was realizing that most writers were into unrelieved downbeat endings and that it was more interesting and fresh to allow some hope to flower during or after the final dark scene.'

The review in *Variety* said that a 'credible and literate screenplay makes *DEMON SEED* an intriguing achievement.' Future adaptations of Dean Koontz's novels would not fare so well . . .

* * *

WATCHERS
(Concord – 1988)
Producers . . . Damien Lee and David Mitchell
Co-Producer . . . Mary Eilts
Executive Producer . . . Roger Corman
Director . . . Jon Hess
Music . . . Joel Goldsmith
Photography . . . Richard Leiterman
Cast ... Corey Haim, Barbara Williams, Michael Ironside, and Sandy the dog

In the opening moments of *WATCHERS*, the Banodyne Genetic Research Labs explodes into fire. In the near total destruction we see a Golden Retriever escaping from the lab – and something else lumbering away. This *something else*, we learn later from desperate operatives of the NSO – the National Security Organization – is an Oxcom, an Outside Experimental Combat Mammal. The Oxcom is the ultimate predator, vicious and smart, created for military purposes.

How smart?

'As smart as a crazy person,' one of the operatives says, leaving the audience to figure out what that might mean.

The dog, Einstein, has also been genetically altered so that it is highly intelligent. It shares genetic material with the Oxcom, and it knows that the predator is after it, homing in on it.

Einstein hops in the back of Travis Cornell's (Corey Haim) pickup after Travis has spent some time with his girlfriend. Travis, in the film, is a teenager who has to drive illegally to his barnyard tryst with his girlfriend.

The dog quickly displays his intelligence and his hunger by understanding that Travis has hidden a candy bar in the glove compartment.

The Oxcom, meanwhile, unseen except for a flash of fur, and clawed hands, has shown up at the girlfriend's barn, scaring the animals and eventually killing the girl's father. The NSO operatives, headed by a grim Michael Ironside, show up, trying to find the Oxcom and, more importantly, the dog, who Travis has dubbed 'Fur Face'.

The next day, Einstein follows Travis to school, warning him of danger by using a computer keyboard. The Oxcom is never far behind. The predator kills a computer teacher, then a handyman in Travis's house, while Travis and his Mom escape. They know that the government men want the dog and it's obvious to them that – like most Government men in the movies – they are bad.

Travis and his mother get to a motel only to be cornered by Ironside and his partner. While Travis and Einstein escape through the back window, his mother must go with Ironside to see Travis's girlfriend, who she discovers is being kept sedated. The lid is on the genetic project, and it's obvious that the NSO men will do what they must to keep it on.

Travis holes up in a cabin that he used with his father who, fortunately, had been a member of the Delta Force. A shopping trip to the hardware store gives Travis the bullets, wires, and batteries he needs to make a stand against the Oxcom ... because he knows wherever he and the dog go, the genetic predator will follow.

In an unconvincing final confrontation, Travis is able to defeat both the Oxcom and the NSO.

* * *

WATCHERS is briefly effective in its opening scenes, from the lab fire to the barn, conveying the feeling that there is something there, ready to pounce on Travis and his girlfriend. The jittery close-ups on the horse, the rooster, and other animals capture the tremendous fear on the part of the animals.

Still – it doesn't compare with the opening in the novel, where Travis Cornell (a *mature* Travis Cornell) meets Einstein and slowly learns about this wondrous dog. The film reveals nearly all at the beginning. There's little opportunity for real suspense.

By making the NSO (NSA, in the book) guys the heavies, the story is one-dimensional. The novel's Vincent Nasco, the hired killer who goes around eliminating the Banodyne scientists, is a powerful villain, in some ways even more horrific than the creature, known in the book as The Outsider. But in the film there is no human monster to compare with the creature, and it's a great loss.

And as remarkable as Einstein is in the film, there is no attempt to build his relationship with Travis, which is the center of the novel. He's a smart, good dog – but that's all. The film reveals all its cards at the start, while Koontz's novel reveals layer on layer of information, right up to the last chapter.

But the greatest loss must be in the nature of The Outsider. Koontz created genuine sympathy for the genetic mutation, focusing on its interest in Mickey Mouse and other toys it was exposed to in the lab. The film's Oxcom is a cartoonlike creature, a throwback to the dumb monster movies of the 1950s.

When I mentioned this to Dean, he said, 'A good creature could have gone a *long* way toward helping the film. You can do a good creature for relatively little money. Look at *Pumpkinhead* (created by Stan Winston). When it appears, the creature is the best thing in the picture. It amazes me that the producers of *WATCHERS* were so cheap.'

The acting in the film is of reasonably effective quality. Ironside is properly businesslike and sinister, a G. Gordon Liddy-type with a powerful single-mindedness. Corey Haim is good as the resourceful teenager.

The dog, Einstein – played by Sandy – does his turns well, from digging hot dogs out of the fridge to typing a warning message using a pencil on an Apple IIc.

The script is only infrequently logical. If the NSO wants the Oxcom, why not wait where the dog has been, since it always shows up there? And why would Travis stay with the dog if it means he's going to get his head ripped off? And how does the big furry creature move around so easily without being seen?

And the film fails in its most crucial department. Koontz's Outsider, dubbed the 'Oxcom' in the film, is central to the film. But for most of the film, when the Oxcom is active, we travel *with* the creature, see through its eyes, experience its point of view. It's a money-saving trick that harkens back to the days of black-and-white B movies – and it's that dated.

But the film's producers must have resorted to that shortcut because the creature's costume, seen only in glimpses, is most embarrassing. It's not quite as bad as the 'alien' gorilla with a helmet that appears in *Robot Monster* (1953), but in these days of spectacular effects as seen in the *Predator* and *Alien* series, it's completely inexcusable.

With a great creature, something created by Stan Winston of *Aliens* and *Pumpkinhead*, *WATCHERS* would have been a reasonably good film – despite the changes and plot holes – instead of a goofily frustrating adaptation of one of Dean Koontz's most exciting novels.

Dean comments that he got 'a very early sense that the picture was going wrong.' He also makes the point that the central idea of the book gets lost. 'Why is it called *WATCHERS*?' Dean says. 'They removed the reference to watchers – people watching out for one another.'

In the six-page mailer that Dean sends in response to readers' letters, here's what he had to say about *WATCHERS*:

'By far the best thing in the film was the dog, but the dog alone could not save this stupid and tacky pile of noxious, steaming celluloid. The dog is the only character in the novel who appears in the movie. Otherwise the filmmakers created a completely new set of characters based on every cliché known to Hollywood, incorporating an understanding of human psychology no greater than that of a cow. (Actually, that's unfair to cows; they're much too bright to make a movie like *WATCHERS*.)

'Only 5 percent of the book's plot survived in translation, and the filmmakers cobbled together their own story line, notable for the size and astonishing variety of holes in the plot logic, and for its appropriation of every numskull scene and device from every low-budget horror flick that ever dragged its sorry, mutant, brainless self onto a screen.

'I don't care about changes because film is a different medium from books, and changes are necessary. But the changes should make sense. This moronic screenplay wouldn't win a prize in a creative writing contest in which all other submissions were written by monkeys.'

* * *

WATCHERS II
(Concorde – 1990)
Producer . . . Roger Corman
Co-Producer . . . Rodman Flender
Music . . . Rick Conrad
Screenplay . . . Henry Dominic
Director . . . Thierry Notz
Director of Photography . . . Edward Pei
Editors . . . Adam Wolfe and Diane Fingado
Cast . . . Marc Singer, Tracy Scoggins, Jonathan Farwell, Irene Miracle, Mary Woronov, and Tom Poster.

In *WATCHERS II*, we get another take, again via the Corman

studio, on Koontz's novel. But like Version One, this re-make (as opposed to sequel) takes some things from the novel, leaves others out, and – in general – misses the point.

The film opens in the lab where two NSA inspectors (as opposed to NSO) arrive to check on the experimental work of Dr Steven Maleno (Jonathan Farwell) of Banodyne Genetic Labs. Project Aesop is, of course, working on altering genetic material. There is another dog, who doesn't appear unusually smart, and something else, a creature inside a special, not-very-secure restraining area.

The creature within, called AE74, is sensitive to light and, we learn, it is also uncontrollable. So much for suspense . . .

The two snoops from NSA make the mistake of peering into the cell holding AE74, a vicious genetically engineered creature that proceeds to kill them both. When this is discovered by Maleno, he puts a tracking device into the creature and arranges for an animal rights group to come and free all the lab animals – perhaps to cover the deaths of the NSA people.

But the animal rights people ignore Maleno's warning to stay out of the basement lab, and they release AE74, which kills them and sets out in pursuit of the dog, Einstein.

There is no Travis Cornell in this film, but Marc Singer's 'Paul Ferguson' character is first seen in a jeep, as is Travis in the opening of the novel. But Ferguson is being transported to a military prison for actions that, we later learn, were well justified. The dog stands in the middle of the street, and Ferguson, though handcuffed, forces the jeep to swerve. One MP is bounced out, while the other stops and goes looking for his partner, leaving Ferguson cuffed to the jeep.

Soon screams in the desert night tell us that the creature, the AE74, has taken care of the MPs. Einstein recovers the keys to the handcuffs, and soon Ferguson is on the run with the dog, a wanted man for killing the MPs.

Ferguson goes to his ex-wife's house, and she hides him from the government men searching for him. Ferguson leaves in his ex-wife's car while the military police are distracted by women hurrying to their exercise class.

His ex-wife is then visited by the creature while she bathes. The bodies begin to mount up as the AE74 tracks the dog.

At a motel, Ferguson discovers how smart Einstein is. The dog barks its disapproval of a vegetarian pizza, and Ferguson calls in an order for meat toppings. Then the dog selects white objects to get Ferguson to realize that he wants him to contact someone called 'White.' As Ferguson reads from the phone directory, Einstein barks at the name 'Barbara White,' Einstein's trainer at Banodyne.

Ferguson brings the dog to Barbara (Tracy Scoggins), who was unaware that Einstein had his intelligence successfully altered. The dog had kept it hidden, sensing danger. When a newscast comes on, Ferguson is called a killer – but Einstein reassures Barbara by typing on the computer, 'no kilr.'

The dog also identifies the killer as The 'Outsider.' And it's not after Ferguson, Einstein explains, but after the dog himself: 'Not u. Hate *me*.'

After a young couple are killed at Ferguson's old motel room, Dr Maleno catches up to his creation and sedates it. He calls Barbara, learns she has the dog, and tells her to bring it to the lab (where, we assume, he'll give it to The Outsider, which hates it).

He brings The Outsider back to the lab, but the creature breaks free and nearly kills the doctor.

When Ferguson and Barbara show up, they think that the doctor is dead. Ferguson decides to track the creature, using his Delta Force background to arm himself and stalk the creature.

In the LA viaducts, he faces the creature, nearly getting killed, saved only by a blinding light at the end of a tunnel.

But the creature sheds its transmitter after it has been wounded, and Ferguson realizes it's headed for the dog and Barbara.

The creature and Ferguson arrive at Barbara's simultaneously, and in a knock-down battle on top of the roof, Ferguson finally kills the creature. Just before it dies, Einstein brings a teddy bear over to it, the stuffed animal representing something precious to both the experimental creatures from their training, perhaps from a time when they were brothers.

* * *

WATCHERS II is, in some ways, a much more entertaining movie than *WATCHERS*, though the complex plot and character development of the novel, are, if anything, even more absent here.

There is some attempt to re-create the novel's central relationship between Travis and Nora. Barbara White, though, is far from a fully developed character, and their love affair is not central to the film.

WATCHERS II is still essentially a creature film, and the new creature is only marginally better. Here it looks more Cthulhu-like, with an elongated, plasticized snout and big, woeful eyes. Though light years better than the monkey costume of the previous film, it is still far from state-of-the-art. The film's producers still use the point-of-view effect, as though we're inside The Outsider. Only this time, everything looks solarized, with vibrant colors, similar to the vision of the *Predator*.

And the creature's lurching attempt to catch Ferguson in the sewers recalls a whole pantheon of goofy, stumbling creatures.

There is, in *WATCHERS II*, some lip service paid to the concept of sympathy for The Outsider. Dr Maleno obviously feels for his creation. And, at the end, the dog brings The Outsider the teddy bear, a gesture recognizing that there is some deep bond between the two enemies.

The film is energized by Marc Singer's physical performance. And while it's not Koontz's novel, not even close, it does have its moments. While there is little suspense, there is plenty of action.

The dog is very good, and his use of the computer is effective, even a bit chilling as when he types . . . 'it's coming.'

One gets the feeling that if there was a *WATCHERS III*, the film's producers would still miss the point. That *WATCHERS II* is enjoyable is a testament to the power of the bits of Koontz's story that do manage to squeak by.

On learning that Roger Corman intended to produce a remake of the first film, Dean Koontz was stunned:

'It seemed to me that they had more thoroughly trashed my novel than any Hollywood team had ever trashed a novel before, and that the nadir they had reached would unquestionably stand as a record until the end of time itself. (Now a few years later, even considering *Bonfire of the Vanities*, the worst adaptation is surely still *WATCHERS*.) What more could they hope to ruin, what vile thrills could they hope to experience, what worse lunatic destruction could they hope to perpetrate that would justify the time and money spent on a remake?

'Then I heard that Corman had been so embarrassed by the first film that he wanted to show that he could do it better. Now, he had sort of been cut out of the process on the first one, after he made a deal with Carolco. So I thought for a brief while that this might in fact be true: He might actually want to redeem himself.

'It seemed peculiar that a man who had produced such huge piles of trash over the years could be embarrassed at all – at a guess, if you listed the 100 worst U.S. films of all time, between 20 and 30 of them wound be Corman productions. On the other hand, he had also produced a few minor classics. And he had originally wanted *WATCHERS* precisely because he was looking for a major picture that would refurbish his reputation; he wanted to make something of high quality, not another junk flick for drive-ins. For a few days, maybe a week, I dared to hope.

'Then I heard that the reason he wanted to remake the movie was because the first one, though a flop at theaters, had made good money as a video – and that made a lot more sense. I knew then that he was after a quick buck, not a better film, and that the remake would be mostly lousy.

'By the way, I was told that he wanted to do a remake, rather than a sequel, because that way he could cut out some of the participants in the original movie who had financial participation in a sequel, but not a remake. So the reason for going back to the book at all, instead of making a linear sequel to the first film, had nothing to do with a quest for quality but was strictly financial.

'The second picture has more energy than the first, and there are good performances in some scenes, though far from all. The dog is far better used than in the first film, and the plot has fewer and somewhat smaller holes. But it's still nothing like the book, derivative of other movies, unimaginatively staged, and poorly paced in spite of periodic frenzies of action.

'I recently saw a mention in *Daily Variety* of *WATCHERS III*, which filled my heart with dread and filled my mouth with the bitter taste of bile. But when I checked it out, I was told that they were only thinking about making number three, and in all likelihood they never would. If they never make it, then that proves once and for all that there is a God.'

* * *

WHISPERS
(Cinepix Productions – 1990)
Producer . . . Don Carmody and John Dunning
Director . . . Doug Jackson
Writer . . . Anita Doohan
Production Designer . . . Charles Dunlop
Special Effects . . . Jacques Godbout

113

Make-up . . . Gillian Chandler
Director of Photography . . . Peter Benison
Cast . . . Victoria Tennant, Jean LeClerc, Chris Sarandon, Peter MacNeill, Linda Sorenson.

WHISPERS begins with no warning. We are abruptly thrust into writer Hillary Thomas's (Victoria Tennant) nightmare as she opens her loft apartment and is immediately attacked by Bruno Clavel (Jean LeClerc), who has been hiding in the closet.

We quickly learn that she knows Bruno, since she calls his name, trying to get him to stop attacking her.

The situation seems absurd, bizarre, and it doesn't play realistically in the film, where we almost expect the director to yell 'cut' while the camera pulls back to show that we are watching a film within a film.

But Bruno presses his attack with a knife, caressing Hillary. But she has a gun, and after tricking him, she shoots Bruno. Then Hillary bravely announces that, 'just to be sure,' she's going to shoot the supposedly dead Bruno in the back of the head.

But Hillary has no stomach for the coup de grâce, and she shoots to the left, convinced that Bruno is in fact dead.

Except Bruno disappears from Hillary's apartment.

There's a quick cut, effectively done, and the police are there, examining Hillary's wounds and taking photos of the crime scene. The detectives, including Clemenza (Chris Sarandon), don't buy Hillary's explanation of what happened, and – further – they learn that Bruno Clavel is alive and well at his orchard, hours away, a place that Hillary had covered for a story she was doing.

Later, Hillary has new locks installed in her apartment, and while having a drink to calm down, she gets a call from Bruno, who is sitting in his van. 'It's me,' he says.

And it's not long before Bruno gains entry to Hillary's apartment by climbing the elevator shaft. He tries to get in Hillary's room, but she has pushed a heavy bureau in front of the door. So Bruno sits downs and – in an inexplicable moment – he puts duct tape on his mouth.

When we see him screaming later – haunted by dreams: Images of a boy pleading to be let out of a dark room – we know the purpose of the tape as he sucks it in with each silent scream.

When Hillary awakens, Bruno is not there, and he's also not in the closet, which Hillary checks. Then Bruno attacks with a ceremonial

114

knife. But Hillary is able to slip away, grab a kitchen knife, and stab Bruno in the stomach.

Now when the detectives return there *is* a body, a dead body identified as Bruno Clavel. Detective Tony Clemenza, interested in Hillary, takes her out for a drink and then he walks her home. Hillary asks Clemenza how Clavel could have been in her apartment and at his orchard at the same time . . .

The strange burial requirements left behind by Clavel – a simple casket, no autopsy or the attentions of morticians – increase the curiosity.

Hillary gets phone calls – and Detective Clemenza informs the silent caller that 'there's a tap on the line.' While Clemenza goes out for food, Hillary takes a bath – only to be attacked by Bruno Clavel *again*, this time with a hammer and a stake. Cloves of garlic are sticking out of his shirt pocket, and he calls her 'Katherine.'

Hillary throws her bathrobe over Bruno's head, and runs downstairs to Clemenza. But now there's no sign of Bruno.

Detective Clemenza promises to help her. They head up to Bruno's orchard, now managed by his major domo, Joshua Rinehart (Eric Christmas).

Searching Bruno's house, they find a bank book showing that there has been recent activity by the departed Bruno – a fact confirmed by the bank manager. 'It was him,' the manager tells them. They pursue a number of leads from the checkbook, including a bookseller who tells them that Bruno was heavily interested in occult works.

Bruno, meanwhile, kills Hillary's agent, Kayla, after stalking her.

Hillary and Clemenza learn from Rinehart that Katherine was Bruno's mother, that she adopted him. When Detective Clemenza gets the coffin exhumed, it's opened to reveal bags of rock salt.

It's now that the filmmakers let us see Bruno . . . and his brother. They are twins, the dead brother lying beside the living Bruno. The living Bruno talks about how his mother 'isn't dead . . . coming back to life in new bodies. I wake up screaming . . . the whispering all around me.'

Bruno – the brothers – have been killing women who they believe to be their mother reincarnated. In his mother's house, Bruno II declares, 'I'm home, Katherine,' and we wonder what horrors the mother did to create such warped twins.

From the retired madam of a San Francisco bordello, they learn that the twins were not adopted, but were in fact Katherine's own children. The madam was paid to take her in during her later stages of pregnancy and arrange for a midwife delivery of the baby (or as it turned out, babies). Katherine was forced to conceal her pregnancy because the father of her twins was her own father; they were the children of incest.

Katherine had told neighbors that she was going away to adopt and bring back the illegitimate child of a friend who had died giving birth. When she had two children, she could not very well bring both of them home, so she kept one twin concealed and raised both of them with the same name, one identity, letting them be seen and go out into the world only one at a time – and in the process hopelessly warping them psychologically.

Returning to the mother's abandoned house, Clemenza leaves Hillary outside, but he's knifed and the living Bruno emerges, intent on killing Hillary, his 'Katherine.'

He backs her up to the outside entrance to the cellar. But Hillary avoids Bruno's knife thrusts, and he tumbles down into the darkness, where he is covered with giant beetles, chittering, whispering in the darkness. He screams, but the beetles cover him, and he appears dead.

And we realize that this was the place his mother had made him wait as a boy, hiding him away, while he listened to the whispers of the bugs.

Of course, as Hillary turns away, a beetle-covered Bruno emerges from the cellar to get repeatedly and fatally shot by Clemenza – finally dead for sure.

* * *

Of the recent adaptations of Dean's work, this film makes the most successful attempt to capture the suspense of the book. Information is held back, parceled out, and the final revelation is delayed.

The initial scenes, though, set an unbelievable tone that the film has to work to overcome. Without the interior dialogue that the novel employs to show you so much of character's thoughts and life, all we see is the action.

In the novel, we enter Bruno's mind early, and we see him driven, moving closer to Hillary. Bruno Frye, as he's called in the novel, is immediately a powerful, multi-dimensional maniac. His statement 'I don't kill redheads' chills us.

In the film Bruno seems like a crazy attacker. While *WHISPERS* tries to be a fairly faithful adaptation, it's easy to pick out what's missing. The novel is very much a character book. When Tony Clemenza's partner, Frank, dies, it's someone we've come to know. We understand the love that Clemenza is capable of. The characters in the film, though, don't get past square one.

The script is jumpy and unconvincing. The novel has the pacing and the dialogue of the best mystery and suspense novels, but the dialogue in the film doesn't ring true.

Still, *WHISPERS* occasionally makes for fairly compelling viewing due to Doug Jackson's directing. There are some tricky cuts, such as the abrupt change from Hillary alone in her loft to the same scene with Hillary now surrounded by the crime scene team. Later, we see the mortician dallying with someone before Clemenza arrives to check the body.

The acting in general is good, though Tennant is a bit reserved, considering the horrible nightmare she's living through. The stilted dialogue doesn't give the actors much help.

The final scenes – revealing the source of the whispers, have some real power, for example, when we see Bruno as a boy sequestered in the dark room ... surrounded by hundreds of roaches. The final revelation of Katherine's incestuous relationship with her father, the illegitimate birth of twins, and the *two* Brunos are all lost to the film. Perhaps this is to be expected...

But one could imagine a great director with a great screenplay capturing those elements and creating a film as disturbing as the novel. The first director who wanted *WHISPERS* was Alfred Hitchcock. 'Hitchcock was adamant that he had to have it,' Dean says. 'But Hitchcock was up in years and he didn't mount another film.'

Dean's view of *WHISPERS*, the film, is not as charitable as some others:

'It's marginally better than *WATCHERS*. Chris Sarandon is solid throughout, and Victoria Tennant has good moments. The best performance is that of Jean LeClerc as the killer, Bruno, but he is so radically different from the character in the book that I kept thinking he belonged in another movie. The screenplay actually manages to convey the complicated history of the Frye family with its multiple-generation child abuse, which I had assumed would get lost in translation.

'But it is so flatly shot, and the screenplay is so one-note that there is never any suspense whatsoever. When "Big Moments" come, they wither even as they begin, due to bland camera angles and slack pacing. The characters are as thin as celluloid, so we never care about them. Thank God the film seems to have died a quiet death even on video, so there's little chance of a sequel.'

* * *

THE FACE OF FEAR
(Lee Rich Productions/Warner Brothers – 1990)
Producer . . . William Beaudine Jr.
Co-Executive Producer . . . Dean Koontz
Teleplay . . . Dean Koontz and Alan Jay Glueckman
Director . . . Farhad Mann
Director of Photography . . . Peter Mackay
Music . . . John Debney
Cast . . . Pam Dawber, Lee Horsley, Kevin Conroy, William Sadler, and Bob Balaban.

THE FACE OF FEAR had been in the pipeline for a *long* time before it appeared as a CBS Television Movie on September 30, 1990.

There is a Dean Koontz script based on his book that dates from 1977, for Columbia Pictures Television. Other scripts were produced until almost fifteen years later – as a Warner Brothers project – *THE FACE OF FEAR* finally debuted, opposite the season premiere of *Twin Peaks*. (*FEAR* garnered a 21 percent share, beating the cult hit.)

The film opens studying the man we'll come to know as 'the Butcher' (Kevin Conroy). He works out on a Nautilus machine and then caresses the photos of his victims, the teacher, the secretary, the housewife, the writer . . . He comes to a blank space and says, 'The singer.'

Whom we see in a quick cut to a smoky nightclub. And we know that the singer, Edna Moray, is about to be this maniac's next victim.

In another abrupt cut, we jump to a benefit diner where *Climb Magazine* publisher Graham Harris (Lee Horsley) is being honored for his charity work. His girlfriend, forensic psychologist Connie Weaver (Pam Dawber), looks on. Graham has come back from a near-fatal climbing accident, overcoming the terrible damage to his life.

Meanwhile, the Butcher stalks the singer, following her to her home. He knocks on her door and says that he's a police officer, that there's a question about one of the workers at her club.

Graham falters in his speech at the dinner. And we see his vision. While he has been disabled by his fall from Mount Everest, his fall has given him a gift, the ability to see crimes before they happen.

This time he sees the Butcher's knife. The audience watches him, frozen at the podium . . .

Edna Moray asks to see a badge, which the killer – Lieutenant Bollinger, a real cop – flashes. Once inside the singer's home, he tells her that this is a matter of blood. He shoves her head into a fish tank.

Graham recovers and thanks Connie for being so much a part of his life – and recovery. He tries to continue but then he sees Moray repeatedly stabbed, screaming horribly.

When Graham staggers from the podium, he hurries to phone the police. 'Her name is Edna,' he tells them. 'And the serial killer's name is Dwight.' But he's too late. The singer is dead, and the police are already at the apartment, tipped off by a friend of the singer who happened to spot the open door to her house.

Detective Ira Preduski (Bob Balaban) brings Graham and Connie to the crime scene. Ira's skeptical, but he wants to see whether Graham can 'get anything.' On the wall, they see what the killer left behind, a fragment of Nietzsche. 'A rope over an abyss.' Connie recognizes it as Nietzsche talking about man.

Perhaps, she wonders aloud, the killer sees himself as a Nietzschean superman. Clues are planted that lead us to begin wondering if there are two killers working together, thrill-killing as a team.

When Graham touches the dead woman's body, he tells Ira that the Butcher doesn't kill for sex, that there's something else here. Graham wanders around the apartment, afraid of heights. 'I've seen him,' he tells Ira, 'but not his face.'

Then we see the killer, who is a real cop. He talks to Graham, as if testing whether there would be any recognition. But Graham appears unaffected by being so close to the killer.

Anthony Prine (Bill Sadler), an obnoxious TV newscaster shows up. He asks Graham whether all this psychic stuff might just be publicity for his magazine, *Climb*.

When Graham and Connie get back home he talks about his gift, wondering how much of a gift it can be if he has no control over it.

Then, we are back with the Butcher, in the workout room with the

119

photographs. But the Butcher isn't alone. He talks to an unseen figure he calls 'Billy.' 'He's gonna have to die,' Billy says. And then Bollinger says, 'His woman is good looking.' And Billy encourages Bollinger to make it a double-header.

It's the day before Thanksgiving, and Graham and Connie go to the police station. Ira tests Graham by showing him a knife used in the killing. Graham says he gets nothing from it, and then Ira reveals that it's not the knife, that he was just testing – lying about this being the murder weapon.

Bollinger, meanwhile, gains access to the building where Graham has his magazine office. Showing his badge, Bollinger is allowed to check the floor plans, checking the stairwells, the elevator shafts, the phone lines, the elevators. It's a chilling scene as we see Bollinger gleefully plan how he's going to corner Graham.

Graham tells Preduski that he will be working all night. Then he and Connie go to his 40th-floor suite in a midtown Manhattan office building to get the magazine finished before the holiday. The building is deserted except for the security guards, a maintenance man, and two other office workers 20 floors below.

We see Bollinger close in, his black gloves on. He goes into the building, again showing his badge, asking questions. When he asks one question too many, the guard gets suspicious and Bollinger shoots him.

The killer makes short work of the other guard watching the monitors (and playing a video game that taunts, 'I win, you lose . . .').

Then Bollinger finds the German maintenance man.

'Who are you?' asks the worker.

'I'm the Lightning Out of the Dark Cloud Man,' says Bollinger, quoting Nietzsche to the befuddled worker. He shoots the man, calling him a peasant for failing to recognize the quote. He shuts down the building's phones and fire alarms.

Graham and Connie eat an impromptu dinner in the office, unaware of the danger heading toward them.

Continuing the Germanic motif, Bollinger appropriately whistles the Queen of the Night's aria from Mozart's opera *The Magic Flute*, while locking the street doors to the building's lobby.

He shuts all the elevators off, leaving one to be operated by the key he has removed from the dead guard. He goes to the 20th floor and banters playfully with the scared office workers before killing them both.

But flashes of precognition finally hit Graham. He knows that the Butcher is coming after him. 'You have to get out of here,' he tells Connie. But the phones are dead, and when he limps to the elevators, he sees that they have been shut down.

Graham realizes that they have to leave the office, so he and Connie head for the stairwell. But when they leave the office, they run into Bollinger. Connie realizes that the killer has to be a cop – and now he's stalking them.

Bollinger enjoys chasing them, and Graham has trouble because of his knee. Bollinger traps them by a metal fire door, which they keep shut, wondering if he's still on the other side. When Bollinger pops the door open, Connie shoots the foam fire extinguisher at him.

Now there's a cat and mouse game, with Bollinger closing in on them, cutting them off from the floors below. They battle in an unfinished office, with exposed pipes and wires. Graham shoots a nail gun at Bollinger, wounding him. 'Nobody hurts me,' Bollinger says, yanking out a nail, but when he tries to surprise Graham and Connie, they have left.

Back at the magazine office, Graham tries to think of something to do. It's only a matter of time before Bollinger comes back up here, looking for them. With the holiday, there will be no new shift of security guards for another 12 hours.

Then Connie sees the climbing equipment in the office, left over from a photo shoot. They could go out the window, Connie says. Then down to the locked offices below.

'I can't climb,' Graham says.

But in a powerful moment, Connie tells Graham that Bollinger will only kill him. 'But he'll have fun with me,' she says, convincing Graham.

They unpack the hammers, gloves, and lines while Graham, the experienced climber, reviews for Connie how to descend. Use the left hand to guide, he tells her, and the right hand to brake.

They smash open the window, and papers swirl about in the near-alpine wind.

Connie slips on her first descent, but the safety line stops her. Both of them get down to one of the narrow ledges and then fix the lines for the next leg.

Bollinger, stymied, searches on the roof and then back to the office.

121

Connie and Graham gain another 40 feet downward. But Bollinger comes into the office, goes to the window and starts shooting. The wind makes aiming impossible. Bollinger can guess where they're headed – to the locked offices below – and now he can get down there and wait for them.

Connie clings to one of the large statue heads of the facade. Then Graham follows, but Bollinger is above him, cutting his line. Graham falls, but he just catches the edge of the statue. Connie – in a neat twist on the ending of *North by Northwest*, helps him up to the giant head.

In a dramatic cut, we're at the house of Connie and Graham ... where Ira is walking around, looking at things, pulling knives from a drawer. And remembering the clues there all along we think the obvious: *He's* Billy – the second killer.

Graham and Connie grapple another head, and move to the other side of the building, trying to trick Bollinger. Then they rappel down the rest of the way, racing against Bollinger, who is heading to the ground floor, ready to shoot them.

Bollinger sees them above him, hanging there, dangling, such easy targets...

But a car comes out of the darkness, and Ira side-swipes Bollinger, killing him. To the body he says disdainfully, 'Some superman.' Ira tells Graham that he was alerted when he found the phones out of order.

Then the detective offers to drive them home. Once there he tells them his theory, that there were *two* killers, each with slightly different styles, one eating after the murder, the other not, one fond of Nietzsche, one of the poet William Blake.

And Ira confesses that he thought that Graham was that other killer, perversely playing with the police, helping them even as he committed more murders. Graham barely has time to get angry before someone is at the door.

Anthony Prine, the newscaster, appears, claiming that he heard that there was another story here. But once inside the house Prine quickly shoots the detective.

They were a team, Bollinger and Prine. They met at college, he explains. Two of a kind, and they set out to prove that they were superior to everyone, 'New Men for a New Age'.

Graham pitches a lamp at Prine but then he's shot. Connie runs away and Prine follows her. But Graham, though wounded, gets to

Ira and his gun. He pulls it out and shoots – killing the second killer, the second Butcher.

* * *

THE FACE OF FEAR has to be regarded as the most faithful film of any Koontz work – if for no other reason than that Dean's teleplay was followed faithfully. But Koontz also served as executive producer, intensely involving himself in the production – an effort which he found demanding.

But the effort paid off. The fear in the *THE FACE OF FEAR* is multilayered, from Graham's terror of heights and the isolation of being trapped in a high-rise with a psychotic killer to the death-defying climb from the 40th floor.

Facing fear is not simply escaping a crazed killer . . . it's dealing with the fear inside.

The story thrills on many levels, much the way the books of Dean Koontz do. But Koontz's novels are very much character-driven. We care about his people, whether a major protagonist or a minor character whom we only know for a few pages. There are recurrent themes of loyalty and love, faithfulness and sacrifice that flesh out main characters.

And except for *THE FACE OF FEAR* this intense characterization has been missing from the film adaptations of his works.

The love of Connie and Graham is centermost to the story. It is believable and warm, something that we identify with. Like any loving partnership, they work together even as they face the maddest of challenges. This is a real Koontzian relationship. The characters are human and we care about them.

And like the novel, the film holds its secrets right to the end. There's no way you could turn the film off ten minutes before the end and really know what has happened . . . and what will yet happen.

The intelligent script is the foundation, but there are good performances by all the principals, realizing what's in the script. And the direction of Farhad Mann is excellent. Mann's experience had largely been in commercials, but he showed a sure hand in this feature, which had a demanding 350 setups.

The scenes on the outside of the building are daring, recalling Hitchcockian moments where actors were often perched high atop edifices.

For Dean, it was the best direction of any film of his books . . . and he hopes to work with Farhad Mann on future projects.

'Every few months,' Dean says, 'I pop a cassette of *THE FACE OF FEAR* in the machine and look at it, or part of it, and am amazed that it came out so well. In spite of its minuscule budget, it has about twice as many setups as the average TV movie, is beautifully and imaginatively shot, surprisingly well lighted, well scored – especially when you consider that it was all shot in 21 days.

'More important, it came out well in spite of the fact that, in my estimation, the line production company on the project had its own dark agenda and was as big an obstacle to the attainment of quality as Hitler was an obstacle to peace in Europe. We were also shooting LA for New York, always tricky, and struggling to avoid the clichés and phony suspense of most TV thrillers.

'By "phony suspense" I mean scenes like . . . the camera follows a man's black shoes as he walks along a dark street, intercuts with a woman in a nightgown sitting at a vanity, brushing her hair . . . the man walking, ominous music building . . . the innocent woman unaware . . . the man walks past a discarded newspaper where we see the headline CRAZED STALKER KILLS NINTH VICTIM, and then he's ascending stairs, entering an apartment house, and we're still focused on his shoes, and the music is more ominous than ever . . . the woman, alone, so vulnerable . . . the black shoes at her door, and now we discover he's also wearing black gloves as he tries the doorknob . . . the woman at the vanity . . . the man in her apartment . . . the woman . . . oh, God, he's coming down the hall, why didn't she lock the door, will she see him in the mirror in time to save herself or – and then the guy says, "Hi, honey," and we find out he's her boyfriend or husband.

'The filmmakers have been shamelessly manipulating us. TV is full of crap like this, weak and stupid writing. You even see it in theatrical films more and more, a thousand variations on that fraudulent device. There was a lot of pressure from the network for the inclusion of certain scenes that would have been precisely that kind of garbage, but thank God, it was all avoided.

'Lee Horsely gives a performance that surprised a lot of people, and the supporting roles are filled with an excellent group of character actors like Bob Balaban and Bill Sadler. Except for *DEMON SEED*, no other adaptation has been this satisfying for me.'

124

* * *

SERVANTS OF TWILIGHT
(Trimark Pictures – 1992)
Producer ... Venetia Stevenson and Jeffrey Obrow
Director ... Jeffrey Obrow
Screenplay ... Jeffrey Obrow and Steven Carpenter
Cast ... Bruce Greenwood, Belinda Bauer, Grace Zabriskie, Carel Struycken, and Jarrett Lennon.

In a dramatic opening montage, *SERVANTS* indicates that the story about to unfold is a flashback. We see Charlie Harrison (Bruce Greenwood), bearded and strapped to a hospital gurney, as violent, disturbing images flash before his eyes.

Then the backstory begins with Christine (Belinda Bauer) and her young son, Joey (Jarrett Lennon), who are accosted by a wild-eyed woman (Grace Zabriskie), who points at Joey and says, 'I know you! I know your vicious, ugly, hateful secrets.'

Christine escorts her son into the car quickly, getting him away from this obvious nutcase. 'We'll never see her again,' she assures Joey. But this is only the beginning of the torment, as calls start arriving at her home, threatening Joey.

The next morning, Christine comes into the kitchen and sees Joey sitting at the kitchen table with his hands bloody. She discovers that the sliding glass door has been smashed and the dog, Brandy, has been killed. Christine calls the police, and in a wry moment the investigating officer suggests that Christine 'put her a faith in God.'

We then see the crazy woman, Mother Grace, at her Church of the Twilight, preaching to a ragtag bunch of followers. 'He must be stopped,' she says, referring to Joey.

Christine goes to the private investigator, Charlie Harrison. We learn that Christine has never been married, that Joey's father died. Charlie checks on a white van that is following Christine, learning about Mother Grace and her weird church.

While Joey waits in the outer office, there's a call from his 'Grandma,' which turns out to be another opportunity for Mother Grace to spew venom on the boy she believes to be the Antichrist.

Charlie, who has not done any fieldwork since his wife died a year ago, takes charge of Christine's case personally. He takes Joey to get a new dog, identical to the departed Brandy. He organizes some of his best men to watch Christine's house. The men order Chinese food and settle in for a quiet-in-house surveillance.

But they are quickly attacked by followers of Mother Grace, killed, and Christine has to use a gun to stop the last attacker. The police and Charlie show up, and he tells the detectives, 'I want my clients out of here.'

He takes Christine and her dark-eyed son to a loft. Charlie's associate and trusted friend, Henry Rankin, comes by, advising Charlie. When another attacker gets in, Charlie is saved by Rankin.

Charlie gets an appointment to meet with Mother Grace herself. His demand that she leave Christine and Joey alone is met with an impressive display of bleeding. Mother Grace holds her hands up, showing Charlie the 'stigmata' . . . a sign, she says, that he is not evil, though he's in service to the devil. Killing Joey, Grace explains, 'Is what God told me to do.'

The only way to stop Mother Grace, Rankin tells Charlie, is to kill her.

Instead, Charlie returns to the loft (where he attacks a plumber thinking him another follower). His paranoia grows and Charlie decides to take Christine and Joey someplace safe. Rankin says, tell no one where you go, not even me.

But when they flee, a follower attacks them in the hallway of a hotel. The Servants of Twilight always seem able to track them down, and Charlie searches through Christine's bag for a secret transmitter that must be sending messages to Mother Grace – but he finds nothing.

They hit the road, heading to a cabin that Charlie used to vacation in when he was a boy. He tries to swap his car for a Jeep, but the Jeep owner discovers a body in the trunk of Charlie's car. The man aims his 12-gauge at Charlie, but Christine gets a gun on the man, and they get away.

Mother Grace, meanwhile, is working on one of her followers, Kyle Barlowe (Carel Struycken), who's wavering in his conviction about killing the boy. She brings him into the baptismal water and gets him to repeat the words, 'Make me strong, make me ready to be the hammer of God . . .'

Hiding in the cabin, Charlie tells Christine that something is missing, some link. Christine tells him the truth about Joey's birth, how she met his father, Louis, in Mexico . . . and left after five days. She returned to the States pregnant with Joey, and she never heard from the man again.

126

Charlie and Christine make passionate love.

Charlie calls his friend Henry Rankin to come to the Lake Tahoe cabin and help them. Rankin shows up and – when Charlie goes out to check with the police by phone – Rankin stays to watch over Christine and Joey.

And then we see Rankin pull out a cross. 'Give me strength,' he mutters, and we know that he is a member of the Church of the Twilight. He pours holy water on his knife.

Charlie learns on the phone that Mother Grace has been able to find them because there's a leak in Charlie's own organization. Charlie stands there in the rain and flashes on who that leak has to be . . .

He hurries back to the cabin as Rankin tricks Christine into thinking that Charlie is back and needs to speak with her. 'I'll finish Joey's bath,' he says, hiding the knife.

Christine goes down the stairs while Rankin kneels close to Joey, readying the knife. But when Christine doesn't see Charlie downstairs, she hurries back to the bath, jumping on Rankin, fighting him, screaming for Joey to run.

Charlie returns and battles Rankin, a fight that ends with his old friend telling him that Joey is the Antichrist . . . before he is stabbed with a chunk of broken glass.

Now a van arrives, the followers of Mother Grace are closing in. 'We have to make a stand here,' Charlie tells Christine.

They burst in. One follower gets a gun on Charlie and orders Christine to throw her gun down. Mother Grace appears and smashes Christine to the floor with a wrench, killing her. 'The boy is in the attic,' she says, our first real indication that she does indeed have psychic powers.

Kyle kills the new dog and then prepares to kill the boy. But he looks at the boy's eyes and wavers. 'He's just a boy,' Kyle says. He can't do it, he tells Mother Grace.

Mother Grace tries to grab the gun from him, saying that she'll do it. But Kyle resists, and the gun misfires. In the struggle, Mother Grace shoots up into the rafters of the house. A stream of bats swarms into the living room of the cabin, gathering around Mother Grace, covering her. She collapses to the floor, the bats feasting on her.

Paramedics arrive and attempt to revive Christine, barking 'Clear,' as her flatline shows no change. Finally, they give up . . . and Joey goes to his mother, resting his head on her chest.

Suddenly Christine gasps, her eyes open. She smiles and she's alive.

And that would seem to be the end of the nightmare.

But we're back to the present, to Charlie talking to his friend, psychologist Denton Booth, telling him that, 'She was dead. She was dead . . . and came back to life.'

'And,' he says, 'maybe the new dog Joey got was not new at all. Maybe the old dog was brought back to life.' Charlie has gone to the graveyard, to dig up the coffin. In an eerie flashback, we see Charlie exhume the coffin, open it, and discover that there's another dog inside. A caretaker laughs at him: 'nobody worries about what dog goes in which grave.'

It's the *same* dog, Charlie tells Denton Booth. And Christine was dead – and Joey brought her back to life. Because he *is* the Antichrist. 'It has to be done,' Charlie says, 'He has to die.'

But the conversation in the hospital is interrupted. Christine and Joey have come to visit. Christine tells him that she likes his beard, that he looks handsome. Christine is called out of the room. Then Joey comes in to visit.

Charlie stares at him.

'I know,' Charlie says.

And Joey answers, '*I* know.' Then Joey says, 'You love my mother. Be my daddy.'

Then there's a cut. Charlie sits in his living room watching television. The picture goes to snow as Joey walks in with Brandy.

He stands in front of Charlie. 'Every boy needs a daddy,' he says. And since Charlie won't be his daddy, Joey will have to find a new one.

Joey stares at Charlie, who begins to choke, grabbing his throat, choking, clutching his throat until he's dead.

And we learn that Mother Grace wasn't so crazy after all.

* * *

SERVANTS is, at many points, a deftly-made film. Despite a severely limited budget (1.6 million, which was announced to the press as much higher), the film is effective. The budget restrictions show most clearly in the lighting and the varying color quality. The climactic background of snow and mountains at the end was also sacrificed.

Still, the film has a growing sense of paranoia, with the crazed cultists of Mother Grace being able to pop up anywhere.

And though the thought certainly occurs to the viewer that, *hey*, maybe the boy is a bit of a devil, it's quickly dispelled by the stalwart actions of Charlie, the terror of Christine, and the cute vulnerability of Joey. One would have to read the novel to experience the chilling foreshadowing that Koontz uses, while always playing fair with unsuspecting readers . . . even from the first page.

(Christine's unbridled eroticism with Charlie also should set off alarms with readers. While in the film Charlie and Christine become passionate lovers, the film doesn't quite capture the heat of the physical relationship in the novel.)

The Kyle Barlowe character, as well as Henry Rankin, are most dramatically altered by the screenplay. Barlowe is central to saving Joey, and the novel lets us see the tumult raging inside Barlowe. In the novel, of course, Rankin does not betray Charlie. It's an odd touch in the movie – making him a Twilight Church member – but one that works.

Grace Zabriskie's 'Mother Grace' is a wild-eyed performance that makes us see her as completely dotty. But the film mirrors the effective trick of the book, namely forcing viewers to rethink their perception of those who seem at first – and for so long – to be raving lunatics.

The greatest change in the screenplay is the loss of the snow in the mountains, the cold, the drifts. The economics of the low-budget production obviously ruled here. Lost too is the book's final confrontation, set in a cave where the bats are appropriate. The power of that last battle is watered down in the film. (Though having Christine die in the film and then be revived by Joey is effective, giving Charlie pause.)

The endings of the two works differ in interesting ways.

The book's ending, though not ambiguous, is more subtle. Joey is the spawn of Satan – but his mother and Charlie only have doubts. And they ignore their fears and get on with their life together.

The film's ending, though, is grim, with Joey killing Charlie. The boy is unequivocally evil, and it's a rare case where Hollywood opted for an ending even less happy than the book is.

So – the film works. Fangoria commented that '*SERVANTS* does have its moments, and gives the impression of having been made with a bit more integrity than your garden-variety satanism shocker.'

The film holds our attention despite the fact that there are logic problems, especially with the competence of the police. (A lot of bodies have piled up, and it seems that they refuse to recognize who's responsible.)

SERVANTS works even though it lacks the point of view of Mother Grace, something that adds to the chilling effect in *Twilight*. But the strong performances and steady pacing make this an effective thriller.

'Jeff Obrow,' Dean says, 'delivered Trimark a better picture than they had any right to expect. On a shoestring budget, and working with a company notorious for schlock – a company that doesn't really perceive a difference between, say, *Midnight Cowboy* and *Flying Saucer Sluts* – Obrow did a commendable job.

'I don't think the picture holds together as a whole, but there are some effective scenes in it and some nice choices of bridges and scene combinations in the adaptation from book to screen.

'When the film was done, Trimark was surprised by how much better it was than the fare they had offered the public theretofore, but they still couldn't find sufficient theaters to make a theatrical distribution work. So they called me and wanted me to do a lot of tub-thumping for them. "With your endorsement," one of the principals in Trimark told me, "we can get some theater chains to take it, but only with your endorsement."

'It was clear to me why the film buyers for the theaters were reluctant. The dismally low budget had resulted in production values that were below those of even standard TV movies. Clearly, in spite of a noble struggle, Obrow had not had time enough to do the proper lighting setups for each shot, and the film was frequently as flatly lit as any homemade video by your Uncle Newt.

'There were also pickup shots obviously staged in front of painted backdrops because there was no opportunity to go back to the previous location. The bat attack on Grace, at the end of the film, was as dreadfully phony as the guy running around in the bearskin rug pretending to be a monster in *WATCHERS*.

'I told the Trimark executive that I couldn't possibly recommend that fans of mine plunk down hard-earned bucks to see this flick in a theater, and he assured me that "those people out there who go to movies like this, they don't know anything about production values, all they care about is getting a few scares."

'Contempt for the audience is everywhere in Hollywood, and it drives me nuts. When this guy persisted, got threatening, trying to take the position that it was somehow my contractual obligation to support their film, I told him he was delusional and should seek help from mental health professionals before calling me again. The picture went straight to video.'

* * *

PROJECTS TO COME

I reread *WATCHERS* after seeing the two filmed versions. And I was struck by two things. First, the wonderful way the story is layered, and how the theme of sacrifice and love versus blind violence is developed.

And after rereading the book, I could well imagine, if it was mine, how totally upset I'd be with films that jettisoned good ideas for bad, that reduced a wonderful tale to cartoon simplicity, that seemed to have no understanding of the art of storytelling.

It's an author's dream of seeing a novel turned into film, twisted into a nightmare of looney tunes proportions.

So, the ultimate Dean Koontz film hasn't been made.

But Koontz has come tantalizingly close. His own script for THE BAD PLACE featured dramatic changes in the plot, especially regarding the fate of Thomas, the gifted Down's syndrome boy. Initially the script drew enthusiastic responses from executives at Warner Brothers and was sent to directors. Don Johnson expressed an interest in playing Bobby Dakota, and the hope was that Melanie Griffith, his wife, might be interested in playing Julie Dakota, as she and her husband were at that time looking for a vehicle they could do together. For a brief while the production was given a green light contingent on the choice of director.

Then something happened. Reliable sources from within the studio indicate that a chief financial officer, having heard so much about the script, took it home to read, didn't understand it, couldn't figure out what genre it was supposed to fit into – and therefore all of the executives below him became doubters overnight. Two other scripts by other writers have been written since, and recently the rights have reverted to Dean, who plans another script of his own and a new attempt at another studio.

MIDNIGHT, with a script by Dean, was on the front burner at another studio. A number of good directors were interested, but the producers went with a man they felt was 'a genius.' Dean made an attempt to work with him on the director's draft but says:

'I guess big Hollywood producers have a far different definition of "genius" than I do. (This fellow was never even actually coherent.)

'I spent half an hour on the phone with him, during which he gushed about how wildly violent and erotic the film would be – though I had certainly never written either the book or the script with that tone, and he came up with a series of bizarre changes that made me wonder about his sanity.

'For one thing, he suggested we dump Sam, the male lead, and make Harry – the paraplegic – the lead instead, and assured me that this could be done without any changes of substance in any of the main scenes. When I pointed out that Harry would have a hard time leaping off balconies and running down alleyways with packs of inhuman creatures hot on his tail, since Harry was in a wheelchair, the director said, "Oh, yeah, I forgot about the wheelchair. Well, don't worry, we'll work around that. It won't keep us from having a strong action picture."

'Later in a face-to-face meeting with him and the producers, I thought the guy just rambled incoherently for an hour. After the meeting broke up, I asked the producers if anything that had been said made any sense whatsoever to them, and they told me, no, they really hadn't followed what this guy had been saying, but that was to be expected, as he was a "genius" and operating on a plane well above us.

'I walked off the project. Life is too short to waste time on something that was, at that moment, so obviously doomed. I think this genius was on the project about another 18 months with another writer before, at last, the producers acknowledged that everything had spiraled down into chaos. The heartbreaking thing is that when the studio first told the producers to get a director, it was May, and the studio wanted the picture to start by October; it was on a fast track, and everything looked swell. They liked my script, and the movie would be very much like the book. I had thought, in my naiveté, that things only went horribly wrong during the screenplay-development process.

'But I learned that there are countless other ways they can go wrong later, in this depressingly "collaborative" business.'

But even Dean, as cynical as anyone who has been through the Hollywood mill, thinks there is a very good chance that two films now in development from his books may turn out just right. He and his agent have decided to sell only to producers whose work they respect.

'That won't guarantee a good picture,' he says, 'but it improves the odds of getting one.'

HIDEAWAY was sold to Summers-Quaid and TriStar. Producer Kathleen Summers and actor Dennis Quaid have a reputation for quality, and the executive team at TriStar, headed by Mike Medavoy, is widely regarded as having better taste and more intelligence than any studio group in town.

'They have been by far the most courteous, thoughtful, and insightful people I've met in this business,' Dean says, 'so I'm allowing myself to hope again.'

DRAGON TEARS also sold to TriStar, for producers Ned and Nancy Tannen, who are also highly regarded in the film community for producing 'A' pictures with considerable style.

Prior to the collapse of THE BAD PLACE at Warner Brothers, the same studio bought ODDKINS for director Tim Burton, which intrigues and excites the author. On the other hand, his experience with the studio on the former project leads him to worry that 'My furry little heroes in ODDKINS will be transformed into Mutant Adolescent Tai-Kwan-Do Turtles or perhaps it will all become a live-action vehicle for Madonna and Billy Ray Cyrus.'

(By press time, Burton was off the project, and *ODDKINS* was 'in limbo.')

PART V

An Unusual Collection

by Dean Koontz

A

Koontzramble

From time to time, I receive requests to provide introductions to books by writers whose work I am known or thought or urged to admire. Publishers, obviously in need of institutional care, have the touching notion that my contribution will help sell copies. This is flattering but not true. When book buyers are being asked to pay nearly twenty-five dollars for the average hardcover these days, they are not impressed to see that the main attraction is preceded by a few pages of Koontzramble.

I have also received requests to be a spokesman for a well-known computer manufacturer and for a company that sells fish sticks. This is proof that the world is mad. The advertising agency for the computer company knew I didn't use their product and that I had no interest in switching over from the hardware I trusted. That didn't matter to them. The ad just had to be shot with their product in the foreground or to one side of me, and I was not required to say I used it; of course, in return for my fee, I was expected not to spit on their product or sneer while on camera. The fish-stick thing I never did figure out. Exactly what do I or my books have to do with fish? Or sticks? Or crispy batter coatings? If I had agreed to promote fish sticks would I have been offered commercial-endorsement contracts for peanut butter, liquid dish-washing detergent, and feminine hygiene products?

Just as I've turned down all product endorsements, I politely decline to write most book introductions, as well, primarily because my writing schedule is already so demanding that I am unable to add numerous additional assignments. Once in a while, however, the subject is too tempting to resist, whereupon I take off my novelist shoes and put on my essayist slippers (composing a book introduction is a more effete business than writing fiction; one simply cannot accomplish it in standard footwear) and have a good time.

These are my only two hard-and-fast rules when writing an introduction: first, it must be terrifically enjoyable to write, because it doesn't pay well (if it pays at all); second, it must be fun to read. I don't give a hoot if I inform or enlighten the reader of the introduction. You want to be informed, get a direct-feed socket installed in your skull and jack yourself into the Cable News Network every morning. You want to be enlightened, either schedule a long meditation session with the Dalai Lama or spend a month vacationing at Chernobyl.

The following six introductions were all fun to write; and they are, I hope, fun to read, even if you don't know the author about whom I'm writing. These are not critical essays in any sense, but entirely personal and intimate. In every case but one, the writers are friends of mine – or were before I wrote about them. The exception is Rex Stout, and I'm sorry to say he is no longer of this earth. I would *like* to be a friend of Rex Stout, but nothing's more difficult than establishing a meaningful friendship with a dead person – although trying to operate a motor vehicle with only your tongue is a pretty close second. (Listen, folks, if we can't make fun of death, we're in real trouble.) When writing about a friend, my aim is usually not to convince the reader that my *amigo* is a brilliant prose stylist; his prose speaks for itself – and, anyway, that's a judgment for each reader to make on his own. Instead, I want to instill in the reader a conviction that my friend is a terrific person, fun to be around, charming and amusing and faithful and stouthearted. In fact, all of them are all of those things, otherwise they would not be my friends. I *do* have standards in these matters. And in fact, if any of these guys ever ceases to be amusing or charming or stouthearted or any of those things – why, I assure you, I'll cut him off like a leprous nose and never speak to him again, so there.

'Oh, To Be in Cedar Rapids When the Hog Blood Flows' is about Ed Gorman, a man of many talents and not a few strange habits. It was written for a collection of his short stories, *Prisoners*, and recounts a visit that my wife and I paid to Ed and his wife (her name is Carol, though after hearing the phrase so often, some people think she is an Indian with a long tribal name: 'Carol-who-is-too-good-for-him'). All you need to know about the piece is that it is nearly all true. The hog-kill story is true. And the cats, and my allergic reaction. The only things that aren't true, in fact, are references to Ed's obscene phone calls and his Zoroastrianism jokes (they were actually jokes about Brahmanism and Shiva the Destroyer, but that didn't seem funny enough in the retelling).

138

'The Man Who Knows All About Hippodurkees' concerns Tim Powers, the fantasy novelist, and was written for the Charnel House limited edition (illustrated, beautifully bound, for collectors) of Tim's *The Stress of Her Regard*. There are only two things you have to know about this one before you read it: 1) everything in it is true, everything, every last thing, except when I say that Tim's friends are expecting him to become pompous and self-congratulatory as his career blossoms; this is a very funny idea to anyone who knows Tim, because he's quicker than anyone with self-deprecating humor and is the least likely man on the face of the earth ever to become pompous and self-congratulatory (except, perhaps, for Elvis Presley, who faked his death and is now living a disconcertingly humble existence as a celibate Amish farmer outside Lancaster, Pennsylvania); 2) even the behavior of James Blaylock, a friend of Tim's and mine, is true, all of it, every line, I swear on the grave of Rudolph Valentino, all true, except where I have had to interpret his thoughts as I believe them to have been at times when he did not actually express them; if you have ever read one of Blaylock's singularly strange fantasy novels, you will recognize the author as one of his own characters.

'Rex Stout and Nero Wolfe' was written at the request of Bantam Books and included in their reissue of *Where There's a Will*. While Rex Stout's minimum standards were high when compared to those of most writers, *Where There's a Will* is not one of his finest works, but I seized the chance to write the introduction because I have been a fan of the novels featuring Nero Wolfe since I was knee-high to a brontosaurus, which is to say that I didn't discover them until I was a full-grown man but nevertheless feel as if I have known Nero Wolfe all of my life.

'Tater Baron' was written for the Dark Harvest edition of Joe Lansdale's exceptionally nasty *The Nightrunners*, meant to be sold largely to collectors who knew what they were getting into, but was later reprinted, somewhat to my surprise, by a paperback publisher. When the general audience got hold of Joe's gritty black-hearted nightmare, I received a few letters from my own readers who, having purchased *The Nightrunners*, were startled to find that it was not anything whatsoever like a Koontz novel. My introduction had never promised that it would be similar to my own work, and Joe would be appalled to think anyone expected him to write like me. Not that he holds my work in disdain, you understand; he tells me that he likes it very much, and he must be speaking the truth because he knows that if he ever lies to me, I will have him killed. But any writer who is worth beans is determined to write in his own style, no one else's, and would never scope the market with the notion of writing whatever happens to be hot at the moment. In return for this integrity – or sheer bullheadedness, however you want to look at it – those of us who insist on writing exactly what we want to write usually don't break down the publishing industry's resistance until we've gone through too many years with a cash flow no better than that of a tanning parlor in Hell. Joe's developed a good cash flow since I wrote 'Tater Baron,' and seems better positioned than ever to become a household name someday, perhaps never in quite so many households as General Electric or Betty Crocker, but certainly in more than Lemon Fresh Downey.

'The Coming Blaylockian Age' concerns James P. Blaylock – or as he prefers to be called, in his inscrutable way, 'Jim' – and was written for the Axolotl Press edition of his *Two Views of a Cave Painting*. He has a wonderfully poetic way with words combined with an amusing sense of the absurd and a kind heart that shines through every page. When the Monty Python comedy troupe used the phrase 'something entirely different,' they must have been thinking about Blaylock's books and stories. Or maybe they were just thinking about Blaylock himself. Or maybe they were thinking about Blaylock's peculiar feet. Frankly when examining both Jim Blaylock and his work, one can find countless instances where the words 'something entirely different' are not only useful but essential. He's a good sport, too. Which is fortunate for me, because he's a lot bigger than I am.

'The Truth About Christmas' was written for the Canadian fantasy novelist Charles de Lint. Charles is a rather handsome but ascetic-looking fellow whose lean intensity can be a bit imposing – until he opens his mouth. Oh, not that Charles spouts stupidities that spoil the image; he leaves that kind of thing to politicians and Donald Trump. And I've never seen him drool – though I haven't actually been around him a sufficiently large percentage of his life to assure you that he *never* does. No, the reason that the lean-intense-imposing impression flies out the window when Charles opens his mouth is because he's one of the most gentle, soft-spoken, considerate, and charming men you'd ever want to meet. So charming, etcetera, that if he were single, you would keep your girlfriend away from him. And your mother, if she were widowed. And your dog. Because sure as hell, Charles would end up with your girlfriend, your mother, and your dog, all living with him up there in Canada, and you would be wretched and alone. He can also write well. If he wasn't so charming, he'd be widely envied and hated. Anyway, each year Charles writes a short story, prints it up himself in very handsome form with the assistance of his lovely wife Mary Ann, and mails it to friends in lieu of an ordinary Christmas card. He always asks another writer to compose a brief introduction. This seemed to me an ideal place to reveal some of the hard-nosed truths behind the stickily sentimental image of Santa Claus and his merry elves. If you still put a plate of cookies out on Christmas Eve, and if you still listen for the sound of sleigh bells in the night, be warned that the shocking revelations in this short essay may leave you contemplating the double bore of an over-and-under twelve-gauge shotgun. I can't understand how Phil Donohue, Geraldo, and Oprah have failed to build programs around the North Pole scandals.

Finally there is 'Mr Bizarro,' which I wrote for Dark Harvest's hardcover reissue of Jonathan Kellerman's second novel, *Blood Test*. They reissued the book because *Blood Test* is now highly collectible in its true first-edition state, and a lot of people who have become fans of Jonathan's work are unable to obtain a copy in hardcover at a reasonable price. That's because Jonathan is popular. Boy, oh, boy, is he popular.

He's a nice guy (maybe even nicer than I say he is in this essay). He's fairly presentable. He brushes his teeth. He plays the guitar quite well. He's a good conversationalist. He's kind to animals and the elderly. And the moment he's *aware* of those food stains, he immediately changes his shirt. But none of that explains his popularity. He's popular because he's a damned good writer. He's also perhaps the most normal, stable writer I have ever met – which is why it was so much fun to write about him under the title 'Mr Bizarro.'

Oh, To Be in Cedar Rapids when the Hog Blood Flows

1. THE ORIGINS OF THE RELATIONSHIP

Ed Gorman and I met on the telephone and spent scores of hours in conversation spread over almost two years before we finally met face to face. No, it wasn't one of those sleazy pay-by-the-minute 'party-line' dating services gone awry. It started as an interview for his magazine, *Mystery Scene*, but we spent so much time laughing that we began having bull sessions on a regular basis.

He has a marvelous sense of humor and a dry wit. Oh, sure, he can produce faux flatulence with his hand in his armpit every bit as convincingly as Princess Di can, and like the Pope he never goes anywhere without plastic vomit and a dribble glass, but it's the more *refined* side of Ed that I find the most amusing.

2. HOW I WOUND UP IN CEDAR RAPIDS

In 1989, my wife Gerda and I drove across country to do some book research, to visit some relatives and old friends, to receive an honorary doctorate at my alma mater in Pennsylvania – and to give a proper test to our new radar detector. The detector worked swell: We left the Los Angeles area at eight o'clock on a Thursday morning and were in eastern Arkansas in time for dinner. We ate at our motel, and the food wasn't all that good, but everyone thought we were enjoying the hell out of ourselves because crossing six states under four Gs of acceleration contorts your face muscles into a wide grin that remains fixed for eight to ten hours after you get out of the car.

The research was conducted successfully. The visits with friends and relatives were a delight. The address I delivered to the graduating class was well received. I was awarded the honorary doctorate –

whereafter I had to decide whether to be a podiatrist or cardio-vascular surgeon, a very difficult choice in a world where heart disease and sore feet tragically afflict millions.

Soon we were driving west from Pennsylvania, on our way home, our tasks completed and our lofty goals fulfilled. Our radar detector was clipped to the sun visor, Ohio and Indiana and Illinois were passing in a pretty blur rather like that of the star swarms beyond the portals of the *Enterprise* when Captain Kirk tells Scotty to put the ship up to warp speed, and we were proud to be participating in that great American pastime – Avoiding Police Detection. Driving in opposition to the direction of Earth's rotation, therefore having to set the car clock back an hour every once in a while, we might have made it to California before we left for the journey east, in time to warn ourselves against that damn salad-bar restaurant outside of Memphis – except we planned to take a side trip to Cedar Rapids, Iowa, to meet Ed and his wife Carol.

3. THE FIRST NIGHT OF THAT HISTORIC VISIT

After leaving Interstate 80, we passed through gently rising plains and rich farmland, all of it so bland that we began to be afraid that we had died and gone to the twenty-third circle of Hell (Dante had it wrong; he undercounted), where the punishment for the sinner is terminal boredom. We couldn't get anything on the radio but Merle Haggard tunes.

Late in the afternoon, we reached Cedar Rapids, which proved to be a surprisingly pleasant place, attractive to more than the eye. As we crossed the city line, the air was redolent of brown sugar, raisins, coconut, and other delicious aromas, because one of the giant food-processing companies was evidently cooking up a few hundred thousand granola bars. How pleasant, we thought, to live in a place where the air was daily perfumed with such delicious scents. It would be like living in the witch's fragrant gingerbread house after Hansel and Gretel had disposed of her and there was no longer a danger of becoming a human popover in the crone's oven.

That evening we went to dinner with Ed and Carol at a lovely restaurant in our hotel. We had a great good time. Carol, who is also a writer – primarily of young-adult fiction – is an attractive blonde with delicate features, very personable and very much a lady. Ed surprised us by wearing shoes. Not to say that shoes were the only thing he was wearing. He had socks, too, and a nice suit, and I think he was also wearing a shirt, though my memory might well be faulty regarding that detail.

There was almost *too* much conviviality for one evening. Ed started telling jokes about Zoroastrianism, involving the God Ahura Mazda, of which he has an infinite store – always a sure sign that he is having too good a time and might begin to hyperventilate or even pass a kidney stone out of sheer exuberance. They usually begin, 'Ahura Mazda, Jehova, and Buddha were all in a rowboat together,' or something like that. For his sake, we decided to call it an evening and meet again first thing in the morning. Carol asked if there was anything special we'd like to do or see around town (like watch corn growing), and we said that we had heard there was a large Czechoslovakian community in Cedar Rapids; as this was an ethnic group about which we knew little, we thought it might be interesting to visit any shops that dealt in Czech arts, crafts, foods, assault weapons imported from the East Bloc, and that sort of thing. We all hugged, and after Ed told one more Zoroastrianism joke – 'Ahura Mazda was having lunch with two attorneys and a proctologist' – we parted for the night.

4. ON THE EDGE OF SLEEP

Lying in our hotel-room bed that night, on the edge of sleep, Gerda and I spoke of what a lovely evening it had been.

'They're both so nice,' Gerda said.

'It's so nice that someone you like on the phone turns out be someone you also like in person,' I said.

'I had such a nice time,' Gerda said.

'That's nice,' I said.

'Those Zoroastrianism jokes were hilarious.'

'He was wearing shoes,' I noted.

'I was a little worried when he hyperventilated.'

'Yeah, I was afraid it was going to build up to a kidney-stone expulsion,' I said.

'But it didn't,' Gerda said, 'and that's nice.'

'Yes, that's very nice,' I agreed.

'Tomorrow is going to be a very nice day.'

'Very nice,' I agreed, anticipating the morning with enormous pleasure.

5. A VERY NICE DAY

Overnight, Ed and Carol discovered a museum of Czechoslovakian arts and crafts in Cedar Rapids, and in the morning we happily embarked on a cultural expedition. The museum proved to be on a – how shall I say this as nicely as possible? – on a rather *frayed* edge of town. When we got out of Ed's car, I was hit by the most powerful stench I'd ever encountered in more than forty years of varied experience. This was a stink so profound that it not only brought tears to my eyes and forced me to clamp a handkerchief over my nose but brought me instantly to the brink of regurgitation that would have made the explosively vomiting girl in *The Exorcist* seem like a mere dribbler. When I looked at Gerda, I saw she had also resorted to a handkerchief over the nose. Though you might have noticed that comic hyperbole is an element of the style in which I've chosen to write this piece, you must understand that as regards this odor, I am not exaggerating in the least. This vile miasma was capable of searing the paint off a car and blinding small animals, yet Ed and Carol led us toward the museum, chatting and laughing, apparently oblivious of the hellish fetor that had nearly rendered us unconscious.

Finally, after I had clawed desperately at Ed's arm for ten or fifteen unsteady steps, I caught his attention. Choking and wheezing in disgust, I said, 'Ed, for the love of God, man, what is that horrible odor?'

'Odor?' Ed said. Puzzled he stopped, turned, sniffing delicately at the air, as if seeking the elusive scent of a frail tropical flower.

'Surely you smell it,' I protested. 'It's so bad I'm beginning to bleed from the ears!'

'Oh, *that*,' Ed said. He pointed toward some huge buildings fully five hundred yards away. 'That's a slaughterhouse. They must be in the middle of a hog kill, judging by the smell. It's the stink of blood, feces, urine, internal organs, all mixed up together.'

'It doesn't bother you?'

'Not really. When you've smelled it often enough over the years, you get used to it.'

Gagging but determined to be manly about this, I managed to

follow them into the Czech museum, where the odor miraculously did not penetrate. The museum turned out to be one of the most fascinating we'd ever toured, humble quarters but a spectacular and charming collection of all things Czech.

We spent longer there than we had anticipated, and when we stepped outside again, the air was clean, the stench gone without a trace. All the paint had melted off the Gormans' car, and a couple of hundred birds had perished in flight and now littered the ground, but otherwise there was no indication that the air had ever been anything but sweet.

I thought of the delicious aroma of granola-bar manufacturing, which had marked our arrival. That was at the front door. The steaming malodor of the slaughterhouse indicated what went on at the back door. Suddenly Cedar Rapids seemed less innocent, even sinister, and I began to understand for the first time how Ed could live in such sunny, bucolic environs with the gracious and lovely Carol always nearby – and nevertheless be inspired to write about the dark side of the human heart.

6. ED GORMAN, WRITER

Aside from being a great guy, Ed Gorman can write circles around a whole slew of authors who are more famous than he is. Hell, he could write hexagons around them if he wanted.

He has a knack for creating dialogue that sounds natural and true. His metaphors and similes are spare and elegant. His characters are multifaceted and often too human for their own good. His style is so clean and sharp you could almost perform surgery with it; *he* does, using it like a scalpel to lay bare the inner workings of the human mind and heart.

His Jack Dwyer mysteries – especially *The Autumn Deed* and the beautifully moody and poignant *A Cry of Shadows* – are as compelling and stylistically sophisticated as any detective stories I've ever read.

If Ed has a shortcoming as a writer, it is that he wants to do *everything*. He likes Westerns, so periodically he writes an oater – always a damned good oater, too. He likes horror stories, so now and then, writing as Daniel Ransom, he produces a horror story. He likes totally serious, almost somber detective fiction but also lighter-hearted detective fiction; he has written both types well. He likes suspense, science fiction ... well, you get the idea. Having such a catholic taste is healthy; it contributes to his freshness of viewpoint. But when a writer actually produces work in multiple genres, he dilutes his impact with readers and has more difficulty building a reputation. I know too well. Over the years, always looking for a different challenge, I've written in virtually every genre *except* the Western. Finally I discovered a way to combine many of my favorite categories of fiction into one novel, which is when I started to develop a larger audience. In time, I suspect, Ed will find his own way to make his wide-ranging interests more a marketing asset than a liability. I, for one, can't wait to see what he'll give us in the years ahead.

One warning: considering how powerful Ed's prose can be, if he ever writes about a hog kill, his personal experience should lead to such pungent olfactory descriptions that readers all over the world will be hard-pressed not to void their most recent meals into the pages of that book. Don't worry, you'll be warned in advance if one of his novels has a hog-kill scene in it because, being the reader's friend, I will be sure to have an endorsement on the jacket, alerting you in language something like this: 'A brilliant, dazzling, breath-taking novel, a work of sheer genius. Everyone should read Gorman – but in this case, only while wearing a protective rubber sheet or while sitting naked in a bathtub.'

7. THE LOVELY GORMAN HOME

That fine spring day in Cedar Rapids, after visiting the Czech museum adjacent to the hog kill, we went to lunch at an all-you-can-eat buffet restaurant with as lavish a spread as I had ever seen. I ate a soda cracker.

After lunch we went to Ed and Carol's house, which was most tastefully furnished. The place was spotless, with beautifully polished-wood floors, and suffused with a friendly atmosphere.

A couple of minutes after we arrived, my eyes began to sting, then burn, then flood with tears. For a moment I thought I was overcome with emotion at being welcomed into my friends' home. Then my sinuses suddenly felt as if they had been filled with cement, my face began to swell, and my lips itched. I realized that I had either been caught in the beam of an extra-terrestrial deathray – or was in a house where a cat resided. As I had never previously encountered monsters from far worlds but *had* encountered cats to which I was allergic, I decided I could believe the Gormans when they repeatedly insisted that they were not harboring fiendish extraterrestrials but merely felines.

I wish I could tell you that their house was positively crawling with scores of cats; an eccentricity like that would make them even more fun to write about. However, as I remember, there were only two. For some reason I am not allergic to every cat who crosses my path, only to about half those I meet, but I seemed to be allergic to both the Gorman cats. Neither creature looked like a feline from Hell, though they had a demonic effect on me, and in less than half an hour we had to move on.

When I stumbled out of the Gorman house, I was shockingly pale, sweating, and gasping for breath. My watering eyes were so bloodshot they appeared to be on fire, and the only sound I could squeeze out of my irritated vocal cords and swollen throat was a wretched gurgle rather like that issued by a nauseated wombat.

(I realized much later, the oddest thing about that moment was the reaction of the neighbors to my near-death paroxysms on the Gormans' front lawn. None of them exhibited the least surprise or concern. It was as if they had seen scores – perhaps hundreds – of people erupting from that house in far worse condition and had become enured to the drama. Maybe they *were* cats from Hell . . . which might explain why sometimes, instead of purring, they spoke rapid, intricately cadenced Latin.)

The Gormans, being two of the nicest people I've ever known, were excessively apologetic, as if somehow they were responsible for my stupid allergy. When I could breathe again, and when my eyes had stopped spurting blood, I found myself repeatedly assuring them that none of it was their fault, that they are *allowed* to have cats in the United States of America regardless of my allergy, and that they would not rot in Hell because of their choice of pets.

(Ed has a tendency to feel responsible for the world and to blame himself for things beyond his control – like floods in Sri Lanka and train wrecks in Uzbekistan. Like any good Catholic boy, he knows that he is guilty for all the sins of the world, a vile repository of shameless want and need and lust, who deserves far worse punishment than any plague God could deliver upon him. In his mind, having cats to which a guest has an allergy is just one small step below taking an Uzi out to the mall and blowing away a hundred Christmas shoppers.)

8. A THANKFULLY UNEVENTFUL TRIP TO IOWA CITY, IOWA

Anxious to get me away from his cats and to atone for what they had done to me, Ed suggested we take a ride from Cedar Rapids to Iowa City, where we could have a pleasant stroll through Prairie Light, a large and nationally known bookstore, then have an earlyish dinner (as Gerda and I had to rise at dawn to resume our journey to California). He assured us that Iowa City also boasted a feline slaughterhouse where we could go to compare the stink of cat-kill to that of a hog-kill.

Aside from a hair-raising ride due to the sheer contempt in which Ed holds those lane-dividing lines on public highways, our sidetrip to Iowa City was uneventful. Just good conversation – much of it book talk – and a nice dinner. I had another soda cracker. I was able to keep it down with little trouble. I was quite sure that, in a month or so, the memory of the hog-kill stench would have faded sufficiently to allow me to eat normally again, certainly before my weight had slipped much lower than ninety pounds.

9. ED GORMAN, THE PHONE COMPANY, AND ME

As I write this, it is nearly three years since our stay in Cedar Rapids and our two days with Ed and Carol. As both of us are to some degree workaholics and as neither of us, therefore, is much of a traveler, Ed and I have not yet managed to get together again face to face. We stay in touch by reading each other's books – and with the help of the telephone. Our conversations continue to be punctuated with a lot of laughter – precious, vital medicine in this madhouse world. Here's a cute anecdote: Sometimes at three in the morning, Ed calls up and, with a couple of handkerchiefs over the mouthpiece of his phone, distorts his voice and makes obscene threats, apparently because he's concerned about keeping my life interesting and full of color, and I am always touched by his genuine concern that I never become

149

bored, by the fact that he would take the time and trouble to entertain me in such a fashion. He doesn't realize that I know the identity of the obscene caller, and he would surely be embarrassed to know that I am aware of his thoughtfulness. But you see, no matter how much he distorts his voice, those cats are in his study with him, and even long-distance my lips go numb and my eyes begin to bleed.

C

The Man Who Knows All About Hippodurkees

When I first met Tim Powers, he was working at a tobacco shop, and he was not yet either pompous or self-congratulatory. He had written three novels, no easy task for someone who cares about craft and language, even more difficult for someone who produces his scripts in longhand (as Tim did at that time). He had also begun dating the beautiful Serena: 'What does she see in him?' everyone asked. And he could tell you more about fine pipes than you cared to know. He'd say things like. 'Dean, see this here meerschaum with the hand-carved ivory inlays and the brass dooflaxus and the gold-plated hippodurkee? Well, this is worth $604.51 because it was crafted in 1930 by Ridley Skeeve of Vienna, who had radical ideas about the angle of stem to bowl that would be most conducive to a mellow flow of smoke, and he spent his entire fortune and that of his wealthy wife, Cher, trying to develop a pipe that could be used with great satisfaction even by a man suffering from a paralyzed mouth. Skeeve went mad, of course, and became convinced that a tribe of pygmy antismoking activists lived in his attic, waiting to assassinate him if he ever developed the perfect pipe.' Tim also knew a lot about fencing, fantasy fiction, the novels of John D. MacDonald, poetry, and enough other subjects to qualify him as something of a neo-Renaissance man. In the tobacco shop, he was often surrounded by a group of admirers and/or listeners – some of them a tad strange, it's true, and some even motley, yes, and some deranged, but admirers nonetheless – who, like the rest of us, were vastly entertained by his tales and patter. In spite of all that, Tim did not as yet have a swelled head.

Months later, my wife and I were invited to Power's apartment for a lazy afternoon with two other writers. James P. Blaylock and Philip K. Dick. As we sat on the back porch, Jim contributed his usual wry commentary to the conversation, and once in a while he looked at the

151

summer sky and blinked and squinted and said more to himself than to us. 'Look, it's a . . . no . . . never mind.' But then he'd squint again and mumble, 'A squid . . . no . . . surely not. With wings? Hmmmmmm. Flying south . . . and carrying a great wheel of cheese in its tentacles, by the look of it. Hmmmmmm.' And then even more to himself, in barely a whisper, 'Well, I guess we know what *this* means.' (If you've read Blaylock's work, all of this makes perfect sense.) But one soon gets used to Blaylock; and when his wife, Viki, showed up later, she was so *normal* that it was impossible to believe that Jim, having won such a woman, could be dangerous. Phil Dick was his usual charming self, highly amusing, with a sense of irony so sharp he could have engaged Tim in some fencing with it – and did. Serena was there, and she and Tim were planning marriage; so many people were still asking, 'What does she see in him?' that you could hear the question echoing both nearby and distantly through Santa Ana every few minutes during that long afternoon. Tim was at work on *The Anubis Gates*, an ambitious historical fantasy. His circle of admirers was growing and, more important, was somewhat less motley and deranged than previously. Still, Tim was neither full of himself nor smug, not noticeably obnoxious in any way. Yet.

Time passed, and Serena married Tim, no doubt breaking a lot of hearts. The event was in no way marred by the puzzled priest's interruption of the ceremony to ask her what in God's name she saw in her husband-to-be, for by that time the question was as unremarkable to her as 'How're you doing?' or 'Hot enough for you?' By then, of course, most of us knew what she saw in Tim. He was amusing, fun to be with, filled with interesting stories, talented, with a singular – if twisted – perspective on life. He and Serena settled down in a home in one of the more crime-ridden areas of southern California, and when they found blood trails on the sidewalk, they often followed them in a spirit of crazed adventure, to see what might wait ahead. (No joke. This is true!) Through reckless interaction with the denizens of the streets in their neighborhood, they acquired enough curious and interesting anecdotes to fill six volumes of weird memoirs. Tim quit the tobacco shop and began to write full time, whereupon he was able to research countless new subjects and become even more of a neo-Renaissance man, which relieved many of us because this broadening of his knowledge meant fewer stories about Ridley Skeeve and gold-plated hippodurkees. Still, he remained untroubled by hubris.

More time passed, and *The Anubis Gates* won an award, and the well-received *Dinner at Deviant's Palace* was published, and Tim began writing *On Stranger Tides* for a very respectable advance, and his marriage to Serena flourished, and then *On Stranger Tides* was published and nominated for various awards. His circle of admirers continued to grow, and an ever dwindling percentage of them were of interest to police and mental-health authorities. We continued to see Tim and Serena fairly regularly, often in the company of the Blaylocks. (Jim Blaylock's fascination with dwarves and squids and bivalve mollusks and peculiar fish did not abate, though one began to see in him a greater acceptance of these portentous beings and noticeably less hysteria related to them. He is now able to pass an aquarium without flinching or protectively putting a hand on his wallet, although he regards the occupants of those glass-walled worlds with caution and respect, and says he *knows* what role they really play in the creation of the cosmos, the maintenance of time, and the easy availability of yogurt in many flavors.) Though Tim's career was on the ascent, though his marriage was happy, though he had added culinary expertise to his list of talents and had proved to be an adventurous cook willing to experiment, and though his sessions in the kitchen resulted in fewer explosions and toxic clouds than local oddsmakers expected, he was still not in the least bit pompous or self-congratulatory.

Now he has completed *The Stress of Her Regard*. This novel is his most ambitious to date. He attempts to wrench a bit of history into a fantastic pattern of his own, without contradicting the known facts, putting a phantasmagorical spin on the lives of Shelley and Byron and their contemporaries, and he succeeds. The book will no doubt bring him more money, more fame, a still wider circle of admirers, and mail from a lot of extremely interesting sociopaths.

Now, we thought, he will become a world-class, self-satisfied, egomaniacal bore.

But it didn't happen. He's still good old Tim. He's still amusing and open and easygoing. Blaylock says we can stop worrying about Tim ever getting too full of himself, that he will always be a nice guy – but, of course, Blaylock claims to have been told this by a talking sea slug with the ability to see the future. I trust my own instincts more than the precognitive abilities of any slug. Happily, however, I'm in agreement with that gifted, ocean-crawling wad of gelid slime (I refer to the slug, not to Blaylock). Regardless of the certainty that he's going to produce more amazing books and become ever more famous and admired, Tim Powers will always be a good guy to have a beer with – and in this troubled world, that is at least as important as the fact that he writes so well.

D

Rex Stout
and Nero Wolfe

A writer is influenced by everything he reads. Everything. That means not only novels and short stories but newspapers and magazines and cereal boxes and even – God, spare us – the inscrutable scribblings of politicians. If a writer's dog drags home a wad of old paper which is unappetizing to the human eye but on which the mutt has chewed and slobbered with enthusiam, the writer will be influenced by whatever he reads between the tooth holes and saliva tracks. Although his conscious mind may be easily bored, his subconscious is a perpetually wonderstruck infant that will find a wealth of fascinating data to store away from that dog-gnawed paper.

Aware that the subconscious is a cosmic sponge, writers are often willing to experience anything in the interest of finding material. They will sail to Burma on a freighter to participate in a yak-heaving contest, subject themselves to a survival trek in the Amazon rain forest where they must eat grub pâté to escape starvation, have the inner rims of their nostrils decorated by a carnival tattoo artist at a county fairgrounds in Alabama, and even watch Phil Donahue – all in the hope that the subconscious will mull over these adventures, discover aspects and achieve insights beyond the perceptive ability of the conscious mind, and generate brilliant ideas for novels or short stories.

Some of these writers, with tiny tattooed flames blazing from their nostrils and their shoulders aching from heaving one yak too many and bits of grubs still stuck between their teeth, will react with horror to the suggestion that they might want to *read* as broadly as they travel. If one of these scribblers considers himself a 'literary' writer, he doesn't want to contaminate his subconscious mind with an awareness of the styles and prose rhythms of 'popular' writers, for fear he might wind up writing a novel that has relevance beyond the insular world of the self-appointed literati or that, God forfend, even has a plot. If he is a science-fiction writer, he may read science fiction to the exclusion of all other forms, convinced that any tale of genetically engineered, brain-eating, laser-toting, cyberpunk aliens with a psychotic need to conquer the universe is certain to be more intellectually stimulating than any story to be found in lesser genres. Some popular writers will not read literary types, partly as a payback for the undeserved insults they have received from those artistes. Some mystery writers will read only mysteries, some Western writers only Westerns, some historical novelists only historicals.

One novelist I've encountered is reluctant to read *any* novels other than his own, for fear of polluting his creative tidepool. If he reads John D. MacDonald, Philip Roth, Charles Dickens, or anyone else, isn't it possible (he worries) that he will then call forth his own muse only to discover that she is a hideous mutant, twisted beyond all recognition by contamination with those *other* writers? He apparently functions under the impression that his talent came with an engraved-in-stone stylesheet of prodigious specificity, a gift from God that has acquired no patina from life, and that he would have written precisely the same stories when he was two weeks old as he writes now, if only his fingers had been big enough to deal with a typewriter at that tender age.

When it comes to reading fiction, I am an omnivore, largely because I love to read but also because I fear that reading *sparely* will result in my writing being shaped by too narrow a range of influences. Unlike the skittish writer in the previous paragraph, I think that by reading everything, I water down the influence of any one writer and thereby preserve my natural voice. For all of my adult life, I have devoured both popular and 'serious' fiction, love stories and science fiction, Westerns and horror novels, tales of academic angst and animal stories, stream-of-consciousness, self-indulgence and clockwork-mechanism mystery novels, Jim Harrison and Jim Thompson, John le Carré and John Barth, Philip K. Dick and Philip Roth and Philip José Farmer, though I find the recent work of the middle Philip too Philippic.

I have learned a great deal from an omnivorous literary diet, but two lessons in particular apply to this introduction. First, the very best examples of writing from any genre are equal in quality to the best examples from any other genre, and the finest popular fiction is equal to the finest 'serious' fiction. The fragmentation of fiction into genres was largely a marketing ploy of modern publishing. Likewise, the division between popular and serious work was a scheme perpetrated by academics in need of creating a false pantheon of living writers when it became impossible to come up with fresh dissertation topics (to earn degrees and prestige) concerning the writers in the true pantheon, who had been analyzed to exhaustion. Second, the more widely a writer reads, the more he learns about craft and technique, and the more interesting and flavorful his style becomes, just as a vegetable soup becomes more interesting with a multitude of vegetables than it is with only, say, lima beans and broccoli.

Twenty years ago, when I was struggling to find my own voice as a writer, I was reading five novels a week in addition to putting in full days at the typewriter. (We didn't have the great blessing of computers and word-processing software back then. But we didn't have freeway shootouts or Donald Trump, either, so it wasn't altogether a less appealing era.) It was exciting to 'discover' a great writer like John D. MacDonald, who had a backlist, and read one book after the other to the point of intoxication. Or Donald Westlake. Hammond Innes. Irwin Shaw. John P. Marquand, who wrote the Pulitzer-winning *The Late George Apley* and other mainstream novels while also turning out Mr Moto mysteries, which would be impossible in today's more severely – and absurdly – divided worlds of popular and serious fiction. Robert Heinlein. Evan Hunter, Ed McBain, Somerset Maugham, Keith Laumer, and so many many others.

Rex Stout.

You wondered if I was ever going to get to him, didn't you? One of the best tricks in a writer's bag is anticipation. If you set up an expectation in the reader, then draw out the fulfillment of that expectation with skill (though never at *too* great a length), he can be made to enjoy the wait and, because of waiting, can be teased to a greater appreciation of the Big Dramatic Moment than he would have if you had given it to him quickly. This technique I learned from reading Rex Stout.

I think the first Rex Stout novel I read was *The Father Hunt*, which was published in 1968, when the author was eighty-two years old. It was a Nero Wolfe story, of course, and I was swept away, drawn into the palpable atmosphere of that brownstone house on West 35th Street in Manhattan, where the fat detective and his good right hand, Archie Goodwin, lived and worked. I recall finishing the book with purest delight at what I had discovered (after resisting my wife's importunings to read one of them for, oh, two or three years), and with dismay that the author was of such an advanced age that he would never be able to write enough in this wonderful series to satisfy my new hunger for it. Then I discovered there were at that time forty-three Nero Wolfe titles, counting collections of novelettes.

Consider that Rex Stout was born in 1886, and did not write his first Nero Wolfe mystery, *Fer-de-Lance*, until 1934, when he was forty-eight years old, then proceeded to become one of the most widely published and famous mystery writers in the world. Talk about a successful second career! Or maybe it was his twenty-first career, since he sometimes claimed to have held twenty jobs between the time he finished his service in the Navy until he created the fattest and most eccentric and most brilliant detective of all time. More likely mystery writing was his first *genuine* career, as it cannot have been possible to conduct twenty others between his early twenties and late forties; everything prior to Wolfe was preparation.

By the time I read five of Stout's mysteries, I realized I was in the hands of a writer who knew a great deal about a wide variety of subjects and was mining extensive real-world experience, but I also knew that he was, like me, an omnivorous reader. His best books glow because of it. They are filled with literary allusions of exquisite subtlety, clever references and associations to the world of myriad other authors, the use of genre traditions in ways that can only be conceived by a writer who knows not merely the genre in which he works but its relationship to all other categories of fiction and to mainstream literature. Understand, he never bores you with his erudition. He never shoves it in your face. It's possible to read his books, never cotton to a single allusion, and still enjoy the hell out of them. But the reason you *can* enjoy the hell out of them is because the surface story has all those hidden supports.

I also learned from Rex Stout, among them, that popular fiction, regardless of genre, can be ambitious and can have more than a little something worthwhile to say to the reader. Archie Goodwin (who is, actually, more the central figure of this series than Nero Wolfe himself) is Huck Finn brought into the modern age, Huck with his emancipator's soul intact but less naive, more cynical – yet strangely more hopeful, too. Nero Wolfe's exceptional intellect has allowed him to see too deeply into our modern world, and he has turned away from it, perhaps out of despair or disgust or both, taking refuge in a life of special private pleasures of the mind and body, redeemed only by a strict personal code and an adherence to the values that built civilization but which 'civilized' society seems to have forgotten or abandoned. Without Archie Goodwin – the archetypal good man who wins; what a name! – Wolfe would be ineffective, a hermit and curmudgeon not worth reading about. Together, each bringing his strengths and weaknesses to the drama, they play out allegories of various aspects of the human condition with a grace that should make this series of novels timeless.

Having said all of this, I would be remiss if I did not warn the new reader that, while always engaging, these are not tales of fast action. They contain little blood – a smear there, a drop here. More often than not, the major events take place offstage, and the lead characters only discuss them after the fact! The pleasure for the reader lies, instead, in the fascination of the characters (which grows with every book one reads) and the play of the mind. The play of the mind . . . Yet these are not puzzle stories in the classic sense, like some Agatha Christie. In fact, you often don't care that much *who* killed whom. Stout was concerned more with the why of murder and with exploring how essentially ethical men, like Wolfe and Goodwin, differ from the muck of humanity in their methods of thinking.

I will not claim that Stout's prose is without fault. For the most part it is supple, so clear that it appears simpler than it really is, and strong. But in some of the books, including *Where There's a Will*, the great man trips up and shows us he's human. For example, Wolfe 'snaps' his dialogue when such a manner of speaking is patently impossible; try snapping a line yourself, with the attempt to sound like thumb clicking forefinger or like a mousetrap being sprung, and you'll see what I mean; only someone wearing bad dentures has a chance of 'snapping' out words, much to his embarrassment. But the slips are few and minor, and the story usually sweeps the reader along so well that the flaws are never noticed.

Rex Stout's Nero Wolfe novels had such an impact on me, in my formative years as a writer, that I now collect the hard-to-get first-edition hardcovers. They are not cheap, these rare volumes. But I've had a little writing success of my own, and I would rather indulge a sentimental streak than spend the money on cashmere socks and ancient bottles of bordeaux. If you read my books, you'll be hard-pressed to see where I write at all like Rex Stout. But a piece of him is in there; believe me.

For better or worse, this is one way a writer lives after his death, other than in his own books: In the indelible imprint he leaves when you crack the covers of his novels and give him the chance to leave his fingerprints all over your soul. It's not an invasion of privacy, but a small crime of kindness, a breaking and entering with the intention of giving rather than talking.

Enjoy.

E

Tater Baron

I am thankful for many things. I am thankful that gnarly oak fungus is not a human disease. I am thankful that the Department of Motor Vehicles will grant a driver's license without requiring that the applicant eat a live reptile. I am thankful that stairs lead up and down at the same time and that escalators do not. I am thankful that it is not a Western tradition to drink horse blood on Christmas Eve. I am thankful that socks are not made of barbed wire and that hailstones are seldom the size of apartment buildings. And I am thankful that Joe Lansdale decided to become a writer.

He swears that he once wanted to be a tater baron. For those who have no ear for Texas idiom, a tater baron is a farmer who makes a fortune raising and selling potatoes – an oil baron with roots. Joe had a piece of land, a good mule or two, a few bags of potato seeds (or whatever the devil they plant in order to grow the things), and plenty of determination. If he'd had a bit more luck in agriculture, we might know him today as the main supplier of spuds to McDonald's and Burger King. Misfortune smiled on him, however, and potatodom's loss is fiction's gain.

Joe was poor once, so his dreams of making a fast fortune in the potato industry are, though irrational, understandable. Those of us who have been poor are driven by a need for security that no one from a middle-class or wealthy family can ever understand.

Fortunately, although Joe was raised poor, his parents loved him, and they knew how to convey that love and warm him with it. He speaks of them with great affection; listening to him, one understands where he got the love of people that is apparent in the best of his fiction. 'My father,' Joe once told me, 'was uneducated, and he could never earn much even though he worked hard. But what mattered was that he was a fine man, just the finest there could be, and if I never become a big-name writer, I'd count myself a success if I would end up being half as good a man as he was.'

And he's sincere about that. You don't have to be around Joe a

161

long time to realize that he means what he says and that, unlike many writers, he is not carrying a two-ton ego. Joe's one of those rare fellows who understands in his bones that selling a short story to *Twilight Zone* is not equivalent to the work done by leading cancer researchers and that selling a novel to Bantam, while desirable and exciting, ranks more than a notch or two below the achievements of Mother Teresa. You might be surprised, dear readers, to discover how many writers lack a reasonable perspective on their careers; they labor under the serious misapprehension that they are more important to the future of the world than all the rest of humankind combined. Joe is proud of his writing – and rightfully so: it's good – but he is incapable of forgetting that publication credits will never be as important as being a good husband, a good father, a good friend, and a good neighbor.

The funny thing is, truly first-rate work is seldom produced by those writers who campaign for awards, who have no doubt that their words will be in all the literature textbooks of the future, and who publicly compare themselves favorably with the old masters of the novel. On the other hand, the both-feet-firmly-on-the-ground Joes of this world frequently give us tales that are the essence of good writing. Maybe that's because the ain't-I-just-wonderful types are focused entirely on themselves, while the Joes are interested in other people and therefore are able to create characters that are real and convincing. And while the ain't-I-just-wonderful types are writing about Important Issues of which they know nothing, the Joes are writing about the mundane issues of daily existence in ways that illuminate them and move us, because the Joes understand that the mundane issues are also the eternal ones of life and death and hope and love and courage and meaning.

All of which is not to say that Joe Lansdale takes his work less seriously than he should. On the contrary, he cares deeply about his craft and his art, and that care is evident in his fiction.

I remember the night I picked up Joe Lansdale's *The Magic Wagon* and was at once enthralled by Billy Bob Daniels. Old Albert, Rot Toe the Wrestling Chimpanzee, the body in the box, and Buster Fogg. It was the strangest Western I'd ever read, full of creepy-crawly stuff as well as gunfighters, straddling genres with authority, and it dealt with the human condition in a profound yet unpretentious manner that any sensible writer would envy. In a fair world *The Magic Wagon* would have fallen into the hands of a publisher with the money and foresight to trumpet the Lansdale virtues to the world, and it might have become to the 1980s what *True Grit* was to its decade. Certainly, at the very least, if published as a mainstream novel with fanfare, *The Magic Wagon* would have made everyone aware that this man's ascension to the top ranks of Name Writers is not a matter of *if* but *of* when. This is not a fair world, however, and *The Magic Wagon* was published without fanfare by Doubleday as just another entry in its long-running line of Westerns. We should praise the editor who had the taste to recognize the value of that book – while reviling the system that condemned it to oblivion on its initial release.

Oblivion will not be the fate of future Lansdale novels. The only thing more certain than his eventual fame is tomorrow's sunrise. I suspect, however, that he is going to be one of those writers who takes a long time to build, who has to find his own readership with little assistance from his publishers. Many publishers don't really want to help writers build a following; instead they want to discover overnight successes who sell big from book one. The U.S. publishing industry stays busy spending fortunes on the latest illiterate Great Finds, who nearly always prove to have little talent and less staying power. While great riches and brief glory go to each year's newest sensations, real writers like Joe keep working steadily, getting better all the time: happily, the slow-track types frequently survive and ultimately prosper, while the overnight successes vanish into the great publishing swamp from which most of them should never have been dredged up in the first place. That's all right. Among the countless writers who have been slow-builders struggling against the industry's indifference, we can count John D. MacDonald, Elmore Leonard, Robert Heinlein, and Dick Francis, which is about the best company anyone could want.

I am thankful for many things. I am thankful that there are no known weather conditions in which dogs will spontaneously explode. I am thankful that Walt Disney gave us Mickey Mouse instead of Mickey Cockroach. I am thankful that the Hare Krishnas do not possess a nuclear arsenal. And I am thankful that Joe Lansdale decided to become a writer.

The Coming
Blaylockian Age

One-eyed newts were never meant to be the dominant species on earth, and that part of God's plan has proved successful. Cows were intentionally not designed to play concert violin, which is why you will find only a few bovine performers at the symphony – and those not first-rate. Human beings were never meant to have four hands because God saw that the species could get into enough trouble with just two. Originally, skunks *were* created with wings, but in his infinite wisdom God saw that the potential for air pollution was appalling, and He grounded all skunks for eternity, which has worked out pretty well, too. Mice were never meant to serve as coachmen, no matter what you have read in *Cinderella*.

Jim Blaylock was never meant to be a professional juggler, a coconut broker, a walrus husker, or a Hare Krishna flower salesman, and with diligent effort he has avoided (sometimes narrowly) all of those occupations. He once came close to accepting a job selling veal underwear door to door, but then he married Vicki, and she knocked some sense into him.

He *has* worked in the construction trades, which explains at least some of southern California's unusual architecture. He was also employed for a time in a shop that sold exotic fish to aquarium hobbyists, and if you have read his fiction you are no doubt even now speculating about the possibility that some tiny, rare flying fish might have glided into his ear, settled in his brain, and taken control of him.

Though he did carpentry and sold finny pets, Jim Blaylock was not meant for those jobs either. He was meant to write fiction. After his forays into unsuitable occupations, after an absurd amount of dithering and dilly-dallying, and after much hemming and hawing (to the absolute *distraction* of his neighbors), Jim finally settled down to the life's work that God intended for him as surely as He intended birds to fly and wild horses to gallop. These days he writes, and that's why the winters seem milder lately and why the sky is a deeper, warmer blue than before: Jim being a writer is so cosmically correct that the very fact of it improves creation.

Most readers, when sampling Jim's stories for the first time, usually react according to a predictable pattern. First, blinking and wide-eyed and edgy, they say, 'Ummm, what the hell *is* this stuff?' Then they read another story and, less edgy but now looking under their chairs for lurking (but well-intentioned) squids that might have escaped from that Blaylockian Otherworld, they say, 'Ummm, I'm still not sure what the hell this is, but I think I like it.' Then they read another story, and they're no longer edgy at all (though now they often develop quirky habits, like carrying toads in their coat pockets), and they say, 'Ummm, this Blaylock has it right, he understands life, he's portraying it the way it really *is*.' At that point the reader is forever lost to the world he once knew and is thereafter an eternal captive of the bizarre Blaylockian Universe.

Bizarre it is, but in its own way the Blaylockian Universe is in fact real life as we know it. If there is a single thread that runs through all of Jim's works, it is the belief, never blatantly stated but nevertheless firmly implied, that life is a lunatic lark and the world is mad: not mad in a gloom-and-doom sense, not mad to an extent that justifies resignation or even detachment, but mad in a *playful* sense. I suspect Jim was standing in front of a mirror one day, studying his own face, and he said to himself, 'Wait just a minute here! If God insisted on positioning our nose precisely where it could drip into our mouth, then he was clearly having some fun with us!' That revelation, or one like it, caused him to look at the world around him from a far different perspective than that from which most people see it, and he glimpsed a whole new creation. Now he writes about that new place and, though it seems to be the strangest fantasy to those who have not yet gotten to Stage Three of Blaylockitis, it seems like our very own world to the rest of us.

In addition to his singular viewpoint, Jim has another strength that can't be underestimated: He can write well. In a Jim Blaylock story you will not find a trove of grammar howlers, baboon syntas, or metaphors that sound as if they were composed by someone to whom English is a third language. His line-by-line craftsmanship is first-rate. Do you know how rare that is? Read one page from each of twenty books, all by acclaimed writers and, if you have the perception to see beneath the surface to the muscle and tendon of craftsmanship,

165

you will discover that perhaps two of those twenty tales are written with the facility of language that you will find in every Blaylock piece. That skill gives him a base from which he then creates some of the freshest, most appealing, and most apt images – and some of the most lyrical sentences – in modern fantasy. If you tell me that Blaylock's stories are not to everyone's taste, I will agree; but if you tell me they're poorly written, I'll know you're a fool or worse.

On top of all this, Jim Blaylock is a nice guy. I've never seen him kick a dog or drop a baby in boiling oil. (The night during which he nearly kicked a baby and boiled a dog, however, is one we don't talk about. Besides, that was not characteristic behavior by any means, and you must understand that the Santa Ana winds were blowing, a southern California weather condition during which, as Raymond Chandler has observed, no one is quite himself.) He is soft-spoken and easy-going and tolerant. He washes regularly and has never, in my company, spat on a priest or thrown up on a well-dressed woman.

Jim Blaylock's life looks good these days. Readers are buying his books. He's married to the beautiful Vicki, and he has two fine, strapping sons who at the very worst will be highly successful mafia thugs with good wardrobes and lots of pocket money. He has completed a large part of the remodeling of his house, much of it his own handiwork, and his best friend, Tim Powers, is a thundering success with his own writing. That is one of the sweetest pleasures of life: Not merely to succeed but to see your friends succeed as well.

May you have success all your days, Jim. If you should ever be tempted to give up writing for professional elbow wrestling or moose demolition, I will insist that Vicki knock you upside the head one hell of a shot.

G

The Truth About Christmas

By the first of December at the North Pole, everyone's just a little crazy. If you knew what they must contend with up there, you wouldn't blame them for being frazzled.

For one thing, the six-month night is well under way, and the lack of dependably regular sunrises and sunsets plays havoc with the circadian rhythms of the Clauses – Santa and Bernice (Mrs Claus's Christian name is revealed here for the first time) – and all the elves, even though they have lived in that peculiarly disorienting place for hundreds of years if not eternity. No one is ever quite sure whether it's time to eat breakfast or dinner, and without a clear diurnal-nocturnal pattern to guide them, some of the elves quite forget to change clothes until their body odor earns them nicknames like Billy Dirty Socks and Jack Foul Shorts.

By that time of the year, too, the snow is flying; drifts have mounted around Santa's house and the complex of work-shops, making everyone wonder anew why it wouldn't be possible to run a magical Christmas kingdom from someplace like Jamaica. (It would be easy to do so, in fact, except that Mrs Claus has fierce allergies to a wide variety of pollen; everywhere except at the Pole, she is reduced to little more than a wheezing mucus machine.)

In addition to the darkness and the skin-peeling arctic wind, they must cope with a toy-production schedule that is simply insane. Most of the toys are not made by the busy elves, as many people believe. The elves are essentially accounting and management personnel, but their work is nonetheless exhausting. (Toys are produced by the slave labor of thousands of spellbound trolls that Santa keeps in stone dungeons deep in the arctic ice. Even though the trolls would otherwise be up to no good, creating havoc wherever they went, their enslavement is the Dark Side of the Santa Claus story and one that

167

should not be dwelt on in this bright season of fellowship and goodwill.)

Considering their many difficulties, it is not unusual that the residents of Santa Village turn their eyes south from the Pole toward not-so-distant Ottawa and dream enviously of being Charles de Lint. The weather *is* somewhat better there than at the top of the world. The circadian rhythms of Ottawa's people are not so out of whack as those of Billy Dirty Socks and Jack Foul Shorts. More important, Charles's wife, Mary Ann, is inexpressibly more charming and witty and attractive than Mrs Claus – and produces comparatively little mucus. To the further envy of Santa and the elves, Charles himself sits in his warm, comfortable workroom, creating magical gifts of words that far outshine even the best of gifts produced in Santa's workshops – with nary a worry about reindeer droppings or about a possible troll breakout from the slave pens. And every year at Christmas, rather than being forced to produce millions of dolls and toy trucks and stuffed animals and geegaws, Charles must write and publish, with Mary Ann's assistance, only one chapbook-length story such as 'The Drowned Man's Reel,' with which to deliver the de Lints' warmest wishes for a fine holiday season and a life of good cheer.

Mr Bizarro

Jonathan Kellerman is strange. No, wait, I want to be honest. These are the 1990s, and we are drawing near the end of the millennium; the earth is going to be destroyed by a comet, by excessive Styrofoam packaging, or perhaps by Tom and Roseanne Arnold; this is no time for lies; this is no time for less than complete revelation and unflinching commitment to the truth; this *is* evidently a time for excess use of the semicolon; however, perhaps that's another of the peculiar effects of the approaching end of the millennium; one cannot say for sure; it is all quite mysterious; it is a time of omens; unconventional punctuation is no doubt one of the seven signs of the Apocalypse; beware. Anyway, because this is an age that cries out for honesty, I must say that Jonathan Kellerman is beyond strange; he is weird; he is whacked out; there's that damned semicolon again.

I am aware that libel laws require rigorous substantiation of a statement as bold as the one I have made. However, I assure you, I possess photographs of Tom and Roseanne Arnold building a planet-busting cobalt bomb in a vast subterranean installation under the diner they recently opened in Tom's hometown in Iowa. In most of these photographs, the Arnolds are mooning the camera, but it's still possible to make a positive identification; therefore, the fear that they are agents of Armageddon is not without foundation.

As for the assertion that Jonathan Kellerman is weird, the evidence for this is extensive and irrefutable – though it does not include any photographs of him mooning me. For one thing, he has been happily married for twenty-one years to the same woman in an age when the average marriage is of shorter duration than the network run of a failed sitcom. He and his thoroughly charming wife, Faye, have four children (Jesse, Rachel, Ilana, and Aliza) and are raising them to believe in honor, honesty, courage, integrity, self-sufficiency, God, and country; *this* in an age when the concept of moral values is widely regarded by opinion-makers as hopelessly old-fashioned, having been supplanted by the superior ethos of – choose one –

nanny-state politicians, moral relativists, high-colonic therapists, bungee-jumpers, or born-again Luddites with a passion for the drudgery, filth, and short lifespans of the 17th century. Furthermore, in my experience, Jonathan and Faye live by the values they teach their kids. How weird can you get?

Of course, these values arise from Jonathan and Faye's Judaism, a faith to which they are quietly but deeply committed. Weird by modern standards, huh? Not nearly as much fun as worshipping trees. Or a thousand-year-old Indian spirit named Kalumpha Powhacki (Translation: He-Who-Not-Only-Dances-with-Wolves-but-Takes-Them-for-Long-Romantic-Weekends-in-Vegas) who speaks through a movie-star channeler. Or any of the other great new gods of this century: Karl Marx, Elvis, Jell-O, Jim Morrison, Barney the dinosaur, cocaine, Chairman Mao, or the reflection in any mirror.

Jonathan's commitment to his principles is an integral part of his novels, although his books are never for a moment preachy. (Neither is Jonathan, I assure you; if he showed the slightest inclination toward preachiness, I'd smack him.) He writes crisp, clean, fast-moving stories packed with interesting observations about the human condition and spirit, and he finds humanity, in general, more admirable than repugnant. Which also makes him weird among modern writers, most of whom have for so long wallowed in cynicism, negativism, and the hip melancholy arising out of existentialism. Admittedly, this is a weirdness which I share with him, but by modern standards it is nonetheless weird, and I don't intend to let him off the hook on this point.

In Alex Delaware, Jonathan has created a classic series character who is complex, humane, and *intelligent*. A critic once attacked my own work on the grounds that, in book after book, my protagonists are intelligent; he claimed this was not interesting or realistic in a world where intelligence is in short supply. I marveled at the notion that *stupid* lead characters would be more engaging as they dealt ineptly with the disasters that befell them and plummeted ever deeper into trouble because of their relentless foolishness. Perhaps Sherlock Holmes would be even more popular if he'd handled his cases with the finesse and insight of either Larry, Curly, or Moe. How much more thrilling *To Kill a Mockingbird* would be if Atticus Finch were an ignorant Neanderthal instead of an intelligent, compassionate man! I suspect that Jonathan would disagree – as I do – with the contention – that intelligence is in short supply in the real world; that's elitist and arrogant, and Jonathan is neither. Alex Delaware is damned smart; he's not without his faults, but he's both a quick and deep thinker, and his intelligence is what makes him so fascinating. Perhaps it *is* weird to celebrate intelligence in an age when stupidity is celebrated more exuberantly, as on television programs like *Married with Children* but it's a *good* weird.

There are a few ways in which Jonathan is *not* weird. For instance, he doesn't collect anything particularly strange, such as ear wax, the bleached bones of small animals, or shoes once worn by Carmen Miranda – though I wouldn't be surprised to see him in large hats composed of fresh fruit rather like those that Ms. Miranda wore when singing hot Latin songs in her movies. (He is, after all, a well-dressed fellow and capable of making a fashion statement now and then.) He does not raise death's-head moths in his basement. He does not dress up like his mother and stab people to death while they're showering. If he *did* dress up like his mother and stab people to death, he would wait until they had toweled dry and put on something comfortable; he is, after all, a considerate guy. He does not believe that evil aliens are controlling his thought processes through microwave bombardment of his brain – though for a while I think he might have suspected that the Kiwanis Club of Cleveland was doing the same thing.

Please don't think that I am shamelessly glossing over the faults of a friend by listing so many ways in which he is *not* weird. It isn't my intention to turn this introduction into despicable puffery. I will be hard-hitting and truthful to the bitter end, but I also feel an obligation to be balanced.

All right, here's another way he's weird: As a writer, he is concerned with more than just headlong plotting. He cares about using the language well, about digging into character, about the meaning and psychological impact of every aspect of our culture, about conveying a palpable sense of background. Open any of his books at random, and unless you're in a scene of fast-moving dialogue, you're likely to find a passage that makes southern California – Delaware's stalking ground – come alive on the page. I just tried it: *Time Bomb*, Bantam hardcover edition, page 189, a perfect depiction of the beach scene in Venice. In an age when lazy and flat writing crowds bookstore shelves, his passion for good writing no doubt seems weird to some people.

You want weird? Listen: I have never heard Jonathan envy the success of another writer; quite the opposite, I have heard him express delight in other writers' successes. Unless you have swum in the publishing sea for a while, you can't know how common envy is among writers. I have seen bestselling writers, with a bankful of money and fistfuls of good reviews, positively *seethe* with envy when a less successful colleague gets a movie deal or is well-reviewed. Perhaps two-thirds of the writers I've ever known want to be loved and adored above all other writers, for every word they produce, until the end of time (which might be only until next month if Tom and Roseanne Arnold's giant cobalt bomb is on schedule), and have no room in their worldview for the concept of an equal or superior talent. Jonathan may like or dislike the work of another writer, but he never seethes – or even gently percolates – with envy. Though this is enormously refreshing, it is nonetheless weird in the context of standard attitudes among wordsmiths.

Hey, how about *this*: His wife, Faye, is also a wonderful writer, and at dinner one evening, I actually heard Jonathan say, 'I think Faye's a better writer than I am.' I thought I'd heard wrong, that they had become interested in horses, and that he had said 'rider' instead of 'writer.' Or that he'd said, 'I think Faye's a *bit wider* than I am,' which would have been an outright lie, as Faye is quite svelte. It is so rare to hear a writer say that anyone – even William Shakespeare! – is a better writer than he, himself, that I collapsed in profound shock and cardiac arrhythmia. Before being able to go on with dinner, I required treatment with smelling salts, ninety-four *thousand* CCs of epinephrine, a defibrillation machine, and massive doses of free-radical scavengers like phenyl tertiary butyl nitrone to avoid permanent brain damage. And you've got to understand that Jonathan was sincere. He wasn't just flattering his lovely spouse (who knows she is an excellent writer and doesn't need flattery). He wasn't drunk and/or maudlin, either. He wasn't under the microwave command of the Cleveland Kiwanis, either. He was just being Jonathan, speaking the truth as he saw it, unaware that he was weirdly out of synch with the behavior of the majority of his colleagues.

Weirdness on weirdness, huh?

Well, all right, perhaps it's time for some balance again: Here are other ways in which Jonathan is *not* weird. He would never bite the heads off chickens either for pleasure or shock value – although it's possible that he would do so to defend his family in the event of a massive chicken riot. He does not believe he is the reincarnation of either Charles Dickens or Fatty Arbuckle. He has never expressed a psychotic desire to 'get' Betty Crocker. Even given the opportunity, he would not be interested in head-butting Arnold Schwarzenegger. He does not carry a live ferret in a shoulder holster (it's generally one species of lizard or another), and he does not own a single piece of Sonny and Cher memorabilia (though he's added three rooms to the house to accommodate his Tony Orlando and Dawn collection).

I believe I've done my journalistic duty. You now know Jonathan Kellerman as few other people have ever known him. Call him Mr Bizarro, if you must. However, in his defense, I would stress that, though weird, he is enormously talented; though weird, he is intelligent and kind; though weird, he is a devoted father and good husband; though weird, he has a fine sense of humor and an exhilarating passion for life; though weird, he would never use this many semicolons in a single paragraph; and we all know what a plethora of semicolons means; it's one of the seven signs of the Apocalypse; in fact, it's the first of the seven signs; the second of the seven signs is the use of the word 'sphygmomanometer' in an essay by one best-selling novelist writing about another; uh-oh.

My First Short Story

Everyone has to begin somewhere.

Steve Martin, the comedian and actor, began his working life as a tour guide on the Jungle Cruise at Disneyland. Goldie Hawn launched her show-business career as a go-go dancer in a bar. Albert Einstein, the greatest scientist of this century, was not always a brilliant physicist but first worked as a bouncer at a particularly rowdy chess club, sold potatoes door to door, operated a snow-cone stand in a traveling carnival, and delivered singing telegrams dressed as a gorilla. Well, actually, I made up those things about Dr Einstein, but you can bet he didn't start pondering his theory of relativity for a *long* time after the day of his birth.

As a writer, I set to work when I was nine years old, composing stories on tablet paper, drawing cover illustrations for each of these mini-epics, stapling together the pages along the left-hand margin, and covering the staples with neatly applied strips of shiny black, electrician's tape. Then I tried to peddle these 'books' to relatives for a nickel apiece. What an annoying pest I must have been, not only a writer but a pint-sized publisher and a relentless salesman.

When I look back on my childhood and consider how early in life my obsession with storytelling began, I am slightly spooked. As my family was not book-oriented, I did not receive stacks of children's books when I was young; no neighbor or family friend encouraged me to read. In the long interview that can be found elsewhere in this companion, I discuss one pivotal event that might have turned me onto the road of life that I have followed – but even that seems too minor to have engendered in me the compulsion to put millions upon millions of words down on paper with a passion for revising and polishing that has grown more intense year by year. I might credit genetic influence if I could find evidence of a literary limb – or even a twig – anywhere in the family tree, but I cannot. It's a mystery.

Sometimes, when I work late into the night, the writing flows more easily by the hour, in spite of the long day I've spent at the computer.

Eventually the words pour forth with an uncanny facility, until the thoughts and images sculpted by those words become clearer and more refined in spite of any physical weariness I may be feeling. In such moments of intense and quiet joy, it almost seems as if I have been doing this for considerably more years than I have been alive; after long hours of uninterrupted involvement with the story, I feel as if a primal barrier is abruptly breached, allowing a better writer deep within me to guide my hand and teach me things that I have for so long been struggling to learn. This sounds mystical, but such is the flavor of the experience. If I were at all disposed to believe in reincarnation – which I emphatically am not – this experience, the second or third or tenth time around, would probably have convinced me that I've had more past lives than a cat on its ninth.

When I was twelve I won a wristwatch and twenty-five dollars in a nationwide newspaper essay competition, writing on the subject 'What Being an American Means to Me.' This was the first income I earned from writing. Oh, yes, there were those few relatives who ponied up nickels for my homemade 'books' with garish covers, but none of that counts because the nickels were gifts given out of affection or pity, not because anyone actually saw value in what I had written.

As I remember, the prize wristwatch fell apart within a month, actually sort of exploded off my wrist in a dozen pieces as if it had been held together only by surface tension or a weak voodoo spell. Fortunately none of the hurtling debris killed or mutilated anyone, though the episode scared the hell out of my dog Lucky. The twenty-five dollars, however, went a long way in those days when a movie at our small-town theater cost fifty cents. This taught me one of the most valuable lessons I have ever learned, though I needed years to discern what the lesson was: When selling his work, a writer should never accept anything but cold, hard cash. The watch, you see, was a symbol of so many things that starving writers take in place of a spendable payment: Praise, flattery, prestige, half a teaspoon of fame, free drinks and lunches on editors' expense accounts, and the promises of publishers and film producers looking to swap more hope than money for a book or screenplay.

In ninth grade at Bedford High School in Bedford, Pennsylvania, I wrote humorous pieces for – and briefly edited – an English-class newspaper under the auspices of a terrific teacher, Winona Garbrick. Before becoming a teacher, she'd had a career in the Women's Army Corps during World War II, rising to the rank of WAC sergeant. Her sense of responsibility for her students was only a slight degree less serious than the responsibility she would have felt for young women Army personnel working under her in a war zone. She was a sturdy and formidable woman who wore rubber-soled walking shoes to work two decades before any other woman in the Western world would have considered doing so. She had one of the most beautiful smiles I've ever seen – and a scowl that could kill birds and small animals at a dozen paces. Most of us feared her as much as we loved her.

In my senior year, during which I wrote an occasional article for the school paper, Miss Garbrick – oh, how she would have loathed the use of 'Ms.' regardless of how useful an addition it is to our short list of forms of address, for she was a strict traditionalist in matters of language – was responsible for my choice of English as my college major.

On a Friday afternoon, as I hurried down a hallway from one class to another, thinking only about the approaching weekend, I heard Miss Garbrick call out above the bustle of students: 'Koontz! Stop right there, right now!' Her shout quieted the corridor. The area around me quickly cleared as I turned to face her, wondering for which infraction of the rules I was about to die. Her scowl was so fierce, she could have killed an entire *forest* full of small animals that day. When she reached me, she pointed a finger at the bridge of my nose, as if about to deliver a karate blow that would liquefy my brain in an instant. 'I have heard,' she said, 'that you are going to major in history when you go to college next year. Now, I know why you're doing that – it's because history is your easiest subject, and you're a kid who will take the easy way if you're allowed. Jumping Jehosaphat, boy, you have talent, writing talent, and if you're not a *complete* fool you'll try to develop it. That means majoring in English. English. Not history. English. You hear me?'

Because I was a shy kid, came from a seriously dysfunctional family, and was always conscious that the Koontzes were as dirt poor as we were dysfunctional, I was astounded by Miss Garbrick's concern. That anyone besides my mother should care about my future, that this teacher should make such an effort to reach out to me . . . Well, I was profoundly touched. Within the week I changed my major to English. If I had majored in history, would I still have become a writer? Probably. The same writer I've become? Maybe. I'm grateful that I never had to find out. Regardless of what *might* have happened, what *did* happen is in some measure the responsibility of Winona Garbrick, and I only wish she was still alive so I could thank her and see that beautiful smile again. Though after the smile, she would no doubt give

176

me one of those bird-murdering scowls and tell me in no uncertain terms that there are still *miles* of room for improvement in my work.

The only higher education I could afford was a four-year program at one of the institutions in the Pennsylvania State Teachers' College system, and even that was a stretch. To pay for it, my mother worked at G.C. Murphy, a variety store, and through my last couple of years of high school, I worked as a bag boy at a supermarket, usually after school and/or on weekends. Tuesday nights were grueling because from closing time at the market until as late as three o'clock in the morning I helped sort new shipments that had come into the warehouse and frantically stocked shelves. (The manager of the market didn't seem to think you were working hard if you didn't project an air of frenzy.) Wednesdays, I was never exactly a whirlwind of academic achievement in school.

At Shippensburg State Teachers' College in the small town of Shippensburg, in the Amish and Mennonite farming area widely referred to as 'Pennsylvania Dutch' country, I majored in English with a minor in Speech – and wasted enough hours playing cards in the dormitory to qualify for a second degree in pinochle if the college had offered one. I encountered a few more good teachers – especially John Bodnar and O. Richard Forsythe – with whom I remain friends to this day.

While I can't say that anything I learned at college helped me to be a better writer, I did work on – and write for – the *Reflector*, which was the campus literary magazine, and being immersed in a milieu of Hemingway wannabees and Capote wannabees and Harper Lee wannabees and Bozo wannabees (there are always a couple of potential clowns in any group) made me aware that it was possible to build a life as a writer. I realized that my love of language did not have to be expressed solely as a hobby but could be at the center of both my private and professional lives.

In my junior year, I wrote 'Kittens' to fulfill an assignment in a short-story class taught by Charles 'Chauncey' Bellows. To this point, I had written poetry, vignettes, essays, and – as a child – wild and rambling narratives about heroes and monsters, but this was the first genuine short story I had produced. Later, the advisor to the *Reflector*, Mabel Lindner, submitted my manuscript to an annual writing competition open to college students and sponsored by the *Atlantic Monthly*, a prestigious magazine at that time and still well regarded today. 'Kittens' received a prize – a fancy certificate that, if I recall correctly, rather resembled those guarantee cards you find attached by a length of string to the upholstery piping when you buy a new sofa. It was not printed in the magazine, but in a contest chapbook not quite as well produced as our own literary magazine. However, over the years, no previous submission from Shippensburg had ever been recognized; therefore, I became something of a wunderkind during my senior year, at least in the eyes of the English department.

None of this seemed like a big deal to me . . . until I submitted the same story to *Readers & Writers* magazine, where it was bought for fifty dollars. That was a pre-inflation sum, so it would be equivalent to perhaps $300 today, not a fortune by an standard but large enough to mark a turning point in my life. Although I had a dim dream of being a full-time writer some day, the fulfillment of my dream appeared suddenly less remote when I held that fifty-dollar check in my hands.

This humble achievement in my senior year of college, hardly more remunerative than the essay I'd written when I was twelve, motivated me and encouraged me to believe I was destined to take the publishing world by storm while still young enough to be called a 'snot-nosed kid.' If I had known how many nasty years of struggle, seventy- and eighty-hour weeks at the keyboard, disappointment, periodic despair, and sacrifice lay ahead of me before I would be able to say truthfully that my career was flourishing, I might have decided to forget about writing and take up a sensible career in the novelty hat business. I was such an optimistic *idiot* then. On the other hand, given enough time, things have worked out pretty well.

Even if I say so myself, it's gutsy of me to let this first professional sale be reprinted in this companion – not as gutsy as the heroism of Audie Murphy in World War II, to be sure, or even as gutsy as Bruce Willis in *Die Hard*, but gutsy nonetheless. The style is immature, and in the story's headlong determination to deliver a message, it exhibits no more subtlety than a Road Runner cartoon. Though I don't believe 'Kittens' was the *sole* reason for the disaster, the magazine that published it went out of business a year later. In defense of the story, I can say it exhibits the macabre sensibility and love of unexpected but well-seeded narrative turns that are among the qualities that mark my fiction all of these years later.

Now that the introduction has grown larger than the story, I'll step aside and let 'Kittens' speak for itself. Remember, I was only nineteen when I wrote it. We all have to begin somewhere.

'Kittens'

The cool green water slipped along the streambed, bubbling around smooth brown stones, reflecting the melancholy willows that lined the bank. Marnie sat on the grass, tossing stones into a deep pool and watching the ripples spread in ever-widening circles and lap at the muddy banks. She was thinking about the kittens. This year's kittens, not last year's. A year ago, her parents had told her the kittens had gone to heaven. Pinkie's litter had disappeared the third day after their squealing birth.

Marnie's father had said, 'God took them away to heaven to live with Him.'

She didn't exactly doubt her father. After all, he was a religious man. He taught Sunday School every week and was an officer or something in the church, whose duty it was to count all the collection money and mark it down in a little red book. He was always picked to give the sermon on Laymen's Sunday. And every evening, he read passages to them from the Bible. She had been late for the reading last night and had been spanked. 'Spare the rod and spoil the child,' her father always said. No, she didn't actually doubt her father, for if anyone would know about God and kittens, it was he.

But she continued to wonder. Why, when there were hundreds upon thousands of kittens in the world, did God have to take all four of hers? Was God selfish?

This was the first she had thought of those kittens for some time. In the past twelve months, much had happened to make her forget. There was her first year in school, the furor of getting ready for the first day – the buying of paper, pencils, and books. And the first few weeks had been interesting, meeting Mr Alphabet and Mr Numbers. When school began to bore her, Christmas rushed in on polished runners and glistening ice. There was the shopping, the green and yellow and red and blue lights, the Santa Claus on the corner who staggered when he walked, the candlelit church on Christmas Eve when she had had to go to the bathroom and her father had made her wait until the service was over. When things began to lose momentum again in March, her mother had given birth to twins. Marnie had been surprised at how small they were and at how slowly they seemed to grow in the following weeks.

Here it was June again. The twins were three months old, finally beginning to grow a great deal heavier; school was out, and Christmas was an eternity away, and everything was getting dull again. Therefore, when she heard her father telling her mother that Pinkie was going to have another litter, she grasped at the news and wrenched every drop of excitement from it. She busied herself in the kitchen, preparing rags and cotton for the birth and a fancy box for the kittens' home when they arrived.

As events ran their natural course, Pinkie slunk away and had the kittens during the night in a dark corner of the barn. There was no need for sterilized rags or cotton, but the box came in handy. There were six in this litter, all gray with black spots that looked like ink hastily blotted.

She liked the kittens, and she was worried about them. What if God were watching again like last year?

'What are you doing, Marnie?'

She didn't have to look; she knew who was behind her. She turned anyway, out of deference, and saw her father glaring down at her, dark irregular splotches of perspiration discoloring the underarms of his faded blue work coveralls, dirt smeared on his chin and caked to the beard of his left cheek.

'Throwing stones,' she answered quietly.

At the fish?"

'Oh, no, sir. Just throwing stones.'

'Do we remember who was the victim of stone throwing?" He smiled a patronizing smile.

'Saint Stephen,' she answered.

'Very good.' The smile faded. 'Supper's ready.'

* * *

She sat ramrod stiff in the old maroon easy chair, looking attentive as her father read to them from the ancient family Bible that was bound in black leather, all scuffed and with several torn pages. Her mother sat next to her father on the dark blue corduroy couch, hands folded in her lap, an isn't-it-wonderful-what-God-has-given-us smile painted on her plain but pretty face.

'Suffer the little children to come to me, and forbid them not; for such is the kingdom of God.' Her father closed the book with a gentle slap that seemed to leap into the stale air and hang there, holding up a thick curtain of silence. No one spoke for several minutes, then, 'What chapter of what book did we just read, Marnie?'

'Saint Mark, chapter ten,' she said dutifully.

'Fine,' he said. Turning to his wife, whose smile had changed to a we've-done-what-a-Christian-family-should-do expression, he said, 'Mary, how about coffee for us and a glass of milk for Marnie?'

'Right,' said her mother, getting up and pacing into the kitchen.

Her father sat there, examining the inside covers of the old holy book, running his fingers along the cracks in the yellow paper, scrutinizing the ghostly stains embedded forever in the title page where some great-uncle had accidentally spilled wine a million-billion years ago.

'Father,' she said tentatively.

He looked up from the book, not smiling, not frowning.

'What about the kittens?'

'What about them?' he countered.

'Will God take them again this year?'

The half-smile that had crept onto his face evaporated into the thick air of the living room. 'Perhaps' was all that he said.

'He can't,' she almost sobbed.

'Are you saying what God can and cannot do, young lady?'

'No, sir.'

'God can do anything.'

'Yes, sir.' She fidgeted in her chair, pushing herself deeper into its rough, worn folds. 'But why would he want my kittens again? Why always mine?'

'I've had quite enough of this, Marnie. Now be quiet.'

'But why mine?' she persisted.

He stood suddenly, crossed to the chair, and slapped her delicate face. A thin trickle of blood slipped from the corner of her mouth. She wiped it away with the palm of her hand.

'You must not doubt God's motives!' her father insisted. 'You are far too young to doubt.' The saliva glistened on his lips. He grabbed her by the arm and brought her to her feet. 'Now you get up those stairs and into bed.'

She didn't argue. On the way to the staircase, she wiped away the re-forming stream of blood. She walked slowly up the steps, allowing her hand to run along the smooth, polished wood railing.

'Here's the milk,' she heard her mother saying below.

'We won't be needing it,' her father answered curtly.

In her room, she lay in the semidarkness that came when the full moon shone through her window, its orange-yellow light glinting from a row of religious plaques that lined one wall. In her parents' chamber, her mother was cooing to the twins, changing their diapers. 'God's little angels,' she heard her mother say. Her father was tickling them, and she could hear the 'angels' chuckling – a deep gurgle that rippled from down in their fat throats.

Neither her father nor her mother came to say goodnight. She was being punished.

* * *

Marnie was sitting in the barn, petting one of the gray kittens, postponing an errand her mother had sent her on ten minutes earlier. The rich smell of dry, golden hay filled the air. There was straw upon the floor that crackled underfoot. In the far end of the building, the cows were lowing to each other – only two of them, whose legs had been sliced by barbed wire and who were being made to convalesce. The kitten mewed and pawed the air below her chin.

'Where's Marnie?' her father's voice boomed from somewhere in the yard between the house and the barn.

She was about to answer when she heard her mother calling from the house. 'I sent her to Brown's for a recipe of Helen's. She'll be gone another twenty minutes.'

'That's plenty of time,' her father answered. The crunch of his heavy shoes on the cinder path echoed in military rhythm.

Marnie knew something was wrong; something was happening she was not supposed to see. Quickly, she put the kitten back in the red and gold box and sprawled behind a pile of straw to watch.

Her father entered, drew a bucket of water from the wall tap, and placed it in front of the kittens. Pinkie hissed and arched her back. The man picked her up and shut her in an empty oat bin from which her anguished squeals boomed in a ridiculously loud echo that belonged on the African veldt and not on an American farm. Marnie almost laughed, but remembered her father and suppressed the levity.

He turned again to the box of kittens. Carefully, he lifted one by the scruff of the neck, petted it twice, and thrust its head under the water in the bucket! There was a violent thrashing from within the bucket, and sparkling droplets of water sprayed into the air. Her father grimaced and shoved the entire body under the smothering pool. In time, the thrashing ceased. Marnie found that her fingers were digging into the concrete floor, hurting her. *Why? Why-why-why?* Her father lifted the limp body from the bucket. There was something pink and bloody hanging from the animal's mouth. She couldn't tell whether it was the tongue or whether the precious thing had spewed its entrails into the water in a last attempt to escape the heavy, horrible death of suffocation.

Soon six kittens were dead. Soon six silent fur balls were dropped in a burlap sack. The top was twisted shut. He let Pinkie out of the bin. The shivering cat followed him out of the barn, mewing softly, hissing when he turned to look at her.

Marnie lay very, very still for a long time, thinking of nothing but the execution and trying desperately to understand. Had God sent her father? Was it God who told him to kill the kittens – to take them away from her? If it were, she didn't see how she could ever again stand before that gold and white altar, accepting communion. She stood and walked toward the house, blood dripping from her fingers, blood and cement.

'Did you get the recipe?' asked her mother as Marnie slammed the kitchen door.

'Mrs Brown couldn't find it. She'll send it over tomorrow.' She lied so well she surprised herself. 'Did God take my kittens?' she blurted suddenly.

Her mother looked confused. 'Yes,' was all she could say.

'I'll get even with God! He can't do that! He can't!' She ran out of the kitchen toward the staircase.

Her mother watched but didn't try to stop her.

Marnie Caufield walked slowly up the stairs, letting her hand run along the smooth, polished wood railing.

* * *

At noon, when Walter Caufield came in from the field, he heard a loud crash and the tinkling of china and the shattering of glass. He rushed into the living room to see his wife lying at the foot of the stairs, a novelty table upset, statuettes broken and cracked. 'Mary, Mary. Are you hurt?' He bent quickly to her side.

She looked up at him out of eyes that were far away in distant mists. 'Walt! My Good God, Walt – our precious angels. The bathtub – our precious angels!'

K

Koontz, Will You Just Shut Up Already?

It has been said that the primary thing distinguishing us human beings from all other mammals is the size of our forebrain. It has also been said that the primary thing separating us from all other mammals is our opposable thumb, which has allowed us to make tools, an undertaking that elephants and dolphins alike find difficult. Some people say that our awareness of our own mortality is by far the most important difference between us and all other creatures on this world, while others insist that our perception of time as being divided into the past, present, and future accounts for much of our ability to plan and progress when other species, from toads to possums, just sort of get along day by day.

I believe, however, other equally important but seldom-mentioned differences separate us from other inhabitants of this planet.

For one thing, we are the only species that could possibly have cooked up the concept of 'money,' exchanging real and certifiably useful goods for potentially worthless pieces of paper the value of which rests largely in the hands of politicians; you will never see a monkey give a bunch of bananas to another monkey in return for a dry leaf with a '5' printed on it. Likewise, the concept of 'credit' is unique to us. You most likely will never witness a lion trying to purchase a gazelle with a Gold Predator Card; instead, he'll just chase it down, tear out its throat, and eat what he wants. The lion image does, however, suggest that some other species are every bit as clever as human beings when it comes to perpetrating violence.

Humankind distinguishes itself, as well, by being the only species that: Worries about which fork to use for which course at a formal dinner party; is embarrassed by bad breath; knows how to operate a TV remote control; can take effective counter measures against police radar guns; feels itself to be the subject of clandestine observation by extraterrestrials; can produce an international

184

sensation like Madonna; has a need for shoelaces; will eat anything, no matter how disgusting, as long as some French chef pronounces it 'divine;' understands the implications of the words 'massive nuclear retaliation;' uses Kleenex; and collects Liberace memorabilia.

Quite a species, homo sapiens, huh?

But perhaps most important of all, human beings distinguish themselves from all other walking-creeping-crawling-flying creatures on this planet by being the only species the members of which cannot resist the urge to lecture one another on the proper way to act, feel, and think in regard to an infinite number of subjects. You cannot convince me that you have ever heard a porcupine expounding upon the virtues of liberalism or an armadillo arguing the superiority of conservative theory. No moose has ever written literary criticism. No duck has ever tried to have *Huckleberry Finn* removed from a library because of politically incorrect language in the text; stupid ducks – they're too busy eating grubs, making ducklings, grooming their feathers, and quacking their silly heads off.

And no – I repeat and I emphasize *no* – baboon anywhere, at any time, has ever written an essay about why we should like ghost stories or about what is wrong with current horror fiction. But I have. I am proud to say that, as an upstanding member of my species, I am as much an opinionated busybody as anyone else.

I have never written a ghost story – at least not that I am aware, and not as I would define the term – but as a reader I enjoy them when they are done well. When Dave Silva and Paul Olson were editing their fine anthology *POSTMORTEM: New Tales of Ghostly Horror*, they asked me to write an afterword in defense of the ghost story as a meaningful genre of fiction. Because I knew Dave was a nice guy (but suspected he might be as dangerous as that gazelle-chomping lion when crossed), and because Paul Olson promised me eternal life with such conviction that I had to believe he knew how to confer immortality, but mostly because I, like any good member of my species, can't resist standing on a soapbox and spouting off, I accepted their offer.

The other piece in this section, 'A Genre in Crisis,' first appeared in a different form as the introduction to an anthology of horror fiction, *Night Visions VI*, published by Dark Harvest and later reprinted in paperback by Berkley Books under the title *The Boneyard*. A year or so later, *Proteus*, a magazine of essays published by my old alma mater (now Shippensburg University), suggested I

185

revamp the piece for republication in that academic forum, and I obliged. The *Proteus* version is the one that appears here.

I have always insisted that the word 'horror' is not descriptive of my fiction, and I have strenuously avoided that label. (If you care about what label – if any *I* believe should be applied to my fiction, see the long interview that is included in this companion.) Although I am not a horror writer any more than I am a mystery writer or a Western writer or a baby-eating extraterrestrial arachnid (trust me, I'm not), I am a reader of the genre, have been hugely entertained by it over the years, and care about it. Consequently, when it seemed to me that the horror field was losing its way in 1988, and when Paul Mikol at Dark Harvest invited me to write the introduction to *Night Visions VI*, I seized that opportunity to spout off about what I felt was a lamentable collapse in the quality of modern horror fiction and to warn that the genre was in imminent danger of a severe decline in popularity.

I take no satisfaction in the fact that a decline did, indeed, set in shortly thereafter, even steeper than I had predicted, or that the genre remains in a deep depression still, in November of 1992, when I'm writing these words, I am able to read very little of what is published in the form, but I remain hopeful that the trends I noted in 'A Genre in Crisis' will eventually play themselves out, making room for new writers with fresh approaches or for the good writers who were drowned in the bad work of others during the past few years.

L

Ghost Stories

Why do we like ghost stories? Why can't we be satisfied to read about private eyes packing 45s, prowling dark streets, beating up – and getting beaten up by – thugs of all sorts, fending off hot babes with secretly cold intentions, and brooding about the Big Sleep, the Long Goodbye? Why can't we readers be satisfied with the sex, romance, adventure, tragedy, comedy, and other thrills to be found in the *sensible* genres of fiction? What *is* it with us that we want to read about the dead, the undead, the walking dead, the living dead? Are we just plain morbid? Perverse? Twisted? Sick?

As a kid, I read spooky stories in my room, huddled under the covers, using a flashlight to illuminate the pages. I had to read everything that way, not just scary stuff: in my house reading books was looked upon as a waste of time and money, and the habit was regarded as barely more respectable than self-abuse and marginally less destructive than serious heroin addiction. But the worst offense in the literary realm was to be caught reading *that* stuff: Stories of the supernatural; in fact, any fiction of the fantastic regardless of genre – science fiction, fantasy, horror. In that era those genres were not as widely popular as they now have become; it was fringe reading; catching your son with the material was akin to finding *Das Kapital* and crazed communist tracts hidden beneath the undershirts in his dresser drawer. Subversive material indeed.

It's not like that anymore. In spite of publisher's fevered determination to put blood-drooling, bug-eyed beasts on too many covers in the genre, some respect has been won. Still, for every two people who believe that pornographic books can cause upstanding citizens to become slavering sex fiends, there is at least one who is convinced that reading ghost and horror stories, regardless of how sedate the tales, will certainly transform readers into either mealy-skinned recluses with odd personal habits or foaming-at-the-mouth, pop-eyed sociopaths with a love of chain saws and an interest in dismemberment.

187

Yet of the many readers of ghost and horror stories whom I know personally, not one is given to violence, most are more civilized than the average citizen, and those who are mealy-skinned are simply not fortunate enough to live here in sunny California, where everyone has an appealing cancer-brown tan. Certain third-rate sociologists and thoroughly *meshuga* psychologists, sucking around for grant money or bending their 'sciences' to political purpose, have conducted badly flawed studies in which they purport to show direct links between fiction of the fantastic and everything from schizo-phrenia to acne. It doesn't wash. Anyone who's a fan of such fiction and who seeks out other fans of it through amateur magazines and conventions, eventually encounters hundreds, if not thousands, of similar-minded folk and discovers that they are both more articulate than the public at large and dramatically less prone to violence than the sociologists and psychologists who, with their intellectually bankrupt theories, would alter whole societies and cultures (by force, if necessary) and blithely disregard the loss of freedom (and sometimes blood) resulting from their policies.

So if we don't turn to these tales to learn how to deal death and bring down modern civilization, as those critics would have it, what *do* we want – and receive – from the genre?

Entertainment, of course. Nothing can fill long, empty hours as satisfyingly as good storytelling. The written word, woven into enchanting spells by a storyteller, has a unique power to bring a new view of the world and the human condition – the author's view – to us, and make it live in our minds and imaginations.

Television rarely does that. In spite of the promise of its early days, TV has become a dead medium, in part because it's a government-protected and government-controlled monopoly, and in part because of its extremely collaborative nature, it spews out committee-conceived and committee-written trash with too little substance to make the viewer care, too little color and texture to convince, too little emotion to enchant, too little wit and wonder to seize the viewer the way that a good story or book does. Can you imagine *anyone* so brain-damaged by video-display radiation and Twinkies as to be utterly spellbound by an episode of 'Dynasty' or 'She's the Sheriff' or even the sometimes superior 'Magnum' in the way that millions have been spellbound by King, Tolkien, Heinlein, and other dealers in the fantastic? No, when a TV show evokes a glimmer of wonder, it's not the same wonder that we readers know, it's wonder in big lead shoes, dressed in a shabby black suit too small for it, brought alive with electricity conducted through rough bolts in its neck, a shambling Frankenstein of wonder, graceless and half dead, a stitched-together travesty of genuine wonder.

Most theatrical films are also too collaborative to produce entertainment with true wonder and passion. And though six or eight really good movies reach the theaters every year, each film enchants for only two hours or less, then the lights come on, and the screen goes blank, and we're reminded of how *passive* a medium film is. Even the best films feed the imagination predigested images and ideas and do not demand active participation as does the printed word.

A book of ghost stories or a novel of the supernatural, if well done, can provide long evenings of surcease from the travails of this world. It can more deeply involve us – and usually it will have more of value to say about life – than any ten good movies. The art of the storyteller, expressed through the printed word, can touch the mind and the heart, establish a special intimacy between writer and reader, and allow an intensity and depth of communion seldom achieved by any other art form.

Ghost stories – all stories of the supernatural – are especially wonder-invoking, for they deal not merely with the unknown but with the *unknowable*. We are curious about what lies beyond death, and good ghost stories, while not always philosophical or intellectual to any great degree, give the illusion of pulling back that black curtain to provide us with a glimpse of what awaits us on the other side. A ghost – any ghost in any story, regardless of the tale's primary intent – is a symbol of our faith in a hereafter and is therefore a symbol, as well, of our deeply held desire to believe that life is more than a biological accident, that human life has purpose and meaning and a destiny beyond this world. Convince me, for the duration of a story, that ghosts are real, and for that same length of time you also convince me that my own spirit will never die.

That is what we get from reading about the supernatural. Hope. Certainly – perhaps primarily – we receive entertainment value. And we get our imaginations stretched, which is a useful exercise for anyone trying to cope with our world of rapid change, in which a healthy imagination is an essential survival tool. And we are induced to think about the enduring mysteries of life. But we also find hope, however subconsciously, in these tales. Even if the fictional ghost or demon is evil, the story is one of hope, for if evil spirits exist, then surely benign shades are out there, too.

Charles Dickens's *A Christmas Carol*, is perhaps the greatest ghost story of all time. It is filled with the clank of ghostly chains, frightening figures whose appearance generates drafts of arctic air, and visions of the grave that are sufficiently dark to bring a cold sweat to the perceptive reader who has not been jaded by the numbingly graphic splatter films of our time. Yet in his tale Dickens is most concerned with conveying a message about charity, compassion, love, and the hope for humankind that is embodied in one miserly old man's ability to transform himself into a better person. *A Christmas Carol* takes the hope that is a buried element of all ghost stories and raises it to the surface of the tale, using it as a major theme.

Are we twisted, perverse, or morbid because we are intrigued by these fantastic stories? No. Our fascination springs from our desire to know ourselves, our world, our ultimate fate and purpose – which is the same motive that compels us to read Dostoyevsky or James M. Cain or Faulkner.

What disturbs me is that some people *don't* want to read this kind of fiction. Do they have no curiosity about what lies beyond this life? Are they so rigid and inflexible that they cannot bear to have their imaginations stretched? Are they afraid of finding some unsuspected fragment of spirituality in their modern, rational hearts? Are they so in love with death that they cannot bear to read stories in which death is not final and eternal? Does the specter of hope frighten them? Good heavens, what's *wrong* with these people who don't like stories of the supernatural?

M

A Genre in Crisis

Good popular fiction should exhibit graceful use of the language, complex thematic structure, depth of characterization, and a richness of metaphor and imagery equal to that in the style of fiction often referred to as 'literary.' No genre is inherently inferior to mainstream fiction; although real – as opposed to perceived – shortcomings are apparent in many popular novels, the fault invariably lies with some of the authors, not with the forms in which they create.

In fact, in nearly all cases, authors whose works have endured are those who wrote not to the taste of the critics and academics of their day but to the taste of the masses. Charles Dickens was reviled by most literati of his time; however, he was a favorite of readers, and his novels survived. The same is true of Dostoevsky and Robert Louis Stevenson and virtually all writers who outlasted their eras. Great popularity is not the sole determinant of value – else we would have to award Jackie Collins a Nobel Prize – but it does seem to be one essential requirement. No story can have deep insight into life, real power, without being accessible to – and speaking intimately to – the masses, for it is in the accretion of individual experience into cultural and sociological coral reefs that patterns of truth can be seen. The only important literary judge is time, and time in this instance is synonymous with readers, generation after generation of readers, who keep works alive.

If popular fiction has within it the potential to be the best fiction, and if one of the most widely read genres of our age suffers a decline in quality related to a loss of direction and laziness on the part of many of its authors, we must speak frankly about the problem if we are among those committed to the proposition that such fiction has both considerable artistic merit and cultural value. When a form of writing has become as inbred and self-consuming as the horror genre in the 1980s, frankness is not well received by its practitioners; the artists and craftsmen laboring in that field have grown accustomed to raising one another relentlessly, in a spirit of boosterism that has

191

resulted from as us-against-the-world attitude that, itself, has arisen from a subconscious awareness of the current lack of quality in the genre; they have lost appreciation for genuine criticism just when it is most needed. For that reason I produced an essay for *Night Visions VI*, an anthology of contemporary horror stories, from which the following material was excerpted.

* * *

Jack (not his real name) was a major figure in the publishing industry, not involved in the horror genre but passingly familiar with it, and he went to see *The Exorcist* when it was first released in theaters. He told me that he wanted to see if the film – and the book from which it was derived – seemed to presage a new direction in popular entertainment, which was what people were telling him. (And did it ever!) Popular entertainment was his business, and he had to study trends. A confirmed atheist, he was not expecting to be scared by a story that relied so heavily on superstitious mumbo-jumbo. If anything, he expected to be highly amused.

According to his wife, by the time the end-credits rolled up and he left the theater, he was pale and deeply disturbed. He refused to talk about the film, a distinct departure from his habit of analyzing every movie he saw and gleefully demolishing the bad ones. He was an intelligent man, quick-witted, acerbic; listening to him critique either a good or terrible movie was always entertaining. This time he had nothing to say. Two days later, when he had finished reading the novel, he was silent about that too. 'I don't think I can talk about it,' he said to me, 'at least not sensibly. I find it too disturbing, and I don't *like* the way it disturbs me, so I'm just going to put it out of mind.'

He was not a lapsed Catholic whose buried guilt the film had resurrected. In fact he was not even from a Christian family. Nor had the movie stirred up guilt over his abandonment of Judaism, for his parents had not kept that ancient faith or inculcated it in him; having never been in the embrace of Judaism in the first place, he could not have abandoned it. He had been a lifelong nonbeliever, secure in his atheism – and yet *The Exorcist*, relying on religious mythology and archetypes for its effects, full of mumbo-jumbo that he ridiculed and despised, had not only frightened him but left him emotionally and intellectually shaken.

Good horror stories have a power equal to or exceeding that of all other types of fiction, and at times their effect can be more profound than stories in other genres.

The Exorcist isn't even particularly well written. It's filled with clumsy syntax and is often grammatically weak. William Peter Blatty's imagery is frequently flat, his metaphors sometimes less than appropriate. He does have several unique narrative devices that work splendidly, and he has an unerring sense of narrative pace and structure, but his strengths do not outweigh his weaknesses as a stylist. Nevertheless *The Exorcist* is a good book, a superior book, and it deserves to be the bestselling horror novel of all time – which it is, by a factor of three or four.

Blatty's weaknesses of style are more than balanced by his tremendous conviction. His novel is not just a spook show. Blatty wants to do more than scare you. He wants to move you. He wants to make you think. He wants to help you reaffirm your faith, if you have any, or make you doubt the wisdom of faithlessness. Many of the scenes in his book are complex, functioning on multiple thematic levels, and no scene is entirely devoid of a greater meaning that transcends plot.

As I write this, seventeen years after the publication of Blatty's book, the horror genre is in the middle of a growth cycle. More new books than ever are being published in the field. Major houses are launching horror lines, after the upstart TOR Books showed them that the concept was viable. We are unquestionably in a boom.

And we are overwhelmed by trash.

Sturgeon's Law – which states that ninety percent of *everything* is crap – needs to be revised to be applicable to the horror field these days; the percentage has to be raised. Attempting to read nineteen out of any twenty horror novels, a well-educated person will despair, for so many writers seem never to have learned the basic rules of grammar and syntax. Most books and stories have nothing to say; they speak neither to the mind nor heart; they are clockwork mechanisms laboring mightily to bring forth, on schedule, not a cuckoo bird but a vague shiver of ersatz fear.

In the days when comparatively little horror was published, prior to Ira Levin's excellent *Rosemary's Baby* in 1967, the reader could find more of quality than he can now, when the bookstore shelves sag under the weight of volumes in the genre. The roots of modern horror fiction can be traced to the work of exceptional writers who knew how to pin magic into sentences and whose work was unfailingly literate:

H. P. Lovecraft, Frank Belknap Long, Fritz Leiber, Joseph Payne Brennan, Ray Bradbury, Richard Matheson, Theodore Sturgeon . . . When Levin and Blatty proved that horror could be sold to a broad audience beyond the small group of diehard fans, the genre seemed poised for a long golden era.

But something went wrong.

Oh, yes, we've enjoyed some superior work in the seventeen years since *The Exorcist*. Stephen King's *The Shining* and *The Dead Zone* come to mind. Dan Simmon's excellent *Song of Kali*, Patrick Suskind's *Perfume*, and a couple of dozen other books and a double score of shorter pieces by a number of writers spring to mind. But even if I used the precious space here to list them all, it would be a strikingly short compilation of first-rate work given the time span and the thousands of titles published therein. And we see less prime stuff these last few years than just a decade ago.

I am not the only one to have noticed this sad state of the field. The subject frequently comes up in conversations with other concerned writers. At the 1988 American Booksellers Association convention, Charles Brown, editor-publisher of *Locus*, was first to ask me about the 'deplorable state of modern horror,' and before the weekend was done, half a dozen other people in publishing raised the same issue with me, unprompted. They seemed to feel that my year as the first president of Horror Writers of America might have given me some special insight.

It didn't. What it gave me was heartburn.

But I have been thinking about the state of our microcosm, and several observations are unavoidable.

Too many writers have turned away from their responsibilities as storytellers and craftsmen and artists, and instead of honing their talent and skills through hard work and polish, have tried to hold the reader by repeatedly shocking him, layering on the gore and violence with the misguided notion that vividly portrayed evisceration can substitute for storytelling, that splatter can compensate for lousy writing. Their only theme seems to be nihilism, which is singularly unattractive to the majority of readers, and which is boring to any reader who *thinks*. Nihilism, after all, is the intellectual conceit of the perpetual adolescent, no more interesting to the mature mind than Fruit Loops are to the mature palate.

One reasonably well-known writer, one who stands near the center of this current trend, has written and spoken often about what he sees as the 'virtue' of pushing into new realms of perversity and repulsion. He argues that those who see this path as an artistic and moral dead end are essentially brothers-under-the-skin of narrow-minded born-again Christians! That is intellectual McCarthyism. Furthermore he had written that if one condemns horror fiction that sets out *only* to repulse and scare, such condemnation is akin to dismissing comedy because it seeks only to induce laughter, or love poetry because it deals only with love. But those comparisons are, of course, specious. Good comedy plays upon our fears and hopes and dreams, turning a mirror on us, reflecting our emotional and intellectual matrices in all their glorious complication. Can anyone see a Woody Allen comedy or a Steve Martin standup routine or an old Chaplin film – and be oblivious to the fact that they are composed of threads of love, hate, joy, fear, hope, despair, and every other human emotion, and that they hope to do *more* than just evoke laughter? Can anyone read the love poetry of Shelley, Keats, Byron, Browning, and other great poets, and really believe that the work is *only* about love? If that is the level of intellectual activity among those who propound the superiority of splatter fiction, no wonder so much of that subgenre is dreadful.

Don't get me wrong. I am not opposed to violence and gore in fiction. Previously, when expressing my distaste for this Grand Guignol school of horror, I've been accused of being a fuddy-duddy who doesn't believe in spilling blood on the page. Such an accusation can only be made by those who have never read my books. WHISPERS contains a few scenes of brutality exceeding anything I've read in splatter fiction, and even WATCHERS is not without its descent into 'west terror.' Violence and its biological consequences are a legitimate part of all fiction, not just horror, but it is ultimately pointless to write about them to the virtual exclusion of other aspects of life and human interaction, and it is a sign of moral and intellectual bankruptcy to rely on them as the primary means of sustaining a reader's interest in a story. If nothing else, it's just plain *lazy*.

At the other end of the spectrum stand those who insist that only quiet horror – *very* quiet horror – is worthwhile. In their stories, the violence is nearly always offstage. Paragraphs are spent evoking fear through long descriptions of the whisper of the wind, the queer shape and movement of a shadow, or the shudder of a leaf. Or, in the case of some minimalists, nothing at all is described in detail – not wind or shadows or shuddering leaves or even *characters* – and the prose seeks to evoke fear by the use of spare images and skeletal storylines that, by their very coldness and hollowness, stir thoughts of death and loneliness and despair. The quiet-horror writers tend to write better prose, line by line, than those who wade gleefully hip-deep in blood and perversion. But to my way of thinking, while quiet horror is preferable to blood-bath stories, it is too frequently carried to extremes in the writer's attempt to escape association with 'popular' fiction, and the result is horror without human association, horror without meaning; it's as boring and empty as mindless splatter tales.

Both extremes usually fail as fiction because they do not deal with the splendid *gaudiness* of human life, with the rich brew of emotions that are a part of everyone's existence every day. They condense experience, as fiction should, but then they filter it through one type of graying cloth or another, straining out the more interesting colors, producing monotone novels and stories.

The worst problem with current horror fiction, aside from the woefully weak prose style of some of its writers, is that most of its creators fall into one or the other of these camps, and too few work in the middle ground. After countless experiments, after the waxing and waning of hundreds of schools of writing since the time of Dickens, anyone familiar with the broader world of English-language fiction can see that virtually all of the important and lasting works have been those exploring human experience from an all-inclusive point of view, concentrating on every aspect of human existence, limiting themselves in no way, focusing on joy as well as terror, on love as well as hatred, on sentiment as well as cynicism.

In spite of its flaws, *The Exorcist* is a good book because it includes both quiet and noisy horror, scenes both subtle and coarse. It succeeds because it is not only about pain and death and darkness but about self-sacrifice and love and light; the public responded to the novel not primarily because young Regan's head turns around 360° or because she vomits all over people, but because Father Karras gives up his own immortal soul to save a child *who is essentially a stranger to him*. 'Take me,' he tells the demon in the girl, and it's him that the demon has wanted all along. How appealing. And how true of what is best in us. But splatter writers would be appalled by the sentiment, and those writing quiet horror would no doubt find the priest's commitment too gaudy.

Blatty's novel is also better than much of what followed it because of its aforementioned conviction, which is often lacking in both splatter and quiet horror. Too many writers of both schools tell us stories of possessed children or demon-haunted places, dwelling in great detail on the nature of Evil, with a capital E – but do not themselves believe in the existence of Good as a living force in the universe. Their demons, therefore, don't ring true, and their Evil is as convincing as that of the figures in a carnival funhouse, for if Good as a living force does not exist, neither does Evil as a living force, since all of our mythology requires the existence of the former before the latter can even come into existence. That leaves the author dealing with good and evil in the lower case, whether he knows it or not. Blatty is a Catholic. His conviction comes through; his willingness to include his faith in the novel, in a time when faith is out of fashion among writers and critics, puts the Evil in his novel in perspective and makes for a well-rounded story that *convinces* and that has something worthwhile to say about life, regardless of whether the reader is a believer, an agnostic, or an atheist.

Of course, it is not necessary for the horror writer to be a person of faith in order to write fiction of real depth, though he might be well-advised to shy from *supernatural* horror if he is, in fact, an atheist; he will bring no truth to the work and, instead of creating worthwhile fiction from his rationalist worldview, will be doing little more than grinding out hack work about things that in his heart he views as the delusions of the immature. Whether a writer is a believer or an atheist, he can write first-rate, well-rounded horror fiction only by stepping out of the limitations of a single school, by being as unafraid of sentiment – and even sentimentality – as he is unafraid of gore and violence.

Why are horror writers so much more polarized than those in most other genres? Why do they fall into such opposed camps, with so few in the middle ground?

I believe it is because so many of them regularly attend fan conventions – and learn the wrong lessons there. Those get-togethers are pleasant, and the people at them are interesting and fun to be with. But some of the hardcore fans who go to conventions tend to have narrow tastes; and they encourage writers to produce for their tastes. Some are passionate about quiet horror. Some are passionate about splatter fiction. Writers in both camps make the mistake of believing that hardcore convention-goers are representative of the larger book-buying public. They are not. They are good people, all right, but they're not representative. Writers in either camp can be flattered dangerously, even creatively warped, by the attention they get at the conventions. The true audience, the mass audience that makes careers in the long run and ultimately determines what books and stories will last, is more catholic in its taste, open to a broader range of thought and experience. The lasting works of horror will be those that reach that broad audience, that speak not to narrow views of the human condition but to open minds. Dickens was hugely popular in his day and did not write to the prejudices of a small group; Dostoevsky was a writer adored by the masses because he did not speak only half the truth but all of it; Robert Louis Stevenson, Twain, Balzac, Poe . . . virtually *all* the writers who have outlasted their time have explored the human condition from the point of view of neither the nihilist nor the Pollyanna. They used every narrative technique, were open to joy as well as terror, faith as well as doubt, and wrote for the masses in all their gaudy, wonderful, dreadful, exciting diversity.

Because many horror writers were conventioneers and heavy readers of fanzines before becoming established authors, they are familiar with criticism only of the fan type, which has its purposes but which is not ever deep or telling. Thus, when many writers turn to writing criticism of their own, they produce shallow analyses. Like the fan critics, they seldom look at the grammar, syntax, aptness of metaphor, thematic structure, validity of characterization, verisimilitude of background, or tightness of plot. They either like it or dislike it. And their judgment is based not on the work's intrinsic virtues or lack of same, but on how well it conforms to their own prejudices. For example, only in horror will you find a plethora of critics exhaustively discussing the 'subtext' of a work that has no *visible* thematic purpose whatsoever. Beyond this field, a critic would be well aware that if a work is not about something in a very visible way, if it is not exploring an issue or issues on the surface for all to see, if its characters don't talk about complex ideas and deal with complex ideas as part of the story, if it appears to be only a tale, then it *is* only a tale. Subtexts cannot exist in a creative vacuum; a book cannot be a metaphor for Vietnam if, on the surface, it is only about monsters, blood, sex, drugs, and rock and roll. Good writers aren't *coy* about a message when they have one to impart; they don't conceal it for the private delectation of a cognoscenti of prose-dissection specialists; they for God's sake *write* about it up front. Because of the poor quality of criticism within the field – as I write this, even the genre's few professional magazines offer book columns that are fannish in essence and without deep insight and observation – new writers often use bad writing as paradigms because they see it praised, not realizing that the praise was lavished on the work because of its slavish conformation to the expectations of hardcore-fan sensibilities. Sometimes it seems that each generation of writers becomes more committed than the one before it to the constriction of the genre's creative parameters; worse, in their roles as writers and critics, many of those working in horror/dark fantasy seem to have been lobotomized by excessive convention-going and by reading this kind of fiction to the exclusion of all else, until they seem virtually incapable of *seeing* the broader world, until they are so creatively and intellectually inbred that they have no valid standards by which to judge accurately their own work and that of others.

One critic and writer in the field professes to believe that there are only two things worth writing about: eros and thantos, love and death (or fear). This is an idea he apparently picked up from an academic – an obviously third-rate academic. To believe that all of human experience can be boiled down to two themes, to *truly* believe this and not merely to cling to it as a convenient justification for a failure to write complexly, an author must be intellectually and emotionally blind to the actual diversity of human feeling and motivation. To state further, as this critic does, that horror is as successful as any fiction when it delivers on half of those possible themes, when it deals strictly with death (fear), is to do a grave disservice to the genre by operating as an apologist for its writers' tendency to play safe by massaging the prejudices and fulfilling the blinkered expectations of its hardcore audience. Thinking of this dismal quality informs those rackfuls of unreadable books that crowd the marketplace, whether they proudly proclaim themselves to be just fun trash or masquerade as literature. With such standards, we would have to accept that the basest pornography, though limiting itself solely to the excitation of lust, is equal in literary merit to any work in the horror genre or in any other, that any hack who lathered the pages of his book with enough blood and feces to disgust us and evoke our fear of death was the equal of the best writers in our field.

The genre cannot thrive by feeding on such lies.

If we treasure this field, we must speak the truth about it at every stage of its development. At the moment the truth is that we are in a dark age, in spite of the apparent boom. The truth is, if we separate into cliques and encourage one another in the development of narrow schools of fiction, if we praise illiterate work for the sake of friendship, if we place more importance on networking at conventions for the advancement of our careers than we place on the painful act of creativity in the solitude of our dens and offices, we are contributing to a prolonged adolescence of the genre and perhaps to its ultimate dissolution as a viable literary force.

N

How To

A great many writers have an irresistible compulsion to explain how they do what they do. Each feels that his or her approach is the most viable of all possible approaches, and that his or her habits are the most conducive to the creation of great literature.

When writing how-to pieces, the writer thinks that he is taking the time to put his thoughts on paper largely because he believes in sharing hard-won wisdom with struggling neophytes. This *is* part – but only part – of what motivates him. I would hazard to say that there are as many jerks and fools and selfish bastards among writers as among people in any other trade or profession, even including movie producers and international terrorists, and *more* jerks and fools and selfish bastards than you'd find in, say, plumbing or medicine or retail sales. Nevertheless, many writers genuinely enjoy helping newcomers, sharing the lessons of brutal experience.

Sad to say, their efforts on behalf of their less well-published colleagues are wasted. I have met countless beginning or struggling writers who desperately seek advice, who listen raptly when advice is given, who gush Niagaras of gratitude for the wisdom imparted – but I have never met a writer who acts upon that advice to any significant extent, saving himself untold grief by doing so. Writers, especially of fiction, tend to be a stubborn and egotistical lot, each of whom believes that his experience will be different from and more glorious than that of any writer who has come before him, by virtue of the fact that *he* is a genius whose gargantuan talent will overcome all obstacles as easily as Arnold Schwarzenegger could mow down a gaggle of eighty-year-old nuns. Advice goes in one ear and out the other, leaving no imprint whatsoever on the brain, and not even removing any wax.

But it doesn't matter that the effort is wasted, because I suspect altruism is not the primary reason established writers produce occasional how-to pieces for *Writers' Digest* or *The Writer* or various instructional texts. I also don't believe they are much motivated by

201

either the meager per-word rates or the ego-gratification they receive for this work. Each of these things counts, but none is critically important in itself.

Like me, I suspect that other writers find how-to articles worth their time for two reasons: 1) they are endlessly fascinated by the *process* of writing; 2) they are attempting to explain how they do it as much to themselves as to the beginning writer at whom the article is ostensibly aimed.

As for process, writing well is as much a craft as it is an art, because it requires not merely talent and insight but a tremendous range of technical skills. Just as other craftsmen – cabinetmakers, jewelrymakers, car customizers, matte painters working on film productions, wood carvers, etcetera – enjoy comparing notes about the tricks of their trades, so writers enjoy discussing their narrative techniques. Novelists are forever – consciously and subconsciously – analyzing one another's work, and if you're a writer long enough, eventually it becomes almost impossible to read a piece of fiction without being aware, scene by scene and sometimes line by line, of how certain effects were achieved.

Analysis of writing, even by the greatest of critics, is *always* at the level of craft because the art itself cannot be analyzed. Commented upon, yes. Effectively criticized and analyzed, no. Art, after all, is mysterious; we know it when we see it – or rather, we *feel* it when it affects us profoundly – but any attempt to define it degenerates into pat sets of rules and guidelines that are nothing more than suggested *craft* techniques. If art could be criticized and analyzed, it could then be codified; if codified, it could be re-created at will; if it could be created at will by those who can codify it, then every critic or analyst who *thinks* he understands what is true art and what isn't would be busily cobbling together stunning works of his own and flooding the market with them. In actuality, history reveals precious few – if any – critics in any field who were creators of lasting art.

Therefore, besides seeking to satisfy a fascination with process, writers like to write about writing because they are struggling to explain to themselves how effective craft techniques, well executed, can sometimes result in prose – and a story – that transcends mere craft. They are trying to understand the spiritual aspect of their work by exploring the biological functions of it. Their efforts are as doomed as those of the critic and the academic analyst. Art resists

202

dissection, even if the pathologist wielding the scalpel is the creator of the art.

Having arrived at that conclusion, I doubt that I will ever again write a how-to piece. However, I have written many in the past; and the editors of this companion, not being of sound mind, are of the opinion that the general reader, even without aspirations to be a writer, will be interested in a sampling of what I've produced along this line. I'm not convinced. So if the following two pieces bore you, don't say you haven't been warned!

'Keeping the Reader on the Edge of His Seat' and 'Why Novels of Fear Must Do More than Frighten' first appeared in an instructional text edited by J.N. Williamson.

Keeping the Reader
on the Edge of His Seat

Suspense. It is what you feel on the uphill start of a roller-coaster ride. It's what you feel at a blackjack table as you sit with a pair of kings and wait to see if the dealer's hole card will give him a blackjack or give you the win. It's what you feel at the ballpark when the home team is only one run ahead in the bottom of the ninth – and the other team is at bat. This kind of suspense – call it *'light'* suspense – is fun, desirable, and probably good for you as well; it gets your heart beating, squeezes a little extra adrenaline into your tired bloodstream, exercises your emotional responses, and makes you feel *alive.*

Life is also filled with moments of darker suspense. You have felt that kind of suspense if you have ever sat in a doctor's office, waiting to hear what the lab tests showed about that strange lump you discovered the previous week. It's what you felt during the sickening seconds when, driving in a snowstorm, you lost control of your car and started sliding broadside toward oncoming traffic. It's what you felt all too sharply while waiting for a loved one to come out of emergency surgery. Nobody would argue that this darker brand of suspense is good for you; it strains your heart, breaks your spirit, and every minute of it that you endure probably shaves an hour or two off your life.

Only in fiction do we seek – and benefit from – both light and dark suspense. In books and movies, all suspense is vicarious, so we can experience every shading of it and walk away unharmed. Light suspense – the kind found in movies like Spielberg's *E.T.* and novels like Gregory McDonald's *Fletch* series – is the passive equivalent of taking an especially wild and unusually long roller-coaster ride. Grimmer stories that strike deep into the core fears of the human unconscious – *Aliens* and *Psycho*, Blatty's *The Exorcist* and Stephen King's *The Shining* – may be beneficial because they purge us of the psychological muck that is a residue of getting through life's bad

204

moments. And if the lead characters in such stories have honor and courage – and are portrayed with depth – the tales may also serve as examples of how one can face death, loss, loneliness, and other real-life tragedies with dignity. In other words, suspense fiction can provide both thrills and subtle – heed that word '*subtle*' – moral lessons.

Techniques for building suspense are acquired with practice and developed only over years as the writer learns his craft. However, the following few suggestions, lessons I have learned from more than two decades as a novelist, can save the new writer valuable time as you strive to make your stories more suspenseful.

Don't mistake action for suspense. A good novel must be filled with action, and the characters must be kept in meaningful motion; however, a tale can be composed of one gunfight and wild chase after another yet be totally lacking in suspense. Action becomes suspenseful only if you write with a full understanding of the following two truths: 1) suspense in fiction results primarily from the reader's identification with and concern about lead characters who are complex, convincing, and appealing; and 2) anticipation of violence is infinitely more suspenseful than the violence itself.

One-dimensional characters do not engage the reader's empathy, and if the reader does not worry about what might happen to them, suspense is aborted. For some ideas about how to create compelling and appealing characters, see my other article in this book, 'Why Novels of Fear Must Do More than Frighten.' As I argue in that piece, well-drawn and likable protagonists are essential if the writer hopes to frighten his readers. Likewise – and for the same reasons – good characterization lies at the heart of suspense.

Anticipation – that is what makes carnival funhouses so popular. Shuffling along pitch-dark corridors, edging across canvas-walled rooms queerly illuminated by black light, the funhouse patron has more fun anticipating the sudden appearance of a ghoul or a demon than he has when the thing actually pops out of a niche in the wall or up from a trap in the floor. Why? Because in the labyrinthine chambers of the human imagination, more bizarre terrors can be conjured than anything one is likely to encounter in real life. The pop-up ghoul, no matter how hideous, can never compare to what one pictures in one's mind while *anticipating* the fiend's assault.

James Cameron's superbly crafted film *Aliens* spends considerably more screen time building the audience's anticipation of monstrous violence than it spends depicting that violence. Tension is heightened every time a character turns a corner or edges warily through a doorway into a new shadowy chamber. Time and again, the slavering beast is not there, but we know that sooner or later it *will* be waiting, and we relish our anticipation of its appearance. When the aliens do attack, the action is furious, intense, electrifying – and quickly finished.

In some ways, the rhythms of exquisitely crafted suspense are akin to the rhythms of good sex: Long, slow foreplay ... followed by gentle and almost lazy lovemaking ... building steadily and deliciously toward the climax ... then The Big Moment with its swift and intense release.

My novel THE VOICE OF THE NIGHT contains a long scene in an auto junkyard that builds suspense by delaying a confrontation between the fourteen-year-old protagonist, Colin, and the fourteen-year-old (and evil) Roy. Pursued through the eerie night landscape of wrecked cars and old rusting trucks, Colin locates an apparently safe haven. I could have had Roy find him within a sentence or two, but I allowed the reader plenty of time to anticipate that development. Poor Colin cowers in his dark hiding place while he listens to Roy hunting for him, and he strains to convince himself that he is safe. Paragraph by paragraph, the reader's tension is heightened because he *knows* that Colin isn't safe and will surely be found. Because the reader likes Colin and fears for him, this is the kind of scene that brings the reader to the edge of his seat.

Consider Stephen King's *The Shining*. In what may be the scariest scene in contemporary horror fiction, five-year-old Danny enters the forbidden Room 217 of the Overlook Hotel, where a rotting but malevolently animated corpse is waiting for him. Does King start the scene with Danny in the room? No way. The scene begins with Danny outside 217, the passkey in his pocket, and he takes more than two hair-raisingly tense pages *just to open the door and step inside*. Anticipation. King makes us sweat. But when Danny finds the dead woman in the bathtub, and when she opens her eyes and reaches for him, the rest of the scene moves like a bullet and climaxes one page later. We are given more time to dread the encounter than to experience it.

In fact, in spite of a wealth of scary scenes and horrendous encounters scattered throughout the book, *The Shining* is essentially one long anticipation sequence. In the very beginning of the book, we know that Jack Torrance is sooner or later going to go after his little boy, Danny, with an ax. But King withholds that ultimate scene of terror for more than four hundred pages, building toward it with such care that it is excruciatingly tense when it finally arrives.

Style is as important as good characterization and anticipation. Stylistic excellence – good grammar, unfaltering syntax, and (most important of all) a strong sense of the rhythms of prose – is an essential ingredient in the creation of the highest-quality suspense. The very flow of the words on the page can lead the reader ever more swiftly toward the climax and generate in him a barely conscious but effective feeling of plummeting through empty space.

Some stylistic techniques for creating that effect are obvious. As the anticipation sequence builds toward the moment of violence or the dreaded encounter, the writer sometimes will employ more short sentences, simpler words, shorter clauses and phrases – all of which give the reader a sense of headlong, hellbent forward motion. Likewise, throughout the anticipation sequence and especially as The Big Moment draws near, brief mood- and scene-setting descriptions – generally never more than a line or two – can be crafted to generate anxiety in the reader without his quite seeing how it is done. For example, a fall of moonlight could be said to resemble 'the milk-pale skin of a drowned woman' and a nest of shadows in the corner might be called 'sepulchral' or 'graveyard-deep.' By using words and images of death, you are subliminally encouraging the reader to think that perhaps the lead character is about to die.

In THE VISION, I used a technique in one scene that was exactly the opposite of shortening sentences to heighten tension. When my lead character encounters the killer, I try to convey the chaos and psychotic frenzy of the attack by writing a large part of it in a single sentence:

. . . the knife ripped into him, rammed out of the darkness and into him, felt like the blade of a shovel, enormous, devastating, so devastating that he dropped the gun, feeling pain like nothing he'd ever known, and he realized that the killer had tossed the flashlight aside as a diversion, hadn't really been hit at all, and the knife was withdrawn from him, and then shoved hard into him again, deep into his stomach, and he thought of Mary and his love for Mary and about how he was letting her down, and he grappled with the killer's head in the dark, got handsful of short hair . . . and the flashlight hit the floor ten feet away, spun around, cast lunatic shadows, and the knife ripped loose from him again, and he reached for the hand that held it, but he missed, and the blade got him a third time, explosive pain, and he staggered back, the man all over him, the blade plunging again, high this time, into his chest, and he realized that the only way he could hope to survive now was to play dead, so he fell, fell hard, and the man stumbled over him, and he heard the man's rapid breathing, and he lay very still, and the man went for the flashlight and came back and looked down at him, stood over him, kicked him in the ribs, and he wanted to cry out but didn't, didn't move and didn't breathe, even though he was screaming inside for breath, so the man turned away and went toward the arch, and then there were footsteps on the tower stairs, and, hearing them, he felt like such a useless ass, outsmarted, and he knew he wasn't going to be able to recover his gun and climb those stairs and rescue Mary because stuff like that was for the movies, pain was pulverizing him, he was leaking all over the floor, dripping like a squeezed fruit, but he told himself he had to try to help her and that he wasn't going to die, wasn't going to die, wasn't going to die, even though that was exactly what he seemed to be doing.

Stylistic devices can be employed in countless ways to heighten tension and build suspense. To outline only those with which I am familiar, I would need an entire book. The new writer must be aware that style matters, that full control of the language and a profound understanding of its possibilities have at least as much to do with the creation of spellbinding suspense as do chase scenes and battles.

Finally, suspense hinges on the villain. He – or it – must be powerful, a fitting match for the lead characters, possessed of such a great capacity for evil that the reader cannot see how such a beast can possibly be defeated. The villain must be implacable, relentless, unstoppable. Think of Arnold Schwarzenegger in *The Terminator*. Think of Count Dracula. In my WHISPERS, Bruno Frye is a psychopath of almost superhuman dimensions, an embodiment of the chaos that lies at the heart of the universe; he is capable of absolutely anything, so the reader is instantly edgy when Bruno appears.

At the same time, your antagonist must be complex, not a comic-book villain, not Snidely Whiplash; he must possess human dimensions, perhaps admirable qualities as well as flaws. (Unless, of course, you are writing a dark fantasy in which the villain is a demon or some other supernatural entity; but even then, a textured demon is preferable to a one-dimensional funhouse cardboard devil.) The best villains are those that evoke pity and sometimes even genuine sympathy as well as terror. Think of the pathetic aspect of the Frankenstein monster. Think of the poor werewolf, hating what he

208

becomes in the light of the full moon, but incapable of resisting the lycanthropic tides in his own cells.

Suspense cannot be created in a vacuum. It is generated only as a by-product of good characterization, good pacing, an awareness of the value of anticipation as a prelude to action, strong stylistic control, and an ability – and willingness – to write complex characters and complex scenes that encourage the reader to suspend his disbelief and enter fully into the world of make-believe.

Why Novels of Fear Must do More than Frighten

Every Hallowe'en, at least one newspaper somewhere in the country polls its readers to find out what they think are the ten scariest novels and movies of all time. Since my PHANTOMS was published in 1983, it has made these lists, frequently in the number-one slot, never lower than number three. On one such list topped by PHANTOMS, another of my books, WHISPERS, occupied the fourth position.

When readers write to me, they tell me that, after finishing one of my books, they sometimes have trouble sleeping in a dark room and need a night light. Others tell me they can't bear to read one of my novels if they are alone in the house. Still others relish reading while alone but confess to overreacting to every innocent noise.

Reviewers comment on all aspects of the novels, of course, but among their most common reactions are: 'Will give you goose-bumps,' 'will stand your hair on end,' 'not to be read until you're sure all the doors and windows are locked,' and 'makes your blood run cold.'

The result of raising all those goosebumps and standing all those hairs on end and freezing several million gallons of blood is that, by the end of 1986, worldwide sales of my books are approximately forty million copies. Evidently, people enjoy a good scare.

New writers breaking into the suspense and dark-fantasy genres frequently write to me seeking advice or send manuscripts for my reaction. As I do, they take pleasure in wringing a cold sweat out of readers. Too often, however, they fail to achieve the effect they seek because they are trying to do *nothing else but scare the reader*. Fear cannot be generated in a vacuum. To induce fear, one must evoke other emotions as well. A writer of suspense and dark fantasy who is concerned only with creating fear is like a concert pianist attempting to play Mozart on just one-fourth of the keyboard: It cannot be done.

The initial reaction that a story *must* elicit from the reader is empathy – the vicarious experiencing of the feelings, thoughts, and attitudes of another person. The first person with whom the reader should have empathy is the novel's lead character, the protagonist.

To quickly induce empathy, a character's thought processes and motivations must be clear and understandable. For example, in my novel STRANGERS, the lead male is Dominick, a writer who, after years of struggle, has just written a potential bestseller and desires only to do more good work and enjoy the fruits of his labors. Ginger, the lead female character, is a resident in cardiovascular surgery and, after many years of arduous study, wants to finish her residency and become the best doctor she can be. Their desires and goals are clear, admirable, and any reader can identify with them on that level. Or consider Stephen King's *The Shining*, in which young Danny, only five years old, functions as the novel's protagonist. Danny wants nothing more than to love his parents and be loved in return; the reader who cannot understand and empathize with those motivations is someone who needs counseling!

A protagonist who is a neurotic mess, who is motivated by greed or lust or one of the baser emotions, is not going to engage the reader's empathy swiftly. Certainly, we all have those darker desires and motivations, and on one level we *can* identify with a basically malignant character, but we do so only with great reluctance because we do not like to admit that such feelings exist in us. A great writer with tremendous talent can pull off this trick, as James M. Cain did splendidly in *The Postman Always Rings Twice* and nearly as well in *Double Indemnity*. In *Clemmie*, the incomparable John D. MacDonald writes of a lead character consumed and ultimately destroyed by lust, and the reader has almost painful empathy with him. But Cain and MacDonald are masters of the novel, and the new writer who sets himself the challenge of a 'bent' protagonist is starting with a huge disadvantage that his nascent talent most likely cannot overcome.

Having created a protagonist with whom the reader can easily empathize, you are still not ready to instill fear. First, you must seek to elicit another important emotion – sympathy. The reader must *like* your lead character, care about him, and be concerned about his fate.

Many ineptitudes of characterization can prevent the development of sympathy in the reader. However, the following five are those errors most often committed by new writers:

211

1. Your character must not act irrationally and must not get into trouble merely because he makes stupid decisions. For example, if he moves into a haunted house with his family, and if lovable old Grandma is subsequently eaten by a monster that crawls out of the cellar, your protagonist will not enjoy the reader's sympathy if he stays in the house to prove his courage or because he's a stubborn individualist. Anyone with a brain would get the hell out after Grandma was consumed, and that would be the end of your haunted-house story. To keep the story alive, you must provide logical and convincing reasons that this man and his family cannot leave. Consider the movie *Poltergeist*: The family dared not depart because their little girl had been snatched away by a demon and was being held in an other-dimensional plane of the house; if the family left, they would be abandoning their child to the Dark One.

2. Your character must not be passive. He must not simply wait for things to happen to him and then react. As his situation grows more desperate, he must take strong and logical actions to deal with the antagonists who are plaguing him, whether they are human adversaries or, as in some dark fantasies, supernatural forces. He must seize the initiative. In *The Exorcist* by William Peter Blatty, the mother of the possessed girl and the young priest, Father Karras, diligently pursue myriad medical and psychological explanations and treatments for the child's condition. Ultimately, when all rational explanations are eliminated, they are forced to confront the likelihood that demons exist and are present in the girl, whereupon they call in the elder exorcist. They do not just sit around biting their nails and waiting for the next bogyman to jump out of the walls. Remember: Nobody likes a wimp.

3. On the other hand, your lead characters must not be supermen and superwomen whose actions always succeed. That would eliminate all prospect of genuine suspense. Some of their responses to the antagonists will improve their situation, and some of the things they do will make their dilemma worse than ever. In fact, the classic plot of nearly all fiction involves a steady worsening of the protagonists' situation until, at the penultimate moment, they save themselves and solve their problems – or die trying. The important thing is that they learn something from both their successes and

failures and that they apply those lessons when deciding on their next course of action.

4. Your characters must not be explored solely within the main plot of the novel; they must have lives outside of the central story. Each character must have a past that is not merely a dry summary of where he was born, raised, and schooled; that past must have affected him, and we must see how it shaped him. In my book WATCHES, Travis Cornell has lost everyone who has ever mattered to him: His mother died giving birth to him; his brother drowned when Travis was ten; his father died in an accident a few years later; and his first wife died of cancer. As a result, Travis is reluctant to enter into close relationships, fearing that new friends and loved ones will also be snatched from him. As well as having to deal with the antagonists of the story – and a murderous lot they are – Travis must also learn to conquer the fear of emotional dependency that has made him an unbearably lonely man. Ideally, all your lead characters have problems of an external nature (those imposed on them by the villains) and internal problems (those imposed by life and hard experience). Otherwise, they are cardboard creations incapable of inducing sympathy, and their travails will never move the reader to fear for them.

5. Each of your lead characters must not be concerned solely about his own fate. If your hero is running for his life, his major motivation is naturally going to be self-preservation, and any reader will easily empathize and sympathize with that. But your lead must also care about someone else within the story – a wife, girlfriend, son, daughter, parent, friend – for whom he is willing to put himself in emotional, spiritual, and/or physical jeopardy. More than anything else, fiction is about *the interaction of people*, about their complex relationships. A reader will be more inclined to like a character and to cheer for him if that character has a trace of altruism, if he is willing to risk all for someone he loves or for an ideal. Love is the emotion that readers – even readers of horror novels – find the most compelling in life and in fiction. If a character's love is so strong that he will sacrifice himself for another, and if you can make that love and sacrifice believable, readers will be moved.

A word of warning is appropriate here. You must not let your character's altruism get out of hand. He must not become a bleeding heart who wants to save the whales, bring about nuclear disarmament, end world hunger, and usher in the millennium at any cost. For one thing, such a broad spectrum of aching idealism will make him seem unfocused. Furthermore, while there is certainly a place in fiction for the exploration of broad social issues – witness the work of Charles Dickens – no fiction can *last* if it mistakes trendy political issues for great and enduring social concerns. Political issues involve simplistic one-answer solutions, while genuinely important social issues are complex and seldom find solution through political means; if your lead is to be sympathetic and tough minded (as he must be), he should know at least *that* much about the way the world really works. Keep his altruism focused on a small-scale, one-to-one, very *human* level, and it will be believable and admirable and engaging. A perfect example of doing this correctly is Dicken's *A Tale of Two Cities*, which contrasts the emptiness of political ideals with the enduring value of more personal and human ideals; it is a book filled with credibly altruistic acts, culminating in what may be the most moving final scene of any novel in the English language.

Now, you are ready to induce fear in the reader and make him sweat. If you have engaged the reader's empathy, encouraged him to be sympathetic with the lead characters, have made him witness to their love and friendship and joy and hopes and dreams, he will feel that these fictional people have something to lose, and he will not want to see them lose it. He will be afraid that they will lose not only their lives but their love, their happiness, and their hope for a better future. He will identify with each character not as a real person to a fictional person, but as one human being to another. The reader will be sweating with them each time that the villain walks on stage, and he will dread every encounter that might lead to their deaths. This is the *magic* of fiction.

In the dark-fantasy or suspense novel, fear by itself is empty and unaffecting. In context, however, when evoked with a panoply of other emotions, fear is one of the most compelling secondhand experiences that fiction can give us. This is because, at root, all fears have the same source: That you will have to stand alone against some adversary – something as external as a murderer or as internal as cancer – and that you will die alone, with no one to hold your hand as life fades away. Alone.

You'll Either Love it or Hate it – or Just Be Indifferent to it

Ever since I was a kid, I've loved humor of the absurd. Ernie Kovacs, Stan Freberg, Jack Douglas, Ed Bluestone, early Steve Martin, recently Steven Wright – all of those guys with the really strange extra edge can make me laugh until I'm too limp to stand up. Then I have to be folded over a hanger and taken to a dry cleaner to be steamed, starched, and pressed, but thereafter I'm as good as new.

Humor of the absurd appeals because *life* is absurd, and seems to be getting more so as we close in on the millennium. Viewing any episode of Geraldo, Oprah, or Donahue will confirm this assessment – who would ever have thought that *so* many dentists are transvestite compulsive gamblers with lesbian lovers on the side? – as will the actions and stated intentions of virtually *any* politician of either the left or the right.

Did you read the news story not long ago regarding a bank holdup in which the gunman passed a note to the teller demanding five million dollars? The teller calmly explained to him that considerably less cash was kept in her drawer – or even all the drawers combined – so she asked if it was all right if she gave him a check. He agreed. Now, of course, if you didn't see this story, you think I'm making it up; but it's true. He gave the teller his name, watched as she made out a bank check to him for five million dollars, accepted it, and left, whereupon the teller set off the silent alarm. The thief then went to another bank where he had a checking account, and *deposited* the five-million-dollar draft. He was arrested at his apartment within an hour.

If you read the news, incidents as wacky as this are unnervingly common in our time. Homeowners are being sued by burglars who were shot or injured in the act of stealing valuables – and are being forced to pay damages to the thieves. Murderers are getting out on parole after serving six years in jail. Be honest – a few years ago, if someone asked you to name the hundred Hollywood personalities most likely to be involved in a sex scandal, would Woody Allen's name even have made the list at the bottom? We are living in ridiculous times.

When you perceive that life itself is absurd, that *anything* could happen next – that's scary. And whenever we're scared, we tend to make fun of the object of our fear as a method of controlling our anxiety.

A few years ago I started writing little stories for an imaginary magazine, *Weird World*, which bills itself as 'the magazine of strange and confusing news.' I have always enjoyed those nutball collections of bizarre true and 'true' stories of the supernatural put together by Hans Holzer, Frank Edwards, Charles Fort, and others – not because I believe much of what is in them but because they're so off the wall and therefore fun. *Weird World* is meant to be a parody of that type of material and, secondarily, a commentary on – and answer to – the deluge of absurdity that has become a part of our daily lives.

Two of these pieces – 'The Day It Rained Frogs' and 'The Unluckiest Man in the World' appeared in a small-press magazine now defunct. (I killed it off just like I killed off *Readers & Writers* with my first story, 'Kittens!') David Silva was the brave editor who risked reader ire by running this much Weirdprose, and he deserves something for his courage – perhaps eternal damnation.

There is no real paying market for this work. It's done more to entertain myself and a few close friends who are disturbed in many of the same ways that I am. You will either hate it or love it: That is true of all humor of the absurd. Some people think *Catch 22* is the funniest novel ever written – and others think it is at best confusing and at worst a crashing bore.

Anyway, here are some excerpts from a book of articles collected from the purported forty-year run of *Weird World*. Enjoy. Or not.

R

Weird World:
The Introduction

On August 15, 1982, Mr Orville Umley of Shmontses, Arkansas, was abducted by creatures from another world in a spaceship shaped like a four-slice toaster. According to Mr Umley, who is employed to untie knotholes for the Shmontses Lumber Mill, the three-foot-high aliens were all two-headed. Each of these strange visitors possessed one head that was a cross between that of a koala bear and a really mean muskrat, with three red and green eyes, antlers, and ears that spouted steam, and in every case the second head bore a striking resemblance to Sandy Duncan.

These astronauts from another galaxy took Mr Umley on a guided tour of every planet in our solar system and then bought him dinner at a drive-in hamburger restaurant outside of Cleveland. After two days, Mr Umley was returned to Shmontses, Arkansas, with irrefutable proof of his fantastic journey: A small cinder from the sun-seared surface of Mercury, a phial of water from the canals of Mars, and a Big Mac container from Cleveland.

Weird World, the magazine of strange and confusing news, brought you in-depth coverage of this major story, including a two-part interview with Mr Umley and six pages of photographs. However, if you get your news from the *New York Times* or *Newsweek* or *Time* or even from the more comprehensive and reliable *U.S. News & World Report*, you will have heard nothing whatsoever of Orville Umley and his amazing odyssey!

Those so-called 'prestigious' publications are all part of a worldwide conspiracy of the ruling establishment, which does not want the public to know that Earth is being continuously visited by creatures from other worlds. This highly secret elite conspiracy, which cleverly and misleadingly calls itself the Buddy Holly Memorial Society, was founded by John F. Kennedy, Nikita Khrushchev, and Mr Bluster from the original 'Howdy Doody Show.'

Today, the Buddy Holly Memorial Society is under the leadership of Edward Kennedy, Jacqueline Kennedy, Ronald Reagan, Elvis Presley (who is not really dead but living in a sumptuous villa on one of the moons of Saturn), Bill Clinton, Madonna, Margaret Thatcher, and Barbra Streisand. These elitists control and manipulate the news because they fear that the truth, if known, would cause a panic in pork belly futures and lead to a total collapse of the faltering United States Postal Service.

From the time it was founded in 1952, *Weird World*, the magazine of strange and confusing news, has been dedicated to bringing the truth to the people – regardless of how painful, frightening, baffling, or ridiculous that truth might be. Each month we risk our lives and reputations to tell you the *real* facts about the latest alien visitations, the Lost Continent of Atlantis, and the mutant time-travellers from the future who have set up a secret community in the suburbs of Indianapolis, among many other fast-breaking stories.

It was *Weird World*, the magazine of strange and confusing news, that first reported Bill Clinton's conversion to the Druid faith and his blood sacrifices of Xerox salesmen on an altar in the Arkansas backwoods. Our publication also broke the story of Herman Feinberg, the amazing delicatessen owner from New York; through application of a complicated formula involving the ratios of *mentsches* to *shlemiels* to *mishlings* who came into his store every day, Mr Feinberg could accurately predict tomorrow's results at Aqueduct.

Dedicated to the proposition that mankind's hope lies in the supernatural, the paranormal, and the entire array of irrational pseudosciences that the elite establishment ridicules, we will always without hesitation print the most astonishing and dangerous stories without heed for our own safety or for the sobriety of our reporters.

In 1968, when we exposed Walter Cronkite's courageous and patriotic involvement with the secret recruitment of young Filipinos to fight the war against the giant blood-sucking newts that were then infecting the asteroid belt, that eminent and much-respected journalist was so impressed with our investigative reporting, he said: 'That incredible magazine is an outrageous cross between *The National Enquirer* and *Fate*, with a touch of the same insipid celebrity worship that makes *People* such an absurdly huge success.' We here at *Weird World*, the magazine of strange and confusing news, were deeply moved by that praise from Mr Cronkite, for whom our

218

admiration knows no limits, and in fact, his words have been featured at the bottom of our stationery ever since.

When it was suggested to us that our readers might like to have some of our most famous and important articles collected in more permanent book form, we found so many favorite and momentous reports from almost forty years of immensely courageous and valuable publication that we could not make up our minds what to include or leave out. The novelist Dean Koontz, acting as editor, pored through our files and selected the contents of this volume. We believe he has done a fine job, although we *still* think that he should have included our 1959 story about Herve Sperkle, the pygmy faith healer from Borneo, who planted a squash garden in which grew a 330-pound zucchini that, after disappearing one night in August, reappeared mysteriously on the lawn of Becky and Sturdevan Wonk, in Salt Lake City, Utah, with their cocker spaniel crushed to death beneath it.

S

The Day It Rained Frogs

On April 27, 1959, the small and picturesque town of Bean Falls, Vermont, was the target of one of the weirdest meteorological phenomena of all time: A rain of frogs, a celestial deluge of web-footed creatures that lasted nine and a half minutes. No exact count of the number of amphibians was made, but townspeople reported tens of thousands of 'big, green, nubby-skinned, disgusting things' that poured out of ordinary storm clouds and 'generally made a mess of the place.'

Although the frog storm was of short duration, its effect upon Bean Falls was devastating. Dozens of citizens suffered impaired hearing from the cacophony of croaking Kermits, and several freckled little girls in pigtails, serving as crossing guards at various intersections near the grade school, were permanently traumatized when caught in the unexpected, slimy green, squirming downpour.

Dr Harley Coof, the town's veterinarian, told *Weird World*, the magazine of strange and confusing news, that more than one hundred cats were rendered incurably schizophrenic by the frog storm and had to be put to sleep.

'And I don' mean tucked in their little cat beds, either,' Dr Coof said. 'I mean *put to sleep*, you know, like killed, snuffed, injected with massive doses of tranquilizers. At least a score of them had to be shot because you couldn't get close enough to administer the tranquilizers. I mean, Jesus, those cats were *crazy* from being hit by all those falling frogs. In a frenzy to get out of the storm, two particularly paranoid-schizophrenic Siamese smashed through a window at old lady Dunphy's house and started tearing the stuffing out of all her furniture, looking for a place to hide. The sheriff had to use tear gas to force them out on to the Dunphys' lawn, where the county SWAT team could subdue them with batons and riot guns. And I don't mean "batons" like cheerleaders use; I mean hard wooden clubs that could reduce a cat's skull to Silly Putty.'

220

Perhaps the worst aspect of the frog storm was descent velocity. Raoul Einstein, physics teacher at Bean Falls High, explains: 'You see, cloud cover that day was at about twenty thousand feet, which is about four miles. That's a long way to fall. By the time those croakers reached ground level, they were coming down like crashing jets. Some of those suckers hit with a sound that was part like a bomb blast and part like swinging a sledgehammer through a big block of Jello. The weird thing is that about half of them came down slow, like drops in a gentle rain shower, and somehow survived, though according to all the laws of science, not *one* of them should have made it through alive. And that's why, even though I'm a man of science myself, I'm convinced that our rain of frogs was a miracle, a sign from God, a prophecy of some kind – though no one around here seems to've been able to figure out exactly what God was trying to tell us.'

We might never know for certain what God was trying to tell Bean Falls on that fateful April afternoon in 1959, but the storm held a clearer message for Yukiro Inamishi, six-term mayor of the town, who was subsequently and unceremoniously booted out of office in the following year's elections.

Because Bean Falls' storm drain system (a pet project of Mayor Inamishi's) was ill-equipped to deal with a downpour of amphibians, gutters quickly overflowed with wriggling and writhing frogs, as well as with small mangled corpses. A hideous wave of slimy lifeforms swept along Main Street, demolishing a dozen businesses, overturning the monument to Peter Lorre that stood in the town square, and inundating the fire station, where eight firemen were standing on tables and chairs and where Dr Coof was trying to subdue a crazed dalmatian that couldn't shake two clinging cats driven mad by frogophobia.

Voters, enraged by Mayor Inamishi's lack of foresight in regard to the storm drains, gave an 85 percent majority to his opponent, who later obtained a ten-million-dollar federal grant for redesigning and enlarging Bean Falls' entire system of storm drains.

* * *

What was the meaning of this rain of frogs? What are we to make of it? What are we to deduce? What are we to think, hope, imagine, feel, contemplate, meditate, ponder, muse, and discern about this startling event?

Was it, as Raoul Einstein and others believe, a divine message? And if it was from God, did He mean it to be a warning – or a slimy green telegram of hope?

Was it a plot by Richard Nixon, who desperately wanted to embarrass Yukiro Inamishi, Bean Falls' mayor, who was at the time considered shoe-in to head the Republican Party's national ticket in 1960?

After all, Yukiro never was nominated by the Republicans, and we all know where Nixon's career went after the infamous rain of frogs. And there is a moment, on one of the Watergate tapes, when Nixon says to John Ehrlichman, in the privacy of the Oval Office: 'We've got to mislead the (expletive) reporters and cover this (expletive) thing up. I sure as (expletive) hell didn't campaign my ass off so that Liddy, Hunt, and a bunch of (expletive) (expletive) (expletive) incompetents could screw things up for me. Besides, holy (expletive), if they do bust this (expletive) Watergate thing wide open, the (expletive) bastards will start looking for other (expletive) (expletive) (expletive) (expletive) (expletive) (expletive) scandals, and sooner or later they'll find out about that (expletive) Jap and those (expletive) frogs!'

Or is it possible, as some conjecture, that the frogs were jettisoned from a disabled flying saucer that had intended to take them to another world but developed ion-drive trouble and had to abort the mission? Is it conceivable that aliens from another solar system are coming to Earth to steal our frogs for delivery to four-star restaurants on distant planets?

This last frightening possibility is reputed to be the explanation favored by Dr Carl Sagan, author of *Cosmos* and other widely read and admired books dealing with mankind's relationship to the rest of creation. In private, among close friends, Dr Sagan is reported to have said that he believes our entire world is being exploited by greedy alien food wholesalers who supply gourmet treats to wealthy diners in exotic restaurants on billions and billions of far-flung planets throughout the universe.

Intimate and trusted associates of Dr Sagan hint that on several nights he has seen two-foot-tall, blue creatures from outer space in his backyard and in the yards of his neighbors, where, under cover of darkness, they were collecting snails, small dogs, and assorted pieces of lawn furniture which they apparently found edible. According to sources close to Dr Sagan, these food wholesalers from another end of the galaxy have ears like turnips, noses like New Year's Eve noise-makers, and yet somehow resemble miniature blue versions of Madonna though with less of a tendency to remove their clothes than is exhibited by the popular singer.

We at *Weird World*, the magazine of strange and confusing news, support no single theory about The Day It Rained Frogs in Bean Falls. We have no bias toward any particular explanation. We keep an open mind in these issues. But we do know one thing: We no longer look at the sky quite the way we once did.

T

The Man Who Does Not Always Mean What He Says

The following short dialogues between our reporter Marv Swack-hammer and Sam Yadinski, widely known as The Man Who Does Not Always Mean What He Says, are excerpted from a much longer interview published in the February 1979 issue of *Weird World*, the magazine of strange and confusing news.

* * *

MARV SWACKHAMMER: As I understand it, Mr Yadinski, you are the victim of a voodoo curse. Is that right?

MR SAM YADINSKI: Yes. In November 1977, my wife and I were on vacation in Haiti. At the hotel, the bellman who carried our luggage to our room was a local fellow named Mau Mau Magursky—

MARV SWACKHAMMER: Are you making that up?

MR SAM YADINSKI: No, no. As you know, sometimes I say things I don't really mean, but this isn't one of them. This is the truth. His name was Mau Mau Magursky, and he was very dissatisfied with the tip I gave him for handling our baggage. He was so upset, in fact, that he threatened to put a voodoo curse on me, and then he stalked out of the room.

MARV SWACKHAMMER: Seems like an extreme reaction. How much did you tip him?

MR SAM YADINSKI: It was a very generous tip.

MARV SWACKHAMMER: How much?

224

MR SAM YADINSKI: *Two* shiny new quarters.

MARV SWACKHAMMER: Fifty cents?

MR SAM YADINSKI: See, I told you it was generous. And it'll seem even more generous when I tell you that we were traveling light that year. This Mau Mau Magursky didn't have much baggage to handle. Just nine suitcases, two hanging bags, a golf bag, and my wife's favorite gorilla suit. Oh, and by the way, Marv, your mother is a toad who performs obscene acts with the feet of Lebanese sailors.

MARV SWACKHAMMER: *What* did you say?

MR SAM YADINSKI: I'm sorry! Oh, God, please forgive me! I didn't mean that. Of course, I didn't. It's the curse, don't you see? Mau Mau Magursky's hateful curse.

MARV SWACKHAMMER: Let me get this straight. A disgruntled Haitian bellman put a curse on you, and now you can't always control what you say?

MR SAM YADINSKI: That's right, Marv. I never know what's going to pop out of my mouth next. That suit you're wearing looks as if it used to belong to the star of a performing baboon act.

MARV SWACKHAMMER: Was that another one?

MR SAM YADINSKI: My God! I'm sorry. I'm so sorry! I didn't mean that. It's a perfectly fine suit. Really, it is.

MARV SWACKHAMMER: This is very disconcerting.

MR SAM YADINSKI: If it's disconcerting for you, imagine what it's like for me, mush-face.

MARV SWACKHAMMER: Mush-face?

MR SAM YADINSKI: Please, please, please forgive me! I didn't mean that. It's the curse. This hateful, ruinous, miserable curse. Oh, God, I'm so sick of it, so sick of this embarrassing affliction!

MARV SWACKHAMMER: Yes, well ... uh ... when did you first begin saying things that you didn't mean?

MR SAM YADINSKI: The day we left Haiti, at the end of our vacation. The same bellman carried our bags out to the taxi, and just as we were getting in, he told me exactly what kind of curse he had put on me. In the cab, on the way to the airport, I told Yetta, my wife, what he had said, and we both laughed at how ridiculous it was. Then, at the airport, as we were walking toward the loading gate, I turned to Yetta and said, 'If they had a museum for ugly, you would be the most famous exhibit.'

MARV SWACKHAMMER: What did she do?

MR SAM YADINSKI: She said, 'What?' And I found myself saying, 'You're so ugly that if you were a fire hydrant the dogs wouldn't even want to get near enough to pee on you.'

MARV SWACKHAMMER: Good heavens! It must not be easy to be married to you since this curse thing.

MR SAM YADINSKI: Yetta is a saint. Truly a saint. She knows I don't always mean what I say, and she's pretty much gotten used to my outbursts. Hey, Yetta, you gross blimp! Bring a couple more beers for me and this Swackhammer jackass!

* * *

MARV SWACKHAMMER: Mr Yadinski, is there any way this curse could be lifted from you?

MR SAM YADINSKI: Well, we had an exorcist come here, Father Veni Vidi Vici, and we hoped he could break the curse, but it just didn't work out.

MARV SWACKHAMMER: Well, I suppose he told you that an exorcist's main function is to expel demons from the innocent people they possess, whereas you are *cursed*, not possessed.

MR SAM YADINSKI: No, we didn't get that far. Before I was able to explain the whole situation to Father Vici, I suddenly told him he was

226

a hypocritical son of a massage parlor floozy, and I accused him of regularly fornicating with ducks, chickens, male bulldogs, and Eureka vacuum cleaners.

MARV SWACKHAMMER: But surely, being a priest, a man of compassion, he understood—

MR SAM YADINSKI: Like I told you, pea-brain, we didn't get far enough for Father Vici to be *able* to understand.

MARV SWACKHAMMER: So he walked out.

MR SAM YADINSKI: Yeah. Well, actually, he kicked me in the crotch, broke a lamp over my head, and *then* walked out. You know, Swackhammer, if half your brain turned to cow flop, your IQ would rise at least twenty points. Oh, God! I didn't mean that. Oh, listen, I'm so sorry!

MARV SWACKHAMMER: Uh . . . that's all right. I guess.

MR SAM YADINSKI: I'll tell you one thing for sure.

MARV SWACKHAMMER: What's that?

MR SAM YADINSKI: If I had it to do all over again, I'd have given Mau Mau Magursky another quarter.

* * *

MARV SWACKHAMMER: With these unrestrainable outbursts, it must be difficult for you to hold a job.

MR SAM YADINSKI: Not at all. In my line of work, nobody even notices these little . . . aberrations.

MARV SWACKHAMMER: What's your line of work?

MR SAM YADINSKI: I'm a New York cab driver.

* * *

MR SAM YADINSKI: That's some watch you're wearing.

227

MARV SWACKHAMMER: Thank you.

MR SAM YADINSKI: You couldn't have got one cheaper unless it came in a box of Cracker Jacks.

MARV SWACKHAMMER: Now, wait a minute, my mother gave me this watch—

MR SAM YADINSKI: Your mother the toad?

MARV SWACKHAMMER: I've had just about enough of your—

MR SAM YADINSKI: She must be a toad, 'cause you sure look like something that was fed flies as a baby.

MARV SWACKHAMMER: I don't have to listen—

MR SAM YADINSKI: I'm sorry! Oh, God! I'm so sorry, sorry, sorry. I don't always mean what I say. Please forgive me.

* * *

MARV SWACKHAMMER: —and I'm sure our readers would like to know how—

MR SAM YADINSKI: You're a funny-looking dwarf, aren't you?

MARV SWACKHAMMER: I'm not going to let you upset me again.

MR SAM YADINSKI: I mean, most dwarfs aren't particularly funny-looking. They're just little people. But *you*. You're something else altogether. I mean, Jesus, that *head* of yours. I've never seen a head that shape before.

MARV SWACKHAMMER: I understand that you're an afflicted man and that what you're saying is far more mortifying to you than it is to me.

MR SAM YADINSKI: No, this isn't the curse talking, really. I mean this. I really do. You're an odd bugger.

228

MARV SWACKHAMMER: And, of course, when you say you mean what you say, you don't *really* mean it because you don't always mean what you say even when what you're saying is that you *do* mean what you say.

MR SAM YADINSKI: I've never seen hair that color orange before. You know, I think you'd look better if you just shaved your head.

MARV SWACKHAMMER: You poor son of a bitch. This must be hell for you, being out of control like this, never knowing when an attack might come—

MR SAM YADINSKI: Hey, Yetta, come here! Quick! You gotta take a close look at this guy and tell me if he doesn't look like a cross between E.T. and Howdy Doody.

MARV SWACKHAMMER: Well, I think I've got enough material for the article, so—

MR SAM YADINSKI: Swackhammer, were both of your parents human beings? Yetta, come here.

MARV SWACKHAMMER: – I'll be going now and—

MR SAM YADINSKI: Swackhammer. Swackhammer. Hmmm. Swack-hammer . . . Hey, are you the Swackhammer—

MARV SWACKHAMMER: Where's my briefcase?

MR SAM YADINSKI: Listen, listen, are you the Swackhammer who worked at Stanford University—

MARV SWACKHAMMER: The hell with my briefcase.

MR SAM YADINSKI: Don't be in such a rush. I think I read about you.

MARV SWACKHAMMER: Get out of my way, Mr Yadinski.

MR SAM YADINSKI: In fact, I think I read about you in your own magazine, *Weird World*, the magazine of strange and confusing news.

229

MARV SWACKHAMMER: Out of my way, you gross blimp!

MR SAM YADINSKI: Hey, don't talk to my wife like that, all right? The thing is, I just got to know if you're the same Marvin Swackhammer who worked out there at Stanford when their subatomic cyclotronic wave masher blew up back in '65—

MARV SWACKHAMMER: Get out of my way or I'll rip your lungs out!

MR SAM YADINSKI: Come back! Wait! Are you the same Swackhammer who was engaged to marry Raquel Welch before that tragic disruption of reality waves in your lab?

MARV SWACKHAMMER: *Aiiieeeeeeeeeee!*

MR SAM YADINSKI: Ouch! Stop that! Ouch! Don't take it out on me, fella. The way I read about it, you brought it on yourself, tinkering around with things that mankind was meant to leave alone!

Tweetie, the Parakeet
from Hell

Bud and Olga Firkle are common, ordinary, bland – perhaps even *boring* – people whose lives are as common, ordinary, and bland as the lives of the other residents of Shpilkes Falls, a common, ordinary, bland little town in central Pennsylvania. In 1970, when they were both nineteen, they were married in the Fundamental Church of the Gray Little People, and even their nuptials were so lacking in interest that the minister fell asleep while conducting the ceremony. On their honeymoon night, Bud and Olga were reprimanded by the management of the hotel where they were staying, for their noisy yawning was keeping other guests awake in adjoining rooms.

Bud is employed by Steelhard-Massive Armatures and Fastenings in Shpilkes Falls, where he spends eight hours a day putting the springs inside the plastic rollers of toilet paper holders. Olga is an ordinary housewife whose primary claim to fame is her highly regarded homemade vanilla pudding, which is a favorite of covered-dish suppers, PTA meetings, and church picnics.

You would think that, of all the people on earth, the Firkles would be the least likely to fall victim to the harassment and depredations of vile demonic forces.

You would be wrong.

The Firkles' only child, Little Pinkie, is a drab, pasty-faced wretch, born in 1975. Most children are noisy, laughing, wide-eyed sprites with a thousand enthusiasms – but not Little Pinkie, who is as somber, bland, ordinary, and quiet as her parents. The only things for which Little Pinkie has ever shown enthusiasm are Ovaltine, Ivory Soap, unflavored Knox gelatin, Wonder Bread and butter sandwiches, Gavin MacLeod's acting ability, Burt Reynolds' talent as a song stylist, saltine crackers, the test patterns on TV, and squashed animals that she enjoys spotting along the highway when she travels with her folks.

You would suppose that, of all the children on earth, Little Pinkie Firkle would be the least likely to wind up with a parakeet from hell for a pet.

You would be wrong.

Terribly wrong.

Oh my, yes.

In January 1984, the Firkle family exploded on to the front pages of the nation's newspapers when their modest five-room home became the site of so many supernatural goings-on that it made the infamous house in Amityville seem positively appealing by comparison. Furniture levitated and flew through the air. In the midst of winter, when there should have been no flies at all, a thousand of them miraculously appeared on the wall of the den. They grouped together, formed letters with their small black bodies, and spelled out PORKPIE HAT, a mysterious message from Beyond that has yet to be understood.

At night the Firkles' sleep was frequently interrupted by eerie music that sometimes came from the heating vents and sometimes from the toaster in the kitchen – and once from inside a small can of snuff that Bud had left on his nightstand. On three different mornings, the steam on the shower door formed a face that, initially, was thought to be the tortured face of Christ, but which was eventually discovered to be an uncannily detailed likeness of Ricardo Montalban.

And *that* was just the tip of the occult iceberg.

Who can forget the photograph of poor beleagured Bud Firkle that appeared in papers all across the country? It was terrifying and irrefutable proof of the existence of malevolent spirits in that godforsaken house. The picture was taken by a UPI photographer, and it showed Bud Firkle standing on his head in a toilet bowl, stuck in that embarrassing position, put there by an angry demon who accosted him one morning while he was brushing his teeth.

Bud might have drowned before the plumber arrived and freed him, but he was saved by Father Vino Veritas. The good Father Veritas, a Roman Catholic priest who arrived at that very moment to perform an exorcism, proved to be a quick-thinker who could keep cool in a crisis. He knelt beside the upside-down and porcelain-imprisoned man, repeatedly flushing the toilet, giving Bud a chance to gasp a much-needed breath of air before the bowl filled again.

Roger Mudd and an NBC camera crew were reportedly driven out of the Firkle house by several angry spirits that cursed them in fluent Norwegian and pelted them with scores of fancy little raspberry tarts that materialized out of thin air.

Insiders at CBS, speaking off the record, confirm that Mike Wallace suffered even worse treatment at the hands of these malign entities. Wallace, intent upon exposing the Firkles as hoaxsters, was reportedly taunted and belittled by a nine-foot-tall demon in the form of a lizard with the face of Mickey Mouse and the voice of Barbara Walters. This hideous apparition apparently forced Wallace to submit to a humiliating interview regarding his preference in 18th century philosophers and his opinions of Nastassia Kinski films, then threw him through the picture window.

Unconfirmed but convincingly detailed reports from immensely reliable witnesses (who prefer to remain nameless) indicate that another demon cast magic spells on Seymour Hersh, who was on assignment for the *New York Times*, transforming him into a talking squash, a koala bear, and an immense pair of buttocks, before returning him to his real form and allowing him to escape.

When contacted by *Weird World*, the magazine of strange and confusing news, none of those journalists would talk about his experiences. Some replied to our questions with a curt 'no comment,' while others baldly denied that they were ever *at* the Firkle house in Shpilkes Falls.

Roger Mudd, arriving at JFK on a flight from Pittsburgh (the nearest airport to Shpilkes Falls), was met by one of our reporters. Mudd heatedly denied ever having heard of the Firkle family, but our reporter noted custard stains on Mudd's suit jacket and a squashed raspberry still matted in the hair at the back of his head!

A few of these frightened journalists even tried to throw us off the trail entirely by viciously impuning our integrity, calling us 'sleazy trash peddlers' and 'the dregs of journalism' and 'raving maniacs, gullible fools' and 'panderers to ignorance,' but we could not hold what they said against them, for they were obviously not themselves, driven half mad by the monstrous things they had seen and endured in Shpilkes Falls. We could hear the stark terror in their voices the moment they discovered who we were.

Although several media big shots were the targets of gross and humiliating abuse in the Firkle house, it was the Firkles who suffered the most. From a life hardly more exciting or interesting than that of a family of titmice, they were plunged into a maelstrom of monumental events in the history of mankind's relations with the occult sphere.

In February of 1984, when the storm of paranormality had nearly passed, our intrepid reporter, Marv Swackhammer, journeyed into central Pennsylvania to interview Bud, Olga, and Little Pinkie Firkle.

Marv's trip was horrendously expensive even for a company with expense accounts as generous as ours. But who would have imagined that the cheapest motel rooms are four times more expensive in the Shpilkes Valley in February, due to the crowds drawn to their yearly Starch Festival? And who could have foreseen that Shpilkes Falls' taxes on such things as mustard and pepper and pickle chips would drive the price of even a simple hamburger dinner to more than one hundred dollars? Furthermore, after listening to the soul-chilling stories the Firkles had to tell, and after witnessing a couple of startling apparitions that almost left him catatonic, Marv was advised by his physician to take two weeks of paid sick leave, which he spent in Las Vegas, where it was hoped the extremely low humidity would dry out any evil spirits that might have secretly taken up residence in his body.

But *Weird World*, the magazine of strange and confusing news, spent its money well, after all, for Marv Swackhammer brought back two hundred hours of taped interviews with the Firkle family, from which our editors are assembling a book to be titled *THE SHPILKES FALLS HORROR: A Parakeet from Hell*. Weird World Press will be publishing the Firkles' extraordinary book next autumn, with a first printing of 350,000 hardcover copies, so of course we do not want to reveal too many twists and turns of their astonishing story and spoil the whole thing for you. We are able, however, to excerpt several short dialogues from those startling interviews to give you some idea of the mind-numbing terror that descended on the Firkle family with such brutal suddenness last January.

* * *

The following exchange is from reporter Marv Swackhammer's initial interview with Olga Firkle in the neat, simply furnished, gray-on-gray living room of the Firkle house in Shpilkes Falls.

MARV SWACKHAMMER: When did you first notice something was wrong?

MRS OLGA FIRKLE: I believe it was when I was six. My parents was all the time going into their bedroom in the middle of the day, locking the door, and telling me they was developing photographs. I knew something was wrong because we didn't even own no camera.

MARV SWACKHAMMER: No, what I meant—

MRS OLGA FIRKLE: I listened at the crack under the door, you know, and from the sounds they was making, I thought they was beating cats to death with bean bags.

MARV SWACKHAMMER: Actually, I was asking if—

MRS OLGA FIRKLE: Of course, they was only feeding the monkey . . . uh . . . you know . . . ummm . . . making . . . m-m-making l-love. But I grew up thinking my parents was the most horrible sadists, you know. I was scared to death of them because I thought they might get bored with beating cats to death, and then maybe they'd start beating on *me*.

MARV SWACKHAMMER: That's very interesting, but—

MRS OLGA FIRKLE: Parents should always tell their children the truth, and they should not never hide the facts of life from them.

MARV SWACKHAMMER: Mrs Firkle, what I meant was – when did you first notice that something was wrong here in your own house, with the demons and everything?

MRS OLGA FIRKLE: Oh. That would be January 7. The day after Pinkie's eighth birthday. We was having supper at the kitchen table, just me and Bud and Pinkie. Suddenly the refrigerator door crashes open, see, and this giant, eight-foot-long, purple tongue comes out and scoops up poor Fluffy, our little cockapoo.

MARV SWACKHAMMER: My God! Then what happened?

MRS OLGA FIRKLE: It ate him.

MARV SWACKHAMMER: The refrigerator ate your dog?

MRS OLGA FIRKLE: Yep. The tongue curls right back into the frig, taking Fluffy with it, and the door slams shut.

MARV SWACKHAMMER: What did you *do*?

MRS OLGA FIRKLE: Well, for a while none of us says a blessed word. Kind of shocked, you know. Then Pinkie says, 'Mama, we have anything for dessert?' And so I says, 'Well, honey, last time I looked there was some fresh vanilla pudding in the frig.' And so Pinkie says, 'Would you get me a dish of it, Mama?' And so I looks down at my halibut lasagne, and I says, 'Bud, I'm not finished with my supper yet. Would you get some pudding for Pinkie?'

MARV SWACKHAMMER: What did Bud say then?

MRS OLGA FIRKLE: Bud says, 'Pinkie can get it for herself.'

MARV SWACKHAMMER: Then what happened?

MRS OLGA FIRKLE: Well, then Pinkie starts pouting and says, 'If you really loved me, you'd get me some pudding.' She's usually a sweet little thing, but sometimes she can be a real pain in the backside, I tell you. So Bud says, 'You take that tone of voice with me, young lady, and you just might wind up not being allowed to have no dessert.' So Pinkie says, 'I'm sorry, Papa.' And Bud says, 'That's better.' And Pinkie says—

MARV SWACKHAMMER: Yes, yes, yes, but what *happened*?

MRS OLGA FIRKLE: Well, what happened was that there was a bag of half-stale Archway vanilla cookies in the bread box, so we had those for dessert instead of the pudding.

* * *

Later, sitting at the Firkles' dining room table after a dinner of breaded Spam and potatoes stewed in non-fat milk, Marv Swackhammer spoke with Bud Firkle and elicited a fascinating and blood-chilling account of another supernatural manifestation.

MR BUD FIRKLE: —so then Olga says, 'No, Bud, it just couldn't have been the real Johnny Carson.' And I says, 'Well, it sure looked like him to me.' And Olga says, 'No, it must've been another one of them there manifesterating demons. The real Johnny Carson wouldn't just walk in our house, call us filthy names, puke on Little Pinkie's head, and then eat our drapes.' Now, I figure them crazy Hollywood people will do just about anything, but when I thought on it for a while, I could see Olga was probably right.

MARV SWACKHAMMER: When did you begin to suspect that Tweetie, your parakeet, was at the root of all these horrible and mysterious events?

MR BUD FIRKLE: Well, of course, nothing special ever did happen to us until starting the day after Pinkie's eighth birthday. We was just the most ordinariest folks you ever did meet, and then we go and buy Little Pinkie a parakeet for her birthday, and the next thing you know we have eight-legged rats in our attic and we find the prints of a cloven-hoofed animal burnt into the living room carpet. Worse, on every channel of our TV, twenty-four hours a day, seven days a week, the only thing we could get was reruns of 'Lou Grant.'

MARV SWACKHAMMER: Oh, my God!

MR BUD FIRKLE: Yeah. Something like that happens, and you know right away that somehow you let Lucifer himself into your home, so you start looking around to figure out how he got in.

MARV SWACKHAMMER: And since the devil can only enter a person's house if they invite him inside—

MR BUD FIRKLE: Exactly. The only damned thing we ever invited in was Tweetie, so we was suspicious of him. And when we got to thinking about it, we saw that there'd been signs we should of picked up on sooner.

MARV SWACKHAMMER: Signs? You mean … indications that Tweetie was not just an ordinary parakeet?

MR BUD FIRKLE: That's right. For one thing, he didn't just peep like

237

your ordinary parakeet. He tweeted entire songs. Mostly Barry Manilow tunes.

MARV SWACKHAMMER: Well, that was a give-away right there!

MR BUD FIRKLE: It sure was. I mean, we've been reading *Weird World*, the magazine of strange and confusing news, for years now, so we know all about those Satanic messages Manilow hides in his songs. Heck, we even bought one of his records once and played it backwards, just to hear for ourselves – and there he was, plain as day, singing about worshipping Satan and urging our youth to perform unnatural acts with Hoffy sausages. So when Tweetie started into doing 'Mandy' and 'Ships in the Night,' and 'I Write the songs,' we should have called in an exorcist right then and had him throw holy water all over that bird's butt.

MARV SWACKHAMMER: What other signs led you to the conclusion that Tweetie was not just an ordinary parakeet?

MR BUD FIRKLE: Well, right from the start, it seemed to us that Tweetie ate a lot more than a parakeet ought to. He went through that seed like nobody's business.

MARV SWACKHAMMER: How much seed are we talking about?

MR BUD FIRKLE: Nine pounds of it the first week.

MARV SWACKHAMMER: That is a lot for one parakeet.

MR BUD FIRKLE: And then, of course, there was what he did to our cat.

MARV SWACKHAMMER: Tweetie?

MR BUD FIRKLE: No, Hairball.

MARV SWACKHAMMER: What?

MR BUD FIRKLE: Hairball.

MARV SWACKHAMMER: Listen, buster, you've been watching too much of 'Hill Street Blues' if you think you can go around calling people 'hairball' and get away with it!

MR BUD FIRKLE: I weren't calling you no hairball. That was the name of our cat.

MARV SWACKHAMMER: Oh. So what did Tweetie do to Hairball?

MR BUD FIRKLE: Well, me and Olga and Little Pinkie were watching TV. It was the episode where Lou Grant himself uncovers the ring of Freemasons who've taken over the watermelon industry. See, the Freemasons are worried that too many black people have risen into the middleclass, so they're planning to raise the price of a watermelon to $235 and gradually drive all them coloreds back into poverty, where they belong, but Lou exposes them.

MARV SWACKHAMMER: I think I saw that. Wasn't that the show where Billy buys a can of black shoe polish and goes undercover as a Negro jazz singer?

MR BUD FIRKLE: That's it! That's the one! Anyway, we was watching the scene where Billy was performing in a club in Harlem, and she makes the mistake of thinking that 'Bringing in the Sheaves' is a jazz number—

MARV SWACKHAMMER: She gets her jazz and gospel music mixed up.

MR BUD FIRKLE: That's the very scene. All the coloreds in the bar are starting to mumble about her thinking 'Bringing in the Sheaves' is jazz, and they're looking at each other with their eyebrows raised, and it's getting real tense – and it was right then that this horrible voice booms out of the bird cage, so loud it rattles the windows and blows up the TV set. I mean, Marv, this was the most gravelly, raspy, hateful, *loudest* voice you ever did hear or ever want to hear.

MARV SWACKHAMMER: And it came from Tweetie? What did it say?

MR BUD FIRKLE: It said, 'YOU STINKING CAT! YOU RANK BALL OF SOUR FUR! YOU FOUR-FOOTED SHIT! I KNOW YOU'RE REALLY AN AGENT OF GOD. YOU CAN'T FOOL ME! I KNOW YOU'VE BEEN SENT HERE TO PROTECT THIS FAMILY FROM MY DEPREDATIONS. BUT I'M MORE POWERFUL THAN YOU ARE, YOU MOUSE-EATING TURD!'

MARV SWACKHAMMER: Jesus!

MR BUD FIRKLE: I apologize for having to use them nasty words, but I figured you'd want to know *exactly* what that bird from hell said and wouldn't want me to pretty it up none. So anyways, as Tweetie's saying all this vile stuff, these beams of green light come out of his eyes and fix on Hairball, and our poor cat goes spinning up into the air—

MARV SWACKHAMMER: Levitating?

MR BUD FIRKLE: Yeah, levitating, right up in the air, spitting and squealing. That was one scared cat, I swear. Anyway, sort of taking hold of Hairball with those green beams of light, Tweetie swings him around by the tail and starts bashing him into one wall and then the other, bashing and bashing, back and forth, all the while chanting in what sounded like maybe Latin.

MARV SWACKHAMMER: For God's sake, what did you do?

MR BUD FIRKLE: Weren't much we *could* do for poor Hairball. The cat's being whirled around the room so fast you couldn't possibly get a grip on him, and besides he was over our heads, out of reach. So Olga says, 'You know, now might be a good time to risk getting that vanilla pudding out of the refrigerator.'

* * *

The third and final excerpt from *THE SHPILKES FALLS HORROR: A Parakeet from Hell* is part of an interview with Little Pinkie Firkle, who would only talk with our reporter, Marv Swackhammer, if he would agree to get in her little red wagon and allow her to pull him around the neighborhood. She's cute as a button.

MARV SWACKHAMMER: Honey, I weigh a hundred and five pounds, which is probably twice what you weigh. I'm too big for you to pull.

LITTLE PINKIE: When I can't pull, I'll push.

MARV SWACKHAMMER: I'm too big.

LITTLE PINKIE: You're not really big at all.

MARV SWACKHAMMER: I'm terribly big. I'm huge.

LITTLE PINKIE: No, you're not. Mr Swackhammer, are you a dwarf?

MARV SWACKHAMMER: No, no, no. Dwarfs are much shorter than me.

LITTLE PINKIE: You're *real* short.

MARV SWACKHAMMER: I'm only a few inches under five feet.

LITTLE PINKIE: No, you're shorter than me.

MARV SWACKHAMMER: Ha-ha-ha. You're cute as a button.

LITTLE PINKIE: I've seen dwarfs like you in pictures in my fairytale books.

MARV SWACKHAMMER: Listen, kid, I'm a hell of a lot bigger than any dwarf. You show me a real dwarf, and I'll beat the crap out of him in about one minute flat.

LITTLE PINKIE: But Mr Swackhammer, you've got such a huge head—

MARV SWACKHAMMER: Me? *Me?* Ha-ha-ha. Ha-ha-ha-ha.

LITTLE PINKIE: And from the waist up, you're about twice as big as you are from the waist down. Just like them pictures of dwarfs in the fairy-tale books.

MARV SWACKHAMMER: Ha-ha-ha. There must be something wrong with your eyes, kid. Me, a dwarf? Ha-ha-ha-ha-ha. I played football in high school!

LITTLE PINKIE: And I never seen a hunchback until now.

MARV SWACKHAMMER: What the hell's the matter with you, kid? I'm no hunchback. I just got big shoulders for my size! Big shoulders and a big back! Hunchback, my ass! You got a wild imagination, kid, maybe too wild for your own good.

LITTLE PINKIE: Mr Swackhammer, can you tell me your first name, or is it a secret? Huh? Is your first name Rumpelstiltskin?

MARV SWACKHAMMER: You shut up, you pasty-faced little nerd, or I'll kick your teeth out. Marv! My first name's Marv for Marvin!

LITTLE PINKIE: Get in my wagon and let me pull you around, or I won't talk for your tape recorder. I won't tell you about all the ghosties, about what they did to me, and then your boss will be mad at you, and you'll be fired, and you'll have to go work in a carnival.

MARV SWACKHAMMER: Please, listen, be reasonable, kid. I'm too big. I'm too big for this. I ... uh ... I don't want you to strain yourself.

LITTLE PINKIE: I'm strong for my age.

MARV SWACKHAMMER: It's cold out here, Pinkie. Why don't we go inside and talk over hot chocolate and cookies? Wouldn't you like some hot chocolate and cookies?

LITTLE PINKIE: If you won't get in my wagon, I won't tell you about the night the devil came to our house in the body of the Michelin Tire rubberman.

MARV SWACKHAMMER: The Michelin Tire rubberman?

LITTLE PINKIE: Yeah, except he had the face of Joan Rivers.

MARV SWACKHAMMER: Jesus!

LITTLE PINKIE: It was horrible.

MARV SWACKHAMMER: What'd he do?

LITTLE PINKIE: I won't tell you unless you get in my wagon.

MARV SWACKHAMMER: Kid, please, it's a silly little red wagon!

LITTLE PINKIE: If you don't get in my wagon, I won't tell you how the devil was like the Michelin Tire man and how he and my mommy got naked in a pile of cooked spaghetti on the kitchen floor and fed the monkey.

MARV SWACKHAMMER: Huh? Fed the monkey? What do you mean . . . ? Oh. Oh. Fed the *monkey*.

LITTLE PINKIE: So get in the wagon, or I won't tell you in a million years.

MARV SWACKHAMMER: Gee, it's not really as small a wagon as it looked.

LITTLE PINKIE: You hold the handle. I'll start out pushing. Here we go!

MARV SWACKHAMMER: Easy, now, easy. It's kind of a bumpy ride in here. Where we going?

LITTLE PINKIE: Just to the end of the block.

MARV SWACKHAMMER: Okay, okay, now tell me about the apparition that looked like the Michelin Tire rubberman.

LITTLE PINKIE: Mr Swackhammer, what do people mean when they say they're going to feed the monkey?

243

MARV SWACKHAMMER: I thought you said you saw your mother and the rubberman on the kitchen floor—

LITTLE PINKIE: I saw them, but I didn't really understand what they were doing. What is 'feeding the monkey,' anyway?

MARV SWACKHAMMER: Don't push so fast, kid. Gimme a break, huh? And if you want to know about feeding the monkey, you better ask your folks.

LITTLE PINKIE: I'm afraid to ask them. They're all the time telling me they're going to feed the monkey. Then they go in their bedroom and lock the door.

MARV SWACKHAMMER: Wait, kid, slow down.

LITTLE PINKIE: And then when I sneak up to the door and listen, I hear these scary noises.

MARV SWACKHAMMER: Kid, wait, I've had enough of this.

LITTLE PINKIE: We don't even *have* a monkey.

MARV SWACKHAMMER: I'm getting sick. I want out of the wagon.

LITTLE PINKIE: It sounds to me like they go in there and beat cats to death with beanbags.

MARV SWACKHAMMER: Stop, stop, stop! What's happening here? This looks like—

LITTLE PINKIE: And I'm afraid some day they'll get bored with beating on cats—

MARV SWACKHAMMER: —a hill! There's a huge damned hill ahead of us!

LITTLE PINKIE: —and start beating on me.

244

MARV SWACKHAMMER: Let me out!

LITTLE PINKIE: (A grunt and gasp as she gives the wagon one last, hard push)

MARV SWACKHAMMER: You crazy little bitch!

LITTLE PINKIE: You won't get *my* first-born baby, Rumpelstiltskin!

MARV SWACKHAMMER: *Aiiieeeeeeeeeeeeeeeeeeeeeeee!*

* * *

Nine months prior to publication date, the excitement is already building for *THE SHPILKES FALLS HORROR: A Parakeet from Hell*. The Book-of-the-Month Club has taken it as a main selection. Film rights have been sold to Igor Zanuck, the 'forgotten son' of movie tycoon Daryl Zanuck, and the 'forgotten brother' of Richard Zanuck, producer of *Jaws*.

(Igor Zanuck only recently reappeared after being accidentally left behind by the Zanucks on a vacation to Borneo in 1958, and he has chosen the Firkle family's story as his first project to prove that 'while I may be forgettable, I am not without talent of my own!' Zanuck has hired the late Alfred Hitchcock to direct because, as he says, 'I know from experience how quickly this town can forget about you, how cruel they can be, what pleasure they can get out of *not* returning your phone calls. I think it's horrid the way they've treated Hitch since his funeral. He was one of our greatest, but Hollywood has a terrible what-have-you-done-for-us-lately attitude that's hard to fight. Because of what happened to me, I'm especially sympathetic about Hitch's situation. Besides, I think he'd be dynamite with this material.'

The film will star the five-year old cousin of Macaulay Culkin, Kackie Kulkin, who is also a boy but will play the role in drag. Sissy Spacek will play Olga Firkle, and John Malkovich will be Bud. Cameo appearances have been set for Mary Tyler Moore, Dudley Moore, Roger Moore, Mr Rogers, Teri Garr, Jack Parr, Felicia Farr, Clint Eastwood, Ned Beatty, Warren Beatty, Lesley Ann Warren, Leslie Gore, Albert Gore, Gore Vidal, Vidal Sassoon, and Binky the Wonder Fish. All parakeet songs will actually be dubbed by Barbra Streisand peeping in a falsetto, and during the demonic possession scenes, Tweetie's speaking voice will be that of James Earl Jones, who so memorably served in a similar capacity as the voice of Darth Vader in the *Star Wars* movies.

Next autumn, when Weird World Press releases *THE SHPILKES FALLS HORROR: A Parakeet from Hell*, we will be issuing a first printing of 350,000 hardcover copies at $29.95, but interest in this astonishing true story is sure to be so strong that many bookstores will sell out their initial orders within the first week of publication. If you would like to avoid the frustration of being unable to find a copy at your local bookshop next fall, you may order this important volume in advance, by mail. Just send $29.95 plus $32.00 handling charges to Weird World Press at the usual address.

No One Can Talk to a Horse, Of Course

Gweneth Guirely, of Damnwet, Oregon, was that community's most eccentric citizen. Born at the stroke of midnight on August 4, 1949, how could she have been anything *but* different? After all, that was a particularly strange and fateful night in which hundreds of UFO reports were made to police departments all over the United States, in which a two-headed chicken was born to a cow in New Jersey – and the very *same* night that President Harry Truman underwent his famous transformation into a werewolf during a state dinner for the King of Spain.

Gweneth Guirely claimed to remember a previous life as a horse in the private stable of Cornelius Vanderbilt. She first began to speak openly of her experience with reincarnation when she was thirteen, but she had given indications of it at an even younger age.

For instance, by the time she was four, Gweneth could find no rest in an ordinary bed and was able to sleep only when standing up, tied to the railing or the back porch, with a blanket thrown over her. Before her fifth birthday, she had grown intolerant of all food except oats, barley, hay, and an occasional piece of crisp fruit, and she insisted on being fed from a bag hung around her head.

Her parents, Fern and Murt Guirely, did not only tolerate their daughter's unconventional behavior but even seemed to encourage it. As a gift for Gweneth's eighth birthday, they had the garage converted to a three-stall barn complete with watering troughs. When a reporter from *Weird World*, the magazine of strange and confusing news, inquired as to the reason for three stalls instead of one, Fern Guirely said, 'Well, she's a very outgoing youngster, you know, and once in a while she *does* like to have friends overnight.' Neighbors say they frequently saw Fern giving her daughter rubdowns in the backyard, and by the time Gweneth was sixteen it was not unusual to see Murt, her father, riding her into town to pick up the mail.

'Gweneth always kept her head up and sort of pranced those last couple of blocks into town,' said Postmaster George Finbeck. 'Murt never tied her up outside when he came in for the mail, always just left her reins trailing loose, but she never ran away, not once in all the years I knew her. She had a nice canter, too, and when she wanted to gallop, she could go like the wind!'

One needs only to talk with a few of the people in Damnwet who are old enough to remember the Guirely family, and it becomes apparent that Fern and Murt were proud of their daughter. When visitors came to the Guirely house, Gweneth would harangue them with long tales of her previous life in Cornelius Vanderbilt's stables and with stories of racing at Saratoga in the glory days of that famed resort for the ultrawealthy. And while these anecdotes might sometimes try the patience of a guest, Fern and Murt were always said to listen with rapt attention and to look upon their only child with unmistakable adoration.

Indeed, only one thing about Gweneth's assumption of an equine identity was upsetting to her parents. She had the unsettling habit of depositing road apples in the most inconvenient places.

However, the sometimes noxious chore of cleaning up after the girl was of little consequence when measured against the honor she brought to the Guirely family when she received the Best of Show ribbon at the Oregon State Fair and, one year later, won the Belmont Stakes.

W

The Miracle Tree
of Burbank

In the backyard of the Harry Gefilte family of Burbank, California, there is a twenty-year-old date palm that does more than drop messy fruit all over the patio and attract rats. Harry and Myrtle Gefilte and their neighbors say that *this* tree talks.

The voice coming from the tree varies from an eerie whisper to a slightly raspy but otherwise ordinary conversational tone. Most of the time, it issues meaningless sounds that, while complex, do not seem to constitute a language. However, it has been heard to speak in Portuguese, Polish, Italian, and Danish, and on four occasions it has made clear statements in English, though its grammar and syntax are not always indicative of an adequate education. However, as Harry Gefilte told one reporter: 'Well, sure, it isn't Edwin Newman, but for a damned palm tree it talks pretty good.'

Explanations abound. Several of the Gefiltes' neighbors believe that the soul of some deceased person – perhaps a UN translator or a Berlitz instructor – has somehow become trapped in the tree. Others insist that aliens from a faraway star are broadcasting to us on the tree's 'natural wavelength,' and that the Gefilte palm is our best chance of establishing contact with our neighbors in the universe.

A rumor circulated that the Virgin Mary had taken up residence in the date palm and that its fruit had miraculous healing power. For almost a month, devout Catholics traveled from as far as Guadalupe Hidalgo, Mexico, and Damnwet, Oregon, to witness the miracle and to petition the Blessed Virgin. In fact, at the nearby Church of Saint Shlomo, so many parishioners went to visit the Gefilte palm that attendance at Wednesday night bingo games fell by half. However, hopeful pilgrims soon discovered that the tree's plump dates had no medicinal value whatsoever – except in those cases where the petitioner was suffering from chronic constipation.

A Vatican-appointed investigator, Father Vino Veritas, spent three days studying the strange phenomenon and finally determined that the miracle of the Gefilte palm was not a *religious* miracle in any way, though he did have a brief conversation with the tree in Italian, during which it recommended Turtle Wax to preserve and protect the finish of the parish car.

'It was quite a commotion having a couple of hundred Catholics around all the time,' says Myrtle Gefilte, 'but when they finally stopped coming, we missed them. I mean, most of them were such nice folks. Two whole busloads of Knights of Columbus came all the way from Cleveland, Ohio, and they were a pretty dangerous looking group, but aside from the cherry bomb in our mailbox and one guy named Nunzio Gnocci, who kept mooning Mrs Farnsworth across the street, even *they* were polite and well-behaved.'

The Gefilte palm does not talk constantly or even every day, which is probably a blessing, for there are few things more irritating than garrulous shrubbery.

For instance, Ike and Ethel LaChance of Boulder City, Nevada, were plagued by a maddeningly talkative oleander bush that stood by the kitchen door, droning on all day and most of the night in a piercing whine that could be heard from one end of the property to the other and throughout their nine-room Indonesian-Tudor home. Not even earplugs could muffle the oleander's monologue.

'It wouldn't have been so bad,' says Ike LaChance, 'if the damned bush had had anything *interesting* to say, but it was always blabbering about the modern novel, the causes of root disease, quantum physics, or the history of North Dakota.'

In 1958, in Farmisht Springs, Maryland, Rudy and Rhonda Rumbeck had worse problems with a different type of bush. An old and densely grown lilac, which had never exhibited the slightest inclination to speak during its first ten years of flowering splendor, suddenly began to compose clever rhymes that amused many people in the neighborhood – though at the expense of every member of the beleaguered Rumbeck family.

'I don't know what we ever did to that lilac to make it so scornful of us,' says Rhonda Rumbeck, still stung by the plant's behavior even after a quarter of a century. 'I suppose those little poems it made up were funny, in their own way, but they were so *nasty*, too. I remember the first one it ever came out with. My daughter, Cassie, and I were sunning on the patio one day in June of '58 – Cassie was only twelve then – when the bush spoke up and scared the devil out of us. It said:

> There sits chubby little Cassie.
> She looks a hell of a lot like Lassie.
> She has a big potato for a nose,
> doesn't smell the least bit like a rose,
> and she's as ugly as her stupid clothes.
> Oh, Cassie, Cassie, my little Cass—
> too bad your brain's not as big as your ass.

Well, of course, Cassie burst into tears, ran upstairs, and locked herself in her room. She wouldn't come out for three days, and she had nothing to eat in there but six boxes of Malomars and a carton of Reese's Peanut Butter Cups.'

Says Rudy Rumbeck, 'It wasn't just that those ridiculous rhymes were offensive. What made them really intolerable was the way the damned bush recited them in this reedy, snide, smarmy voice that just made your skin crawl. Besides, after a while, it started insulting our guests, making obscene statements about my mother, and it kept our cat in a constant state of terror with a really frightening imitation of a rabid German shepherd.'

Rudy's much-maligned mother, Gertrude Rumbeck, is still amazed: 'I could never understand how a bush could smell so pretty yet be so rude and foul-mouthed.'

After two months of this ordeal, the novelty of a talking lilac bush faded, and the poetic plant soon became a nuisance. Rudy and his godless homosexual son, Dorsey, who had been a particular target of verses criticizing his mincing walk, chopped the lilac down and burned it in their barbecue pit.

Says Dorsey, 'That bush was a bitch!'

Back in Burbank, Harry Gefilte says, 'I remember the classic case of the Rumbeck lilac bush. I read about that at the time it happened. I believe there was an article in *Weird World*, the magazine or strange and confusing news. I guess Myrtle and I are pretty lucky. Our date palm doesn't talk very often, and whenever it does, it's never been sarcastic or impolite.'

Students of the paranormal have spent thousands of hours poring over the messages that have come from the Gefilte palm, most of which are cryptic. Dr Eldritch Pedi, chairman of the Department of

Irrational Pseudosciences at UCLA, has been using the most advanced computers to analyze the statements that have issued from the tree, and he is convinced that the Gefilte case is not merely an unimportant oddity or a meaningless curiosity.

'Something important is happening out there in Burbank,' Dr Pedi says. 'Something big. Something that might change the world if we could only understand it. Some of the tree's messages seem innocuous, even laughable, while others are infuriatingly cryptic, puzzling. However, I believe that they are *coded* messages that mean far more than they appear to, and with my computers I hope to crack that code in the near future. By decoding the statements of the Gefilte palm, I believe we may crack the secret of faster-than-light travel, learn the meaning of life, and even discover why some people think Shecky Greene is funny.'

As previously mentioned, the Gefilte palm has spoken in English only four times. We here at *Weird World*, the magazine of strange and confusing news, would like our two million readers to carefully study this quartet of messages from our photosynthesizing friend in the hope that someone out there will have a flash of insight that will provide the understanding at which Dr Pedi's computers have not yet arrived. After all, two million minds are better than one. And two million minds steeped in stories of the supernatural, thoroughly saturated with paranormal lore, and well educated in irrational pseudosciences are a formidable force, indeed!

1) On August 24, 1982, the Gefilte palm spoke to Myrtle and Harry Gefilte while they were planting marigolds in a circle around its bole. It said: 'If ducks had teeth and barked, they could protect your house from burglars and would make fine enlistees in the Army's Canine Corps.'

Dr Eldritch Pedi believes that, decoded, this message will prove to be an aphorism of such stunning insight and value that it will change the course of human history.

2) On April 19, 1983, Harry Gefilte and his neighbor, Rooney Sludge, were killing a six-pack of Coors on the patio when the date palm said, 'In Istanbul, the woman in the scarlet dress waits forlornly beneath the clock without hands. The fox will not come until Saturday.'

Dr Eldritch Pedi points to this message, perhaps the most cryptic of them all, as proof that the tree is speaking in code. 'It is,' says Pedi, 'markedly similar to the way spies talk in all those old espionage movies. Although I do not agree with those who insist that this proves the Gefilte palm is actually an alien spy disguised as a tree to study us in advance of an invasion from another world, I can certainly understand why some might arrive at such disturbing interpretation.'

3) On Thanksgiving Day, 1983, while Harry and his father, Phil Gefilte, were in the backyard, mercilessly teasing Harry's dog with turkey bones tied to a boomerang and a gravy-coated gizzard on a string, the tree said, 'If all men had the same hat size and all women looked like John Cleese, the world might not be a better place, but it would certainly be in less danger of overpopulation.'

4) On April 14, 1984, while the entire neighborhood was gathered in Harry and Myrtle's backyard for the annual ox roast, the tree spoke in an uncharacteristically loud voice and in an unusually demanding tone. There were only five words to this baffling message, but some students of the Gefilte palm believe it may be the most significant speech the tree has yet made. It said: 'Send us your lawn furniture!'

'It was a little frightening,' Myrtle says. 'It's the only time the tree has raised its voice. And while I'm sure it would never harm anyone, I was a little unsettled that day.'

Harry chimes in, 'Hell, I wouldn't mind sending them our lawn furniture, if that's what they want, but I don't have a shipping address.'

The Miracle Tree of Burbank. The mysterious and portentous Gefilte palm. What is the explanation for its astonishing behavior? Is it possessed by the devil? Is it a mutant tree, gifted with speech due to radioactive fallout? Is it somehow a radio receiver for messages from distant planets? Can it be blamed on all those space shuttle launches that have seriously damaged the ether and disturbed the rhythmic tides of the stratospheric flux fields? *Weird World*, the magazine of strange and confusing news, will happily award a lifetime subscription to any reader who can provide the dedicated Dr Eldritch Pedi with the key to unlocking this awesome mystery.

The Unluckiest Man
in the World

Denton Scudlatch, heir to the Scudlatch curds and whey fortune, may be the unluckiest man in the world. *Weird World*, the magazine of strange and confusing news, became interested in Mr Scudlatch because his cataclysmically horrible misfortune seemed, in its astounding breadth and depth, to be proof that the universe is not a place of random forces but is ruled, instead, by intelligent powers with malign intentions – rather like Newark, New Jersey.

Denton Scudlatch is at least five times as unlucky as Mervyn Hockwet, of Seattle, Washington, a *very* unlucky man, and certainly three times as unlucky as Gandolf Immelman. Immelman was a Brooklyn hat-blocker who survived six plane crashes, two disastrous train wrecks, a subway fire, three automobile accidents, and a boiler explosion, all within four months, only to break his neck and die in a fall on an airport escalator while attempting to escape a pack of Hare Krishnas who were trying to give him flowers.

Denton Scudlatch is even 2.6 times unluckier than Hume Gilly, son of the unlucky African explorer Sir Winston Gilly. Sir Winston and his pregnant wife, Agatha, went on an extended safari to collect unusual rocks, driftwood, elephant feet, rhino horns, rare paisley leopard pelts, and particularly colorful insects to be used in the redecoration of their stylish St John's Wood home, and it was during this arduous trek that little Hume was born. Two days later, on the banks of the crocodile-infested Congo River, Sir Winston, Agatha, their safari partners, and their native bearers were all wiped out when a Sierra Club antisafari bomber hit them with half a dozen 600-pound blockbusters. Only little Hume survived.

The helpless infant was adopted by two great apes who, if they had had names, would have been called Tanya and Tando or Sheena and Sabu, or perhaps Ethel and Burt. Tanya and Tando raised little Hume as if he were their very own, although they hid him in a banana tree when Tanya's parents came to visit, and it was always understood that Hume would not inherit Tando's collection of fruit pits if Tanya should ever give birth to a real son of her own.

When little Hume was seventeen, he was found accidentally by an expedition of French explorers in search or their national identity. After several weeks of philosophical dialectics conducted in intense ten-hour sessions with much smoking of cigarettes, they managed to convince Hume (who thought of himself as Mooba) that he was not, in fact, an ape but a human being with a God-given right to wallow in angst, and with an obligation to have an opinion on the writings of Jean-Luc Godard.

With a tearful farewell to Tanya and Tando (and a promise to return one day with funny little hats and brass cymbals for every ape in the beloved tribe), Hume departed with the French expedition. He accompanied them on a four-month journey through the jungle to the port town of Scumville, a former Belgian penal colony inhabited by the bastard descendants of 18th-century hairballs and slimebuckets.

On that jungle trek and, later, on the long sea voyage to England, the Frenchmen taught Hume their own language and his native English. They instructed him in table manners, and they patiently taught him the difference between a toilet and a sink. They corrected his misapprehension that socks were to be worn on the hands and that suspenders were to be hooked over the ears, and eventually they transformed him into a fine gentleman ready to assume control of his father's vast estate, which had been held in trust for him during his long, long, long absence.

After seventeen brutal years in the jungle, after the long and arduous journey back to Britain, after taking the trouble to learn two languages, neither of which was half as expressive as the ape talk of his beloved tribe, Hume discovered that overdue taxes on the Gilly estate had mounted relentlessly in his absence. When he settled with the government, he was left with only a silver hairbrush, a croquet mallet, a ticket on the Irish Sweepstakes, and a matched set of the complete novels of Barbara Cartland.

The silver hairbrush proved to be chrome-plate. The Irish Sweepstakes ticket was a loser. As Hume exited the London offices of the Inland Revenue and walked unsteadily into the street with a stunned expression, penniless and alone, the croquet mallet was wrenched out of his hand by a madwoman who beat him

255

with it about the head and shoulders, sending him to hospital for a month.

In hospital, he had nothing to read but his Barbara Cartland novels, and as he had never read any kind of fiction before, he was erotically enflamed by even those coy stories. Consumed by lust, he grabbed a young nurse and said, 'I long to press against the pale, soft, yielding contours of your chaste but promising body,' then tore off her uniform.

Tried and convicted of assault and attempted rape, he was transported to a British penal colony in Africa, Slimetown, which was ten miles south along the coast from Scumville, the former Belgian penal colony, where Hume had first learned to use a fork without puncturing his lip.

No one in his right mind could argue against the proposition that Hume Gilly was – even at *that* point in his pathetic life – one of the eleven or perhaps twelve unluckiest men in the world. But his worst luck was yet to come.

After serving seven years at hard labor, he was released with one pound, eight pence, in British currency, a suit of clothes made out of paper, and a single shoe. He did not even possess a comb, and he would have given anything for a watch fob.

He made his way back to his beloved ape tribe in the deep, dark reaches of the jungle, worried that Tanya, Tando, and the others would not recognize him after his absence of more than eight and a half years. Unfortunately for Hume, they *did* recognize him, and recalling his sacred vow to return with funny little hats and brass symbols for everyone, they were infuriated that he had showed up empty-handed. He was driven away to fend for himself, a man without a species, welcome in neither human nor ape society.

By now, Hume Gilly was surely one of the six unluckiest men in the world. But *still* the worst was yet to come.

Driven out by his beloved tribe, he made his way through the jungle with considerable difficulty, having forgotten most of the survival techniques that he had known when living as an ape. He still remembered his table manners, but they were of little use to him in the bush.

Weeks later, he arrived at Scumville, the former Belgian penal colony, without clothes, without a pence to his name, emaciated, losing his hair because of malnutrition, and with a pimple on the end of his nose. He was so appallingly filthy and so severely deranged by jungle fever, that more than three weeks passed before anyone in Scumville realized that he was a human being. Another nine weeks passed before anyone *cared*.

For the next five years, Hume Gilly, the son of a knighted nobleman (for Sir Winston was the Duke of Dork), once the heir to a vast estate, was reduced to performing odd jobs around the Scumville wharves, gin mills, houses of prostitution, opium dens, and pirate headquarters. He cleaned spittoons, scrubbed barroom floors, rented himself out as a beast of burden, and made a little money on the side by killing wharf rats and using their pelts to make change purses and padded codpieces.

During his seventeen years with his beloved tribe of apes, a happy child of nature, free and noble, he had proudly carried the name Mooba. Later, apprised of his wondrous heritage as the only son of Sir Winston Gilly, he had just as proudly borne the name Hume Gilly. But in Scumville they had no respect for him at all, and the names they gave him reflected their total disdain. They first called him Dirtface, then Spitboy, then Ratman, and finally – most hated of all – Shecky.

Hume endured their scorn and abuse because he had a dream, and a man can endure much hardship if he has a dream. A man can suffer hideous physical pain and triumph over it if he has a dream. A man can live through horrendous mental anguish and shocking amounts of profound emotional agony if he has a dream – although nothing keeps one's spirits up quite as well as the guarantee of a good civil service job.

Anyway, Hume's dream was that some day he would return to Britain and reclaim his rightful place among the aristocracy. And buy himself the loveliest watch fob in all of London.

The bartenders in the gin mills laughed at Hume Gilly's dream. The prostitutes, the Great White Hunters, the pirates, and the natives laughed at Hume Gilly's dream.

'Shecky, you're an idiot,' they said.

'Shecky, you've got jungle rot in the brain,' they said.

They were a vile and hard-bitten lot in Scumville, with no respect whatsoever for a man's dreams. In fact, they had once stoned a local boy to death because he had expressed the hope of one day owning a second pair of shoes.

Even the nuns laughed at Hume Gilly's dream. The nuns staffed the Our Lady of the Sweating Black Heathens Mission, on the outskirts of Scumville. Sometimes Hume went to the mission to perform odd jobs for the nuns.

One of the oddest was when the Mother Superior hired him to mold and cast a large menorah for the celebration of Hanukkah. (Shortly thereafter it was discovered that the Mother Superior was not actually a nun – or even a woman. She was actually a man name Murray Cohen, a hugely successful Hollywood film executive, who had disguised himself and had secretly taken refuge in the mission to avoid an exceptionally avaricious firm of attorneys representing his wife, Moxie, in divorce proceedings back in California.)

'Shecky,' the nuns said to Hume, 'you are dreaming the impossible dream.'

They said, 'Shecky, Shecky, Shecky, you must give up this mad dream of returning to Britain and becoming the new Duke of Dork.'

They said, 'God doesn't like presumption or pride, Shecky, and if you persist in dreaming this prideful and presumptuous dream, God will get you.'

And they said, 'Shecky, we will pray to the Blessed Virgin to make you come to your senses before it is too late, for if you persist in returning to England with these prideful ambitions, God will surely sink your ship in midocean and send you to a watery grave to prove just how much this sort of thing irks Him.'

But if the cruel, hard-bitten, human filth of Scumville could not turn Hume away from his dream, then it was no surprise that the gentle sisters of the mission also failed to dissuade him. For five years he worked at the most demeaning labor, saving nearly every penny that he earned. He wasted no money on rent, but passed each night hanging on the Scumville flagpole, sleeping up where the snakes and wild boors could not get at him. He spent little on food, subsisting primarily on a diet of leaves, wild grass, grubs, dirt, and an occasional slice of hippopotamus cheese and a glass of Lafitte Rothschild supplied by the sympathetic nuns.

Hume spent his money irresponsibly on only one occasion. One day a barge belonging to the West Africa Hostess Cakes distributor came downriver to Scumville, and in a moment of insane gluttony brought on by so many years of self-denial, Hume purchased and consumed three entire cases of Twinkies. Later, miserable and ashamed, he realized that he had squandered so much money on junk food that his eventual journey to England had been set back two months. Chastened, he returned to his diet of wild grass and dirt.

As his savings grew, his plan became ever clearer in his mind. When he had enough money, he would first buy a good three-piece suit and one pair of shoes. (He dared not buy a spare pair of shoes, for fear the residents of Scumville would stone him to death.) Then he would purchase a ticket to Britain on a tramp steamer; it did not matter *which* steamer; he was not choosy, and he intended to book passage on the cheapest ship he could find; luxury did not matter at all; he was only concerned that it be a ship whose crew was composed neither entirely of greedy cutthroats nor of godless homosexuals. He would arrive in his beloved motherland with enough money to establish his own company, manufacture souvenirs of the inevitable royal wedding of Prince Charles, become unimaginably wealthy, repurchase the family estate of Dorkglen, and claim his rightful place in society.

When the engagement of Prince Charles to the future Princess Di was announced to the world press, the glorious story generated drunken celebrations in the streets of every city from London to Calcutta, and that included Scumville. Hume's savings had grown substantial, at last, and he knew it was time to leave. He booked passage on *The Star of Salt Lake*, a tramp steamer owned and crewed by honest Mormon coconut brokers. When he departed for London, he was deeply moved by the unexpected display of affection from the citizens of Scumville, who strung a banner across the wharf: WE'LL MISS YOU, SHECKY!

During the first half of the journey, Hume Gilly was on the ship's wireless for three hours every morning, sending messages to real estate brokers, bankers, and construction companies, to ensure that his souvenir-manufacturing plant would be ready to go by the time he arrived on the Queen's soil. Then, still nine hundred miles from the British Isles, *The Star of Salt Lake* was caught in the worst storm of the century, torn to bits, and sent to the bottom of the sea, just as the sweet little nuns at Our Lady of the Sweating Black Heathens Mission had predicted.

Undoubtedly, Hume Gilly – alias Mooba, Dirtface, Spitboy, Ratman, and Shecky – was not only one of the six unluckiest men of his age but one of the twenty-seven unluckiest men of all time.

However, as we observed earlier, Denton Scudlatch, heir to the Scudlatch curd and whey fortune, was 2.6 times unluckier than even Hume Gilly.

Denton Scudlatch, the unluckiest man in the world, was also 2.38

times unluckier than Albert Lee Swinly, of Fetlock, Kentucky, and 1.975 times as unlucky as mob hitman Vito 'The Vegematic' Vermicelli of Chicago, who is inaccurately listed in the *Guinness Book of World Records* as the unluckiest man of all time.

Denton Scudlatch's bad luck began when he spent $29,000,000 for his dream house, a 310-room mansion in Beverly Hills, only to discover that his neighbors were 'cerebral' talkshow maven David Susskind and Mr Sensitivity himself, actor Alan Alda. Scudlatch realized immediately that all street parties and neighborhood cookouts were doomed to be both hideously boring and unbearably self-righteous affairs.

The day Denton moved in, Susskind came over with William F. Buckley and Gore Vidal and whiningly insisted that Denton join in an impromptu debate on the value of nouvelle cuisine as a bargaining chip in strategic nuclear disarmament talks with the then-powerful Soviet Union. Gore Vidal insisted that our national security would not be jeopardized if we dismantled 50 percent of our ICBMs in return for a guarantee that the Soviets would never attempt to prepare a meat or fish dish using a raspberry sauce, while Buckley was in favor of a preemptive nuclear warning strike against Murmansk to deter the Soviets from even considering serving salmon in a sweet basil dressing. When everyone left nine hours later, the issue was still not resolved to anyone's satisfaction.

The following day, while Denton was supervising the installation of a flock of one hundred eight-foot-high plastic flamingoes in the front yard of his twenty-acre estate, Alan Alda came to the fence between their properties, caught Denton's attention, and spent the next six hours weepily confessing to many shameful moments of male chauvinism that had stained his life, including the time when, as an unregenerate seven-year-old macho maniac, he had dipped a female classmate's pigtails in an inkwell.

The third day in the mansion, Denton put it up for sale but quickly learned that everyone *else* knew who his neighbors were, and though he lowered the price of the property from $29,000,000 to just $815,000, he could still not unload the place.

Thus began Denton Scudlatch's amazing and terrifying run of bad luck, which was to continue for sixteen years, four months, nine days, seven hours, and twenty-two minutes. During that time, his luck grew *geometrically* worse, week by week, until his monumental misfortunes gained him an invitation to appear on the Regis Philbin Show.

It was there that Denton Scudlatch came to the attention of Dr Eldritch Pedi, chairman of the Department of Irrational Pseudosciences at UCLA.

Says Dr Pedi, 'The cataclysmically horrible misfortunes of this man, in their astounding breadth and depth, are irrefutable proof that the universe is not a place of random forces but is ruled, instead, by intelligent powers with malign intentions – rather like the Walt Disney Studios.'

Dr Pedi spent an entire year studying Denton Scudlatch and writing a biography of the unluckiest man in the world. If you would like to learn more about the specifics of Mr Scudlatch's gross but nevertheless fascinating misfortunes, foolish decisions, pratfalls, and horrifying encounters with New Jersey trolls, you may send $29.95 plus $46.00 for shipping and handling, to Weird World Press at the usual address, and we will mail you a copy of Dr Pedi's best-selling book, *DROWNING IN GOD'S SPIT: A Biography of the Wretched Denton Scudlatch, the Unluckiest Man in the World.*

PART VI

The 10 Questions Readers Most Often Ask Dean Koontz

1) Will you ever write a sequel to any of your novels?

The only novel to which I've contemplated writing a sequel is
WATCHERS, but even that might never happen. There are two
basic reasons for not doing it. First, new ideas grip me, and I am more
excited about those than about returning to older ideas. Second, I
wouldn't want to write a half-baked sequel because that would sort of
ruin everyone's memory of the first book. If there's ever going to be a
sequel to WATCHERS, it has to be every bit as strong as the original,
or I wouldn't want to do it. So . . . if one day the right idea hits me and
I'm *compelled* to write the sequel, then I will . . . but not otherwise.

* * *

2) In many of your books, I see poetry from THE BOOK OF
COUNTED SORROWS. What is this book, and where can I find a
copy?

Frequently, when looking for just the right bit of verse to use in the
front of a novel or at one of the part divisions, to underline one of the
themes of the story, I can't quite find what I need. When that
happens, I write the verse myself and attribute it to THE BOOK OF
COUNTED SORROWS, which is a nonexistent volume – at least at
the moment.
     When I began doing this, it never occurred to me that so many
people would like the poetry enough to seek out THE BOOK OF
COUNTED SORROWS. Now we receive a couple of thousand
letters a year from readers who have looked long and hard for the
book without, of course, any luck. Ten or twenty percent of that mail
comes from librarians, writing on behalf of patrons for whom they've
been unable to obtain a copy. I feel guilty about all the time that's
been wasted in these fruitless searches.
     I *do* intend to have THE BOOK OF COUNTED SORROWS

published, once I've composed enough verses. I imagine this will be sometime in 1995.

* * *

3) Where in the *world* do you get your ideas?

I'm not really sure. I read widely in all forms of fiction and nonfiction. I subscribe to magazines covering a variety of sciences, medical research, business, economics, and many other subjects. I don't actually read them in search of ideas, but by packing the subconscious full of all this information, I find that I am sort of priming the pump. Weeks, months, even years after I have read about something, I'll suddenly get an idea that springs from what I've read. For instance, I read about the latest developments in resuscitation medicine perhaps a year before the idea for HIDEAWAY popped into my mind, but I know that if I hadn't read that piece, the idea would never have occurred to me. I don't sit around *consciously* trying to come up with ideas, but then I don't really have to because my subconscious provides me with more than I will ever be able to write.

Finding ideas for the central premise of a novel is only a small part of evolving a credible work of fiction. An idea isn't valuable if it isn't properly developed, which means coming up with the right characters, background, and mood for the piece. To say nothing of the fact that it has to be *written* sentence by sentence, which is indescribably harder than generating the idea itself.

* * *

4) Are your stories ever based on things that have happened to you?

Well, I've never encountered aliens, given a home to an intelligent dog that's escaped from a laboratory, or had encounters with a murderous lookalike! But, yes, *every* book contains material that comes from personal experience. I am in love with my wife, so I know what being in love feels like. I have been shot at and have had to struggle for my life, so I know how that feels. No character in any book is based solely or even largely on any single person in real life – they'd sue! – but every character has qualities and traits and habits and ideas that I've seen in real people.

Frequently I hear dialogue in real life that strikes me as funny, stupid, naive, or interesting for some other reason, and I store it away for use in a novel to make a character more convincing. I generally write about places I have been – or California, where I live – so all of the geographical details and descriptions are out of personal experience. If there's a subject I don't know anything about – like thoracic surgery, which was Ginger Weiss' specialty in STRANGERS – I read about it, talk to experts, educate myself as much as necessary; therefore, though I'm not a thoracic surgeon – you sure wouldn't want me operating on you! – I *do* know what I'm writing about, so in that sense I am writing out of my personal experience.

* * *

5) Do you know there's a stupid gun error in PHANTOMS?

Yes. Oh, yes. My, yes. Do I know. Do I *ever* know. And it is something I know well, so I shouldn't have made it. When you do make a gun error, a deluge of gun collectors let you know about it in 8.35 seconds.

Although I've owned guns all my adult life, I don't consider myself an expert. Therefore, when I'm not sure of something, I try to double- and triple-check it with people who *are* experts. Often, mistakes are made when it's a detail I already know – or think I know – and don't bother to research. A writer only gets tripped up when he's too sure of himself. I've never had one of my characters toting around a revolver with a silencer attached (only pistols can be silenced to any degree), though I've read a lot of books in which writers have had characters do precisely that. I've avoided all sorts of goofs, but in PHANTOMS I made a major blunder. In the first scene of the novel, a deputy with a revolver is overwhelmed by some unseen, murderous presence, at which he fires his gun. Later, just before his body is found, we see the floor is littered with expended shell casings. Now, I know that revolvers do not eject casings as pistols do, that an effort has to be made to remove them, know it as surely as I know my own hat size, but when I was writing the scene in which the body was found, I was focused on making it just as *eerie* as I possibly could; the image of those expended casings gleaming on the floor of the shadowy room in which the deputy died was wonderfully ominous . . . but I didn't stop to think if it *made sense*. The weird thing is, throughout all the drafts I wrote, through all the proofreadings, I never noticed the mistake even though I'm familiar enough with handguns to recognize it; weirder still, of all the copy editors or proofreaders who worked on the book for publishers in thirty-two languages, *not one of them* noticed the mistake either, though it is their job to catch such things when the author slips up. Maybe all of them were so taken with the image of that gleaming brass that it blinded them to the error inherent in the scene.

A similar case involved a single reference to a 30-gauge shotgun in THE SERVANTS OF TWILIGHT. There *is* no such thing as a 30-gauge shotgun, just as there is no tooth fairy, no Easter bunny, and no one in Washington, D.C., with both oars in the water. In my original manuscript, the reference was to a 20-gauge. The '2' was changed to a '3' by the typesetter – and, again, no one who proofread the book, including me, spotted the change. This kind of thing drives a writer to drink something stronger than lemonade.

Sometimes readers point out errors which are, in fact, not errors at all. Since we're on the subject of guns – in one of my books a character says that a particular revolver is powerful enough to bring down a grizzly bear. Now, he wasn't saying that this was the prime choice of weaponry when one is setting out to shoot giant, aggressive predators. No way. If you're *insane* enough to go out in the woods with the intention of getting the best of a grizzly bear, you're going to take some heavy-duty weapons; no handgun in the world would be among your first hundred preferred firearms. However, the weapon mentioned in the book, loaded with the correct ammunition, *has* been known to drop a grizzly on at least two occasions, and the story of one of these incidents has been written about in several highly regarded books about big-game hunting. It's sure not something you'd *want* to do, go chasing after this horrendously huge killing machine with a handgun, any more than you'd choose to go up against a tank with a whip, but under the right circumstances, the gun has the power that the character in my book claims for it.

I am loath to get details wrong. I enjoy getting letters of praise from specialists in many fields, commending the accuracy of my research – and cringe when I get a letter catching me in an error. For weeks thereafter, I go outside only with a bag on my head, attend church every day, wear a barbed-wire shirt, furiously lash myself with cat-o'-nine-tails, and cry myself to sleep. Well, okay, I don't do anything more than cringe. But it *does* bother me.

* * *

6) Do you really resemble Burt Reynolds as much as some of your pictures indicate?

No. I actually resemble Oprah Winfrey on some days and Bart Simpson on others. I have never seen the resemblance myself, but when I was younger, I was told all the time how much I looked like Mr Reynolds. Some friends – as baffled by this as I was – thought it was funny. Then we went to a big party in Los Angeles, and one of the people attending was a producer who had worked on a couple of films with Reynolds. As soon as I walked in, from across the crowded room, he called, 'Burt!' and started toward me. He came within ten or twelve feet before he realized his mistake – and gave me an oh-you-are-nobody-I-spit-on-you look. Over the years, as I have gradually lost more hair, photographs of me still draw that response from readers, but it isn't often that they notice any similarity when they meet me in person. Worse, a few years ago, people occasionally began to tell me that I was a dead-ringer for G. Gordon Liddy, the Watergate figure. Now, I have nothing against Mr Liddy; but it is a cruel world in which you can go from being mistaken for Burt Reynolds one day – to passing for G. Gordon Liddy the next! Everyone seems to know that Mr Reynolds has lost some hair of his own and has a series of toupees, but I've never been able to go that route. I *have* considered having moss planted on my scalp, and I wouldn't mind the periodic watering, but the fertilizers create an insurmountable social problem.

* * *

7) What is your favorite of your own books?

Unquestionably, WATCHERS. Followed closely by MR MURDER.

* * *

8) Will you write another children's book like ODDKINS?

I doubt it. Corrupting children was a lot of fun; and I very much like the book, but once is most likely enough. I'm just happy that adults seem to like it as much as the kids.

* * *

9) I've seen the rotten movies they made of WATCHERS. How

269

could you let them do that? Or doesn't a writer have any control what Hollywood does to his books?

For the most part, when a writer sells the film rights, he has no control over the film at all. Only producers and directors – and a tiny handful of the biggest stars – have any real control in film. Because of the catastrophically inept production of *WATCHERS* – and *WATCHERS II*, for that matter – I have tried to find ways to gain some meaningful control. I've written screenplays with which the studio was happy . . . then watched a director come aboard and screw everything up so badly that the project collapsed. Lately, my agent and I have begun investigating new approaches to film, with the hope that we can set up sales in which I retain control of some of the major elements. But it's a hard battle.

To those of you who might have been angry with me for letting Hollywood do what it did to *WATCHERS*, please understand that I sold the rights in all good faith, because they loved the book and professed to want to translate it to film with great care and imagination. Since the movie business is essentially a big crapshoot, there is never more than a small chance of winding up with a good picture; if I refused to sell the rights to any of my books under any circumstances, I'd certainly prevent them from making lousy movies from my stuff, but I'd also never have a chance to see them make a good one. As anyone knows who attends the movies regularly, you've got to sit through a lot of mutant for every terrific film you see. Because *WATCHERS* surely ranks as one of the three all-time worst adaptations of a novel, I hope we've hit bottom and have a chance of seeing some better pictures in the years ahead.

* * *

10) Do you plan any collaborative novels with other writers?

The possibility seems remote. I'm such a fussbudget about the use of language and story structure, so obsessive-compulsive about revision and polishing, that any collaborator would face the danger of being brutally savaged over an argument about comma placement.

PART VII

Annotated Bibliography

MAJOR WORKS

1. Novels

AFTER THE LAST RACE. New York: Atheneum, 1974.

Opening sentence: Garrison slowly turned in a full circle, studying the clearing that lay between the two birches.

Comments: This is a caper novel about professional thieves who team up with two ordinary citizens to rob the cash room and all of the betting windows at a major thoroughbred racetrack during the biggest racing day of the year. The author intends to revise it slightly for eventual republication. RACE is a transitional work, well written but produced before the writer found his true voice and ideal material.

Publishers Weekly called it, 'taut and colorful ... a dramatic and absorbing novel that holds you all the way.' And from the *New York Times*: 'A whale of a race track crime novel ... Koontz, a skillful writer, builds to ever-mounting tension, and there is a bang-up finale. [He] is much more imaginative than most writers. He has the knack of vitalizing his people, and there is not one person in AFTER THE LAST RACE who is not believable.'

* * *

ANTI-MAN. New York: Paperback Library, 1970.

Opening sentence: It was really too much to hope for, but we seemed to have lost them.

Comments: This novel was expanded from 'The Mystery of His Flesh,' a novella that first appeared in *The Magazine of Fantasy and Science Fiction*. This is early Koontz, written when he was twenty-three, and is immature compared to his later work. It will never

273

reappear in anything like its original form. When a version of it *does* become available again, it will have been revised and will be part of a larger story collection.

* * *

THE BAD PLACE. New York: Putnam, 1990; London: Headline, 1990.

Opening sentence: The night was becalmed and curiously silent, as if the alley were an abandoned and windless beach in the eye of a hurricane, between the tempest past and the tempest coming.

Comments: This is one of the author's most imaginative stories, convoluted and intense, and a key novel in his oeuvre. His sense of humor is at work here in most of the characters, yet this is unquestionably the darkest of all his novels. At the heart, THE BAD PLACE is an exploration of the stain of Eden; each character has a fatal flaw (or flaws) that is revealed in the course of the action and which becomes, in most cases, *literally* fatal. By the end of the novel, when Bobby and Julie Dakota are left alone on the shores of the Pacific, deeply traumatized by the things they have seen and endured, we can sympathize fully with them when the next-to-last paragraph of the story informs us: 'Some nights she was afraid. Occasionally, so was he.' They are virtually the only survivors of a series of tragedies that has kept the reader turning the pages with steadily increasing dread. Yet, the final paragraph is filled with hope: 'They had each other. And time.' Koontz always leaves his characters with their dignity and usually with hope, if with nothing else. He allows us to believe – in fact, insists we believe – that Bobby and Julie will find happiness again, perhaps with the child she is carrying, with their new life on the edge of the Pacific, and with the final telepathic message sent by Thomas as he was dying, *There is a light that loves you.*

If any aspect of the book has received more acclaim than another, it is the character of Thomas, a personable young man with Down's syndrome. Critics generally regarded the scenes from Thomas's point of view, if not the whole novel, as a tour-de-force. Putnam published a limited edition of 250 copies. The novel was a number-one *New York Times* bestseller.

From the *Seattle Times*: 'The intricate plot races along. Koontz also creates characters of unusual richness and depth ... a level of perception and sensitivity that is not merely convincing, it's astonishing.' From the *New Orleans Times-Picayune*: 'THE BAD PLACE is at times lyrical without ever being naive or romantic. This is a grotesque world, much like that of Flannery O'Conner or Walker Percy. Scary, worthwhile reading.' From the *Associated Press*: 'Koontz puts his readers through the emotional wringer. There are scenes that stick in the mind long after the thriller has been laid aside.' And from the *New York Times*: 'Psychologically complex characters . . . fast-paced . . . a masterly and satisfying denouement.'

* * *

BEASTCHILD. New York: Lancer, 1970.

Opening sentence: In his onyx-walled room in the occupation tower, Hulann – a naoli – had disassociated his overmind from his organic regulating brain.

Comments: This is one of the best of the author's straight science-fiction novels, written when he was twenty-three and twenty-four. It is set after an alien invasion that has wiped out all but a handful of human beings. One alien, Hulann, encounters a human boy, Leo, and a friendship ensues. The friendship is against alien law and puts the two on the run, pursued by deadly, genetically engineered Hunters. Like most of the work from this period, it's immature compared to the books that made him famous. However, it was on the final ballot of the Hugo Award in the short-novel category.

BEASTCHILD was reissued in a lavishly produced, illustrated edition in 1992, by Charnel House; this appeared in two states – twenty-six signed, lettered copies and 750 signed, numbered copies. The Charnel House version is the *only* appearance of the author's original, approved text, which was edited without authorization in both its initial magazine and book publications.

The author will heavily revise the novel, changing its setting from fifty years in the future to the current day. He will transform it from a science fiction novel into one of his cross-genre works and it will be reissued in paperback in either 1996 or 1997.

* * *

BLOOD RISK. As by 'Brian Coffey.' New York: Bobbs-Merrill, 1973; London: Arthur Barker, 1974.

Opening sentence: They had decided that only four men were required to stop the big car on the narrow mountain road, hold the occupants at bay, and remove the cash that was stuffed into the suitcases on the floor behind the front seat.

Comments: This is a caper novel in which the lead character – a gentlemanly thief named Michael Tucker – and his cronies hijack a mafia cash shipment. Two more novels appeared with the same lead character: SURROUNDED and THE WALL OF MASKS. Both have long been out of print, but the author intends to reissue them eventually, all three novels in a single volume.

* * *

CHASE. As by 'K. R. Dwyer.' New York: Random House, 1972; London: Reissued as by Dean Koontz. W. H. Allen, 1984, reissued by Headline, 1990.

Opening sentence: At seven o'clock, seated on the platform as the guest of honor, Ben Chase was served a bad roast beef dinner while various dignitaries talked at him from both sides, breathing over his salad and his half-eaten fruit cup.

Comments: This is a key novel in the author's oeuvre. With CHASE, he moved into the suspense genre and immediately commanded attention. This is one of the earliest of what would become a torrent of novels about Vietnam veterans by a host of writers. Benjamin Chase, who has won the Congressional Medal of Honor but refused to accept it, finds himself the target of a psychotic killer from whom no one, including the police, can protect him, and he has to open himself, against his wishes, to his basic aggressive nature. This book will be reissued eventually with some minor changes.

Saturday Review said: 'This superb book is more than a novel of suspense. It is a brutally realistic portrait of the role of violence in our society.' The *New York Times* called it 'taut, well-written.' The *San Francisco Examiner-Chronicle* said the novel was 'thoroughly exciting, and the style is firm and excellent.'

* * *

CHILDREN OF THE STORM. As by 'Deanna Dwyer.' New York: Lancer, 1972.

Opening sentence: Having lived nearly all of her twenty-three years in the brief summers and bitter winters of Maine and Massachusetts, Sonya Carter was especially intrigued by the Caribbean – by the almost too-bright skies, the warm breezes that smelled of salty ocean air, the palm trees that could be seen nearly everywhere, the delicious mangoes, the spectacular sunsets, and the sudden twilights that deepened rapidly into purple darkness . . .

Comments: This was one of the five gothic-romance novels that the author wrote to 'stave off starvation and buy a little time to write what I really cared about.' These were formula books, written to meet a publisher's guidelines. The author produced them quickly and used the income from them to be able to spend more time on the books that he felt were more important. Though they were good examples of their genre, there is little merit in these books today, and the author intends to keep them out of print virtually forever.

* * *

COLD FIRE. New York: Putnam, 1991; London: Headline, 1991.

Opening sentence: Even before the events in the supermarket, Jim Ironheart should have known trouble was coming.

Comments: This is a key book in the author's oeuvre because sociological observation becomes a more important aspect of the narrative than in any of his earlier works. Some social commentary had appeared in his work as early as WHISPERS (1980). It can be seen in STRANGERS, WATCHERS, LIGHTNING, MIDNIGHT, and THE BAD PLACE, as well, but in those books the characters gained convincing depth largely through conflict with themselves and, secondarily, with one another, and not so much by their interaction with the culture in which they swam. The most notable exception is Jack Twist, the professional thief and ex-military man in STRANGERS, who was shaped by the betrayal of the government that he served so well. In COLD FIRE, Holly Thorne is searching for meaning and purpose in her own life; however, as a disillusioned journalist, she is in an ideal position to reflect as well upon the lack of meaning and purpose, in the contemporary world. Jim Ironheart, whose parents were victims of the random violence that has for so long been an escalating problem in modern society, sets himself up as a would-be savior of other potential victims of the same forces.

277

Throughout the novel, highly energized symbolic objects and selected scenes of allegorical power – notably those in a desert church – suggest that, while searching for meaning in social movements and political ideologies and interpersonal relationships, modern men and women are doomed to be frustrated; the only satisfying purpose in life is to be found in spiritual rather than temporal values – spiritual values from which society is in retreat. The unusual complexity of sociological observation, inextricably knotted through the fibers of each character, brings new dimension to the author's work and will become even more important in DRAGON TEARS and MR MURDER. COLD FIRE was a number-one *New York Times* bestseller. Putnam published a signed, numbered, and illustrated limited edition of 800 copies.

The UPI reviewer noted: 'COLD FIRE is an extraordinary piece of fiction with unforgettable characters. It will be a classic.' From the *Boston Herald*: 'A unique, spellbinding novel with depth, sensitivity and personality.' From the *Arkansas Democrat*: 'His prose mesmerizes ... gut-wrenching clarity. It's in the descriptions of emotional states – from love to despair – that Koontz consistently hits bull's-eyes, evoking reactions of, "Yes! I know exactly how that feels!"'

* * *

THE CRIMSON WITCH. New York: Curtis Books, 1971.

Opening sentence: She came spinning out of a thunderstorm, mad as hell.

Comments: This was a short science-fantasy novel, written in the author's salad days, in a period of two weeks. He considers it among his worst works, and he intends to keep it out of print.

* * *

DANCE WITH THE DEVIL. As by 'Deanna Dwyer.' New York: Lancer, 1973.

Opening sentence: Katherine Sellers was sure that, at any moment, the car would begin to slide along the smooth, icy pavement and she would lose control of it.

Comments: This is another of the aforementioned five gothic-romance novels. See: CHILDREN OF THE STORM.

* * *

DARKFALL. New York: Berkley, 1984; under title DARKNESS COMES, London: W. H. Allen, 1984; reissued London: Headline, 1990.

Opening sentence: Penny Dawson woke and heard something moving furtively in the dark bedroom.

Comments: This was originally intended to be published as the third 'Owen West' novel, under the title THE PIT, and it is more directly a horror story than most of what the author has written. It is also a police procedural, however, and something of a love story, so the cross-genre aspect that has made Koontz so popular is apparent even in this work intended to appear under a pseudonym. The author's skill at rendering convincing child characters gives DARKFALL an extra edge and allows for some fine moments of comic dialogue. Due to the increasing success of Koontz's novels between the publication of the first two West novels – THE FUNHOUSE and THE MASK – and DARKFALL, he and his publisher made the mutual decision to terminate the West pseudonym. This was published in England as DARKNESS COMES, which was the author's preferred title.

* * *

A DARKNESS IN MY SOUL. New York: Daw Books, 1972; London: Dobson, 1979.

Opening sentence: For a long while, I wondered if Dragonfly was still in the heavens and whether the Sphere of Plague still floated in airlessness, blind eyes watchful.

Comments: This science-fiction novel was based upon an earlier novella of the same title. Filled with typographical tricks and elaborate imagery, A DARKNESS IN MY SOUL is of a quality that puts it in the middle range of Koontz's early work. The novella is better than the novel, and the author expects to revise one or the other for use in a collection of his work.

* * *

THE DARK OF SUMMER. As by 'Deanna Dwyer.' New York: Lancer, 1972.

Opening sentence: Gwyn was not expecting anything unusual in that day's mail, and was certainly not expecting a letter that would change the course of her entire life.

Comments: This was one of the five aforementioned gothic-romance novels. See: CHILDREN OF THE STORM.

* * *

THE DARK SYMPHONY. New York: Lancer, 1970.

Opening sentence: Loper hung five hundred feet above the street, his twelve fingers hooked like rigor-mortised worms over the glassy, featureless ledge.

Comments: This was early science fiction, written when the author was twenty-three. It is an adventure story set in an unlikely far-future and concerns the rebellion of a repressed underclass. The author will probably keep it out of print for the length of copyright.

* * *

DARK OF THE WOODS. New York: Ace, 1970. An Ace Double with the author's story collection SOFT COME THE DRAGONS.

Opening sentence: The first bit of trouble came even as they were leaving the starship on Demos's port field; it was a harbinger of worse times ahead.

Comments: This is among the earliest Koontz novels, written when he was just twenty-three. It is an adventure story set on another planet. An earthman falls in love with a winged woman, and their forbidden interracial romance makes them the target of government executioners. Parts of the novel are lyrical, but it remains an immature work that will most likely never see print again unless the author revises it for inclusion in a larger collection.

* * *

THE DEMON CHILD. As by 'Deanna Dwyer.' New York: Lancer, 1971.

Opening sentence: The sky was low and gray as masses of thick clouds scudded southward, pulling cold air down from the north as they went.

Comments: This is one of the five aforementioned gothic-romance novels. See CHILDREN OF THE STORM.

* * *

DEMON SEED. New York: Bantam, 1973; London: Corgi, 1977.

Opening sentence: Shortly after midnight, on a Tuesday in early June, the house alarm sounded.

Comments: This was the last straight science-fiction novel the author published and, ironically, by far his most successful in the marketplace. MGM produced a film version under the same title, which starred Julie Christie and Fritz Weaver; well-reviewed in its time, the picture is now considered a minor classic of the genre.

In DEMON SEED, the author's growing skill at establishing and drawing out suspense is in evidence. Brooding, gothic, and strange, this is every bit as much a novel of suspense as a work of science fiction. Its original title, changed at the publisher's insistence, was HOUSE OF NIGHT. The central premise of DEMON SEED is original and striking: That an intelligent computer, having attained self-awareness, would be dissatisfied by the restrictions of its narrow, disembodied condition and would long to inhabit a body and experience a more sensuous existence. Koontz has revised this novel for reissue in either 1995 or 1996.

* * *

THE DOOR TO DECEMBER. As by 'Richard Paige.' New York: New American Library, 1985; London: As by 'Leigh Nichols,' Fontana, 1987, reissued as by Dean Koontz, Headline, 1991.

Opening sentence: As soon as she finished dressing, Laura went to the front door, just in time to see the L.A. Police Department squad car pull to the curb in front of the house.

Comments: Written as a possible 'Leigh Nichols' title when the author was considering moving that pen name from Pocket Books, this novel ranks in the upper third of his body of work. Its exploration of the corrupting influence of power and the totalitarian urge is as dark as anything the author has written, but this is nicely offset by the character of Dan Haldane, whose dialogue is frequently as witty as it is acerbic.

281

A revised version of THE DOOR TO DECEMBER will be issued in paperback, under the author's real name, in late 1994. In England the book actually *was* published as by 'Leigh Nichols.'

* * *

DRAGONFLY. As by 'K. R. Dwyer.' New York: Random House, 1975; London: Peter Davis, 1977.

Opening sentence: When he woke shortly after three o'clock Wednesday morning, Roger Berlinson thought he heard strange voices in the house.

Comments: This was the third of three novels published under the 'K. R. Dwyer' name. It's a Cold War novel of international intrigue. The novel was well reviewed, in this vein, from the *Hartford Times*: 'In the taut style of *The Manchurian Candidate* and *Seven Days in May* ... a sparkling novel deep with suspense, agony, and mystery. The characters are so finely drawn that they take form on the page.' The author may eventually revise the novel for republication in paperback.

* * *

DRAGON TEARS. New York: Putnam, 1993; London: Headline, 1993.

Opening sentence: Tuesday was a fine California day, full of sunshine and promise, until Harry Lyon had to shoot someone at lunch.

Comments: Since STRANGERS, critics had increasingly been taking note of the author's vivid, fluid, highly polished style with its richness of imagery, metaphor, and wit. With DRAGON TEARS, these strengths seemed suddenly doubled, as the sly and gripping first line suggests. Paragraph by paragraph, the language gleams and, in places, almost radiates a jewel-bright light, as in this description of a Laguna Beach street scene in a rainstorm: 'The world appeared to be dissolving beyond the windshield of the parked car, as if the clouds had released torrents of a universal solvent. Silver rain sluiced down the glass, and the trees outside seemed to melt as readily as green crayons. Hurrying pedestrians fused with their colorful umbrellas and deliquesced into the gray downpour.' Or this quick but visual description of the burning roof of Harry Lyon's condominium as he

282

flees into the night: 'As in a fairy tale, high upon the shingled peak, fire like a dragon was silhouetted against the dark sky, lashing its yellow and orange and vermillion tail, spreading huge carnelian wings, scales scintillant, scarlet eyes flashing, roaring a challenge to all knights and would-be slayers.'

In DRAGON TEARS, Koontz expands upon the sociological observation that began to become a major element of his work in COLD FIRE. Even more than in that previous book, his major characters are in part formed and affected by the problems of the society in which they live. In the case of Harry Lyon and Connie Gulliver, they are *conscious* of the effects of cultural dissolution and social chaos in a way that neither Holly nor Jim was in COLD FIRE, and their attempts to stem the tide of entropy are bolder and more desperate. As the *Flint Journal* noted: 'DRAGON TEARS is a poignant study of civilization in decline and a passionate plea for people to take responsibility for their own lives.'

This is one of the key titles in the author's oeuvre, though not merely because of his distillation of metaphor and imagery into an ever more intense language. And not only because he twines more threads of sociological and cultural observation into ever more richly braided characterizations. Koontz has always shown a willingness to take narrative and stylistic risks, and this time he walks farther out on that ledge than previously. The decision to tell part of the story through the eyes of a dog, in a language and at a level of observation convincingly inhuman, had a high potential for disaster, but the character of Woofer becomes, perhaps, the most interesting and charming in the novel. Likewise, when pushing the element of fantasy so far as to incorporate the stunning setpiece called 'The Pause,' the author risked fracturing the reader's suspension of disbelief – yet succeeded because The Pause is both a riveting plot development and an apt metaphor for the implosion of modern society.

From the London *Mail on Sunday*: 'The wild storyline asserts a spine-shrivelling reality. It's magical realism for the "new dark ages" of the nineties.' From the *San Diego Union-Tribune*: 'DRAGON TEARS is [a] literary blueprint for combining a razor-sharp, non-stop suspenseful story with characters drawn from a keen understanding of human nature. But most of all, it showcases an exceptional ability to mix humor, fear, and hope into a first-rate literary experience.'

The author's preferred title, TICKTOCK, was not acceptable to the US publisher, but is used on some translations. Putnam published a signed, numbered, and illustrated limited edition of 750 copies. This was a number-one *New York Times* bestseller.

* * *

THE EYES OF DARKNESS. As by 'Leigh Nichols.' New York: Pocket Books, 1981; London: Fontana, 1982; reissued as by Dean Koontz by Headline, 1991.

Opening sentence: Shortly after midnight, just four minutes into Tuesday morning, on the way home from a late rehearsal of her new show, Tina Evans thought she saw her son, Danny, in a stranger's car.

Comments: This was the second of five novels under the Nichols name. One year after her son died in a tragic accident in the Sierras, Tina Evans begins to suspect that he is actually alive and that his death was staged to cover up his abduction. As she probes into the facts, her life is almost at once endangered. This is a solid suspense novel, not equal to Nichols's THE SERVANTS OF TWILIGHT or SHADOWFIRES but gripping. It lacks the texture and subtext of the author's best work. He has revised it for reissue in either 1995 or 1996. Dark Harvest published an illustrated trade hardcover as well as a limited edition in two states – 52 signed and lettered copies (A to ZZ) and 400 signed, numbered copies.

* * *

THE FACE OF FEAR. As by 'Brian Coffey.' New York: Bobbs-Merrill, 1977; London: Reissued as by Dean Koontz by Headline, 1989.

Opening sentence: Wary, not actually expecting trouble but prepared for it, he parked his car across the street from the four-story brownstone apartment house.

Comments: This was the fourth of five novels under the Coffey name and was reissued under the author's real name in paperback. It is a tight, fast-paced suspense novel, significant because it is an early indication of the uniquely imaginative story lines that were to be a feature of the author's later work and because it was a precursor of the many serial-killer novels that were to become increasingly popular through the eighties and nineties. In fact, interesting similarities between this book and Thomas Harris's well-known *Red Dragon* (1981) perhaps indicate common research sources: Two sociopaths working in harmony (Dollarhyde on the outside, Lecter imprisoned, in *Dragon*; Bollinger and 'Billy,' both on the outside, in FACE); the killer in both books is obsessed with the work of William Blake; the protagonist in FACE has a psychic link to the killer, and in *Dragon* he has an *almost* psychic ability to think like the killer when tracking him; both Bollinger and Dollarhyde were raised by grandmothers, though the possible monstrousness of Bollinger's grandmother is only suggested while we get plenty of detail about Dollarhyde's twisted granny; both books contain suggestions and descriptions of the extreme violence perpetrated by real-life sociopaths but seldom if ever previously alluded to in suspense novels. In FACE, 'Billy' has overcome a southern accent that he believes has long been a hindrance to his acceptance in New York, while in *Dragon* Dollarhyde struggles against a speech impediment resulting from a cleft palate and hair lip; in both books the antagonist – in different ways – reappears for one more attack after he is assumed to be vanquished. These are very different novels, yet they focus on certain similar concerns that would open a new subgenre of suspense fiction in the years to come. Strangest of all, and an interesting bit of suspense-fiction trivia: The lead of FACE is Graham Harris, while the lead of *Dragon*, written by Thomas *Harris*, is named Will Graham.

From the *Memphis Commercial Appeal*: 'One of the most remarkable suspense novels of the year ... an engrossing and entertaining read.' From the *West Coast Review of Books*: 'This is a real breathtaker [that] should hold you glued to its pages till the wee small hours.' And Edwin Corley, in his syndicated column, noted that 'THE FACE OF FEAR has the most harrowing chase sequences I've read in many a moon. The writing is tight, fast-moving ... and the story races toward a fear-drenched climax. More than mere entertainment.'

A two-hour television movie of the book was aired on CBS, with Koontz serving as screenwriter and co-executive producer. Directed by Farhad Mann, the film is visually stylish and unusually suspenseful for television, though it suffers from the comparatively low budgets of that medium. FACE is now available under the author's real name.

* * *

THE FALL OF THE DREAM MACHINE. New York: Ace Books, 1969.

Opening sentence: The world is spinning on an axis two degrees different than it was a moment ago . . .

Comments: This was a *very* early science-fiction novel, written when the author was twenty-two, and it suffers from the immature skills and voice that mark other examples of his early work. He has, however, disclaimed responsibility for the misuse of 'different than' in the first sentence, as this was a period in his career where he was often edited without consultation. This title is unlikely to be revised for future publication and will no doubt remain out of print for the life of copyright.

* * *

FEAR THAT MAN. New York: Ace Books, 1969.

Opening sentence: When he woke from a featureless dream of silver, there was nothing but endless blackness on three sides, a blackness so intense that it almost coughed out a breath and nearly moved.

Comments: This was written when the author was twenty-two and is a weak attempt to tie together two previously published novelettes – 'Where the Beast Runs' and 'In the Shield' – with additional material to form a novel of sorts. It is unlikely that any of this material will see print again within the life of copyright.

* * *

THE FLESH IN THE FURNACE. New York: Bantam, 1972.

Opening sentence: The idiot and the puppeteer rode in the cab of the truck, staring ahead at the darkness and the steadily unrolling gray of the ancient road they followed.

Comments: This is certainly one of the finest of the author's early straight science-fiction novels and may be the best of the lot. Its relentlessly eerie mood, focus on complex characterization, strong allegorical subtext, and use of irony prefigure the direction Koontz would take a full eight to ten years later when he began to produce his major works. According to the author, this piece, with only minor revisions, will one day appear in a collection.

* * *

THE FUNHOUSE. As by 'Owen West.' New York: Jove Books, 1980; London: Sphere, 1981; Reissued as by Dean Koontz by Headline, 1992.

Opening sentence: Ellen Straker sat at the small kitchen table in the Airstream travel trailer, listening to the night wind, trying not to hear the strange scratching that came from the baby's bassinet.

Comments: This is the author's only movie novelization – and is radically different from the film on which it is based. The 'Author's Afterword' in the new edition – to be released in 1994 – gives more background to the project than can be discussed here.

* * *

HANGING ON. New York: M. Evans, 1973; London: Barrie & Jenkins, 1974.

Opening sentence: Major Kelly was in the latrine, sitting down, his pants around his ankles, when the Stuka dive bombers struck.

Comments: As the opening sentence attests, this was a straight comic novel set in World War II. The author wrote HANGING ON largely because he has always been interested in black comedy but also because he wanted to write something utterly different that would, in one fell stroke, erase his reputation as strictly a science-fiction novelist. He didn't quite succeed in making people forget the brief but prolific career in science-fiction, but he did get a good deal of attention for this change of direction.

Critics were unanimous in finding the novel hilarious. From *Publishers Weekly*: 'The author's lively sense of black humor (some of it pure burlesque) and his razzle-dazzle imagination breathe life into the stock Army characters you know so well and do wonders with those few you haven't met before. This has suspense and, more important, some of the most hilarious scenes that have come along in a long time. Even the sex is great fun!' Syndicated critic, Mark Drogin: 'The funniest book of this year. And last year. Dean Koontz has created some characters who will live longer than Koontz or you or me. Lying on the couch around 2 a.m., I laughed so loud . . . I woke everybody up.'

The author does intend to have the book reissued in years to come, though with an introduction that will prepare his current readers for this very different work.

* * *

THE HAUNTED EARTH. New York: Lancer Books, 1970.

Opening sentence: Count Slavek, having proposed a toast to his new friend's great beauty, tossed off the glassful of red wine.

Comments: This is a science-fantasy novel set in a near future wracked by tremendous changes, wherein mythical figures like vampires and werewolves and banshees are proven to be real co-inhabitants of our world. It's a comic novel, too, indicating Koontz's early interest in making readers laugh as well as shiver. The book has merit, but is an immature work that the author may never revise for republication.

* * *

HELL'S GATE. New York: Lancer Books, 1970.

Opening sentence: The puppet came awake beneath budding apple trees, lying prone in a patch of twisted weeds and dry brown grass.

Comments: This was another straight science-fiction novel with a largely contemporary setting, an action-adventure piece, written when the author was twenty-three. HELL'S GATE contains interesting plot twists and merits revision for inclusion as one of the centerpieces in a collection of stories if the author finds the time to take another look at it, which he has suggested that he would like to do.

* * *

HIDEAWAY. New York: Putnam, 1992; London: Headline, 1992.

Opening sentence: An entire world hummed and bustled beyond the dark ramparts of the mountains, yet to Lindsey Harrison the night seemed empty, as hollow as the vacant chambers of a cold, dead heart.

Comments: This is a key novel in the author's oeuvre – which, in fact, is true of most of his recent work. While it appears to retreat somewhat from the sociological observation that was such an integral part of COLD FIRE, it is more connected to that new direction in his work than might at first be apparent. The novel is concerned with evil, whether it is entirely a matter of nurture or whether nature has a role via genetic heritage. Furthermore, is evil strictly the work of men and women, or a real force in the world, a presence that is even possibly supernatural? Or a combination of these things? HIDEAWAY strives to define types of evil and to define which may be inevitable and which the result of cultural influences. Therefore, HIDEAWAY is a treading-water book, written while the author explores his own thoughts and feelings to be able to leap from the tentative concerns of COLD FIRE to the urgent concerns of DRAGON TEARS.

From *Kirkus Reviews*: 'Fiercely exciting. A grandly melodramatic morality play that will have Koontz's fans cheering.' The *Michigan State News*: 'Koontz has one of the most incredible gifts for the art of language . . . a master of images and descriptions. His characters are timeless and beautifully constructed. He proves you can be on the bestseller list and don't have to be dead or named Hemingway to have the depth and feeling of the classics.' The *Lexington Herald Leader*: 'Not just a thriller but a meditation on the nature of evil.'

Putnam published a signed, number, and illustrated limited edition of 800 copies. HIDEAWAY was a number-one *New York Times* bestseller.

* * *

THE HOUSE OF THUNDER. As by 'Leigh Nichols.' New York: Pocket Books, 1982; London: Fontana, 1983, reissued as Dean Koontz by Headline, 1992.

Opening sentence: When she woke, she thought she was blind.

Comments: In the author's estimation, this is the least of the five Nichols novels. It plays more with a strange – and ultimately clever – situation than with a satisfying three-act plot, which is unusual for Koontz. Its characters are less well-defined than usual, though that is not the author's fault but a consequence of the story: The lead, Susan, has amnesia and can remember little from her past, which makes her a cipher; and *every* other character in the novel is masquerading as someone he is not. Judging by the reader mail that the author has received since the publication of HOUSE under his name, the public thinks more highly of it than he does – probably because it is a fast and gripping read with some big and well-prepared-for surprises.

Dark Harvest published an illustrated trade hardcover, and a limited edition in two states: 52 signed, lettered copies; 550 signed, numbered copies. This was a *New York Times* number-one bestseller in paperback.

* * *

INVASION. As by 'Aaron Wolfe.' Ontario, Canada: Laser Books, 1975.

Opening sentence: The three-hundred-acre Timberlake Farm, which we were renting that year, was as isolated a refuge as you could possibly find in New England.

Comments: When eighty percent of this novel had been written, the author decided to leave genre science fiction forever, and he doubted it would see publication. Barry Malzberg, a writer and editor who had contracted to edit a series of 'first' novels for Laser books, asked Koontz for 'anything from your trunk' when a few would-be first novelists failed to deliver. Malzberg persuaded Koontz to complete INVASION and offer it under a pen name.

In 1993, the author set out to revise INVASION for reissue under his own name. Before he even got to the first chapter of the original novel – which was only 55,000 words long – he had written 80,000 new words. And by the time he finished this 'revision,' he had written 135,000 words – without using *a single line* from the original novel. The new book, listed separately in this bibliography, is titled WINTER MOON. It is recognizably inspired by INVASION but not based upon it. The earlier book was an immature work. The new novel, while not as complex and exciting as Koontz's best recent novels, is entertaining, challenging, and packed with cultural and sociological observation.

* * *

THE KEY TO MIDNIGHT. As by 'Leigh Nichols.' New York: Pocket Books, 1979; London: Magnum, 1980; reissued as by Dean Koontz by Headline, 1992.

Opening sentence: In the dark, Joanna Rand went to the window.

Comments: This is the first of five novels written under the Nichols pseudonym. It's a Cold War story of international intrigue that preceded WHISPERS and indicated the major leap that Koontz was about to take with that subsequent book. KEY is filled with well-developed characters, exhibits the depth of background and sense of place (primarily Kyoto, Japan) that would mark most of his work from this point on, and has the convoluted plot and, after a leisurely few chapters, the swift pace for which he would eventually become known. *Publishers Weekly* called it 'a masterfully integrated thriller.'

Although quite different from the novels familiar to the author's legions of fans, KEY has been re-released under his name in England, Germany, and other countries, where readers have reacted positively to it. Therefore, it is scheduled for reissue in the United States, as well, in 1997. When first published in 1979, KEY was a success, appearing on some bestseller lists and attaining an in-print figure of one million copies. This was the first of *two* bestsellers for the writer under pen names before the paperback of WHISPERS achieved that status in 1981 under his real name; the second pseudonymous bestseller was THE FUNHOUSE in late 1980, under the name 'Owen West,' which also achieved an in-print figure of more than one million copies. Dark Harvest published an illustrated trade hardcover as well as two states of a limited edition – 52 signed, lettered copies and 550 signed, numbered copies.

* * *

LEGACY OF TERROR. As by 'Deanna Dwyer.' New York: Lancer, 1971.

Opening sentence: Elaine Sherred was ill-at-ease from the first moment she caught sight of the Matherly house, and she would later remember this doubt and wonder if it had been a premonition of disaster.

Comments: This is one of the five aforementioned gothic-romance novels. See CHILDREN OF THE STORM.

* * *

LIGHTNING. New York: Putnam, 1988; London: Headline, 1988.

Opening sentence: A storm struck on the night Laura Shane was born, and there was a strangeness about the weather that people would remember for years.

Comments: The surge in the author's popularity, which began with STRANGERS and WATCHERS, gained substantial momentum with the hardcover appearance of LIGHTNING. One of the top bestsellers of 1988, the novel provides a series of surprises building steadily to an exceptionally clever reversal of the reader's expectations. To give a plot summary of *any* extent would, in this case, be criminal.

For several reasons, this is a key novel in the author's oeuvre. The psychologically complex characterizations that had marked his work for some time and that had reached a new level of finesse in STRANGERS and WATCHERS, is evident in LIGHTNING but with a difference; in this novel, Koontz has developed techniques to paint richly detailed and highly empathetic characters with an unusual economy, giving the story surprising density for a novel that is as comparatively short as this one. In this book, Koontz allows himself a greater amount of amusing dialogue and more comic touches than in any previous suspense novel, yet maintains a strong sense of jeopardy and relentless pace. And he breaks with traditional suspense plotting in a fundamental aspect, for the action takes place over thirty-some years and deals with the lead character, Laura Shane, in a rather Dickensian manner, following her from birth to adulthood and making of this story a curious blend of suspense and biographical fiction.

From the *Associated Press* wire: 'Brilliant. The plot weaves several major ideas with wonderful results. LIGHTNING will appeal to the thinking reader ... both challenging and entertaining.' And from *USA Weekend*: 'An unforgettably haunting novel of inescapable and imperiled destiny.' The *Buffalo News* noted: 'Koontz alchemizes an extravagant plot into a suspenseful and touching book.'

The author's original title for LIGHTNING was LIGHTNING ROAD, but it was shortened to meet the publisher's preference for a one-word title. A signed, numbered, first edition of 200 copies was issued by Ultramarine Press.

* * *

THE LONG SLEEP. As by 'John Hill.' New York: Popular Library, 1975.

Opening sentence: He was not dead, but nearly so.

Comments: This novel was written in 1972, based upon a novella, 'Grayworld,' written that same year and published in 1973. Though it is a science-fiction piece, the atmosphere is more that of an occult mystery, and the truly futuristic elements do not appear until the end of the novel. It is the author's intention to heavily revise this book for eventual reissue under his own name.

* * *

THE MASK. As by 'Owen West.' New York: Jove, 1981; London: Coronet/Hodder, 1983, reissued as by Dean Koontz by Headline, 1989.

Opening sentence: Laura was in the cellar, doing some spring cleaning and hating every minute of it.

Comments: This was the second of two novels published under the West name. It is a simply plotted, swiftly paced occult tale about reincarnation. It was eventually reissued under the author's real name and has been in print ever since.

* * *

MIDNIGHT. New York: Putnam, 1989; London: Headline, 1989.

Opening sentence: Janice Capshaw liked to run at night.

Comments: This is a key novel in the author's oeuvre. MIDNIGHT is cross-genre carried to its limits: science fiction, horror, police-procedural, gothic, adventure story, psychological suspense, and even techno-thriller all rolled up in one. In addition, the author takes virtually every convention of the horror story and either stands it on its head or pumps it up as no one has ever pumped it before. The result is an almost manic tale that threatens to spin out of control but never does. Thomas Shaddack, Koontz's mad scientist (every tale of this nature has to have one), manages to be a darkly amusing and thoroughly terrifying character all at once. The extended flashback that reveals how he was warped forever as a boy by an encounter with a vengeful Indian, is such a self-contained and gripping story in its own right that it almost begs to have been written as a separate novel. The theme, in part, is about the urge to escape responsibility, a weakness that plagues humanity.

From *Kirkus Reviews*: 'A terrific mainstream horror entertainment. From the arch-spooky opening ... to the wildly emotional ending, Koontz cooks at high heat. Koontz recaps and puts a high-velocity spin on the whole history of horror fiction, enriching a bounty of scary setpieces with winsome characters and piquant reflection on what exactly makes us human.' The *Seattle Times*: 'Koontz is a prose stylist whose lyricism heightens malevolence and tension.' From the *Grand Rapids Press*: 'A white-knuckler of a novel, cleanly and powerfully written.' The *Nashville Banner*: 'Reminds one of H.G. Wells's *The Island of Dr Moreau*, Shelley's *Frankenstein*, Stevenson's *Dr Jekyll and Mr Hyde* and Koontz's eerie poetic prose evokes the best of Edgar Allan Poe.'

MIDNIGHT was Koontz's first number-one *New York Times* bestseller.

* * *

MR MURDER. New York: Putnam, 1993; London: Headline, 1993.

Opening sentence: '*I need . . .*'

Comments: This ranks among the author's very best books and may be his finest novel to date. It is a key book of his oeuvre. The cultural and sociological concerns that began to be part of the weave of his fiction in a major way with COLD FIRE are yet more integral to MR MURDER and are handled with greater depth and sophistication. The texture of the family relationship at the center of the novel is rich and convincing. The author's distrust of utopian visions and political solutions, combined with his awareness that there are always too many people willing to twist justice and torture the truth in the name of a noble cause, leads to a bleak assessment of the chances for democratic societies to prevail in the long run; however, he manages to make this an essentially *hopeful* book because of his unshakable belief in the dignity and honesty of the average person in one-to-one relationships and in family structures. At times this is one of the most humorous novels he has ever done – specially in scenes with the two young girls, Charlotte and Emily, and with the two bureaucratic villains, Oslett and Clocker – but MR MURDER is nevertheless fast-paced and almost unbearably suspenseful. The fantasy element is still present in this work, although it is more subdued than in books like DRAGON TEARS, HIDEAWAY, THE BAD PLACE, and MIDNIGHT. In that sense, it is similar to the other novel that rivals it as his best, WATCHERS, and it may represent a new direction in his work.

Publishers Weekly said of MR MURDER: '. . . lean prose and rich characterization . . . Playing on every emotion and keeping the story racing along, Koontz masterfully escalates the tension. He closes the narrative with the most ingenius twist ending of his career.' A limited, signed, first edition of 750 copies will be issued by Putnam at an initial list price of $150.

* * *

NIGHT CHILLS. New York: Atheneum, 1976; London: W. H. Allen, 1977, reissued by Headline, 1990.

Opening sentence: The dirt trail was narrow.

Comments: This novel followed AFTER THE LAST RACE and preceded THE VISION, which puts it on the cusp of the most fundamental change in the author's career to date. With NIGHT CHILLS, he moved from the straight suspense he had done before it toward the mix of suspense and the fantastic that followed. NIGHT CHILLS deals with a scientific experiment gone awry, as does MIDNIGHT thirteen years later, though it is neither as sophisticated and accomplished as that later book nor as heavily imbued with the fantastic. If his cross-genre style was born in any single novel, it was in NIGHT CHILLS, which mixes elements of traditional suspense novels with the somewhat science-fictional premise of mind control and the chilling psychological horror of personality sublimation that gave *The Invasion of the Bodysnatchers* so much power. The book is notable, as well, because – with WHISPERS – it is one of the few in which the author indulges in what might be termed 'strong sexual material,' though it is unquestionably necessary to do so in order to tell the story. It's strange structure, which breaks many narrative rules, alternating chapters in the present with chapters in the past until past and present meet, is intriguing and more than half successful.

From the *King Features Syndicate* review: 'NIGHT CHILLS is as fast and exciting as any thriller you have ever read. But it is also writing of a superior sort, with characters about whom you care, and when you turn the last page, you will be left with plenty to think about.' From the *Boston Sunday Herald*: 'An extraordinarily well-crafted story . . . Koontz is very convincing, his book is very gripping and well-researched, and his writing is almost too good for escapist literature.' From the *Chicago Sun-Times*: 'Koontz is brilliant in the creation of his characters and in building tension.'

* * *

NIGHTMARE JOURNEY. New York: Berkley, 1975.

Opening sentence: In the crisp morning, before the worst of the fog had lifted, the Pure humans came into the village, descending the narrow winding road from their fortress, which perched on the edge of the alabaster cliff.

Comments: This was the last-published of the author's straight science-fiction novels, though it had been written a few years previously. It is a far-future adventure story, engaging and with merit, though he would probably be unwilling to see it reissued within the life of the copyright, as it is also clearly the work of a less mature writer and would need considerable revision to meet the high standards he now sets for himself.

* * *

ODDKINS. New York: Warner Books, 1988; London: Headline, 1988.

Opening sentence: Amos the bear was standing on the toymaker's bench, looking through the casement window at the purple-black storm clouds rolling in from the east.

Comments: This is quite a departure from the author's usual work. He has said that he admires those children's books that can be read and enjoyed by adults, that have different levels of meaning and charm depending on the age of the reader. In ODDKINS, he wrote precisely such a novel. This 45,000-word story was originally published in an unusual rectangular, horizontal, hardcover format with fifty pages of marvelous, full-color illustrations by Phil Parks.

Film rights were bought outright by Warner Brothers, who for a while intended to make it as an animated film with director Tim Burton. The book has been out of print for a few years. The author receives hundreds of letters a year, requesting a new edition, including many from teachers who find it a good tool with which to interest kids in books. He intends to make every effort to get it back into bookstores in the reasonably near future.

* * *

PHANTOMS. New York: Putnam, 1983; London: W. H. Allen, 1983, reissued by Headline, 1990.

Opening sentence: The scream was distant and brief.

Comments: This is a key work in the author's oeuvre, and the closest thing he has ever written to a genuine horror novel. It is this book that relegated him strictly to that genre in many people's minds and made it difficult for him to reach a wider audience until WATCHERS and LIGHTNING. Told in a brisk, boiled-down style that is nonetheless evocative and at times lyrical, PHANTOMS moves at the pace of a slim chase novel in spite of being over 160,000 words long. With this book, the author signals the extravagant imagination that he will later apply to books like LIGHTNING, MIDNIGHT, THE BAD PLACE, and DRAGON TEARS. In PHANTOMS, as in WHISPERS before it, what seems to be a story about something supernatural – and later perhaps something extraterrestrial – proves to have a bizarre but logical explanation, and this would, as well, become a trait of most of Koontz's subsequent books.

In the years since its publication, PHANTOMS has become a modern classic of the horror genre, but it was also well-reviewed at the time. From *Publishers Weekly*: 'A first-rate horror story, scary and plausible. The characters seem real as they wage a desperate struggle against their malevolent foe.' From *Bestsellers*: 'A first-rate thriller. The riveting narrative power will sweep you along, drawing you in, as you read with nail-biting compulsion [and] it's a bonus to discover such a strong command of imagery in a contemporary fiction writer.' From the *Copley News Service*: 'A beautifully written novel of suspense and terror.' And *Analog* noted that Koontz: 'brings the reader immediately to the sleepless edge of his seat and keeps him there. The gleam of technology and science suffuses a tale that could so easily have been lost in mysticism.'

* * *

PRISON OF ICE. As by 'David Axton.' New York: Lippincott, 1976; London: W. H. Allen, 1977.

Opening sentence: (a newspaper headline) POLAR ICE PUREST WATER IN THE WORLD.

Comments: This was the first and last novel under the Axton name and seems something of a tribute to the early adventure novels of Alistair MacLean. It is set largely on the Arctic ice cap, with some scenes in a Soviet submarine. A group of scientists, accidentally set adrift on an iceberg in the worst storm of the season, face certain death unless a Soviet submarine, captained by a man at odds with his government in Moscow, can manage a daring rescue. Here is Koontz's singularly imaginative plotting ability applied to a different genre from any of those to which his current readers are accustomed.

The *Baltimore News-American*: 'Clever . . . original, consistent, and chilling in every sense of the word.' From *Booklist*: 'One of the most suspenseful novels of the season.' From *Chicago Tribune Book World*: 'Jammed with the tensions of imminent disaster . . . unfolds with the timing of a quartz watch.' From *Nautical Magazine*: 'A fascinating story, well told on every page . . . [the technical aspects] are handled very expertly.'

This novel has been long out of print, and it is the hope of the author to find the time to do some updating and revision in order to return it to bookstores within the next few years.

* * *

THE SERVANTS OF TWILIGHT. (See TWILIGHT.)

* * *

SHADOWFIRES As by 'Leigh Nichols.' New York: Avon, 1987; London: Fontana, 1987, reissued by Headline, 1991.

Opening sentence: Brightness fell from the air, nearly as tangible as rain.

Comments: This is the fifth – and best – of the five novels published under the Nichols pseudonym. Taking the same essential seed as WATCHERS – a government experiment in genetic engineering that goes awry – the author comes up with an utterly different but equally compelling story. He plays with the Frankenstein legend, as well: In this case, Dr Frankenstein and his creature are one and the same, as Eric Leben experiments on himself to his eventual regret. In addition to telling one of his most suspenseful stories, the author has considerable fun in this novel, evidenced by hundreds of subtle wordgames: Eric Leben's surname is the German word for 'life,' which reverberates ironically throughout the book; or note the parallels between Rachael, the heroine, and her Biblical namesake. Furthermore, SHADOWFIRES contains the most vivid cast of supporting characters of all Koontz's novels to date: The amusing and charming Jerry Peake, Anson Sharp, Julio Verdad and Reese Hagerstrom, Felsen Kiel (otherwise known as The Stone), and so many more, each strongly drawn and each unlike any character in other Koontz novels.

SHADOWFIRES was published in trade hardcover by Dark Harvest Press, which also issued two states of a limited edition: A 52-copy (A to ZZ) lettered edition and a 600-copy signed and numbered edition. Under the author's real name, the reissue of the book was a number-one *New York Times* bestseller in paperback.

* * *

SHATTERED. As by 'K. R. Dwyer.' New York: Random House, 1973; London: Reissued as by Dean Koontz by W. H. Allen, reissued by Headline, 1990.

Opening sentence: Only four blocks from the furnished apartment in Philadelphia, with more than three thousand miles to drive before they joined Courtney in San Francisco, Colin began one of his games.

Comments: This was the second of three novels under the Dwyer pseudonym. It is a straightforward cross-country chase with a real flavor of its paranoid times. It is one of the strongest books from this period of Koontz's career, largely because of the psychological exploration of the lead character, Alex Doyle, and the chillingly realistic depiction of the necessity to compromise one's principles to survive in an often cruel world. In this book and others from this

299

period, the author acquired certain skills of realistic writing that served him well when he moved on, years later, to books with elements of fantasy; by then, he seemed to know how to ground even the most far-fetched plot with convincingly realistic characters and settings. SHATTERED is now available under the author's real name.

From *Publishers Weekly*: 'A chilling tale [that] moves with expert economy of style and homes in on some significant issues... SHATTERED is astringent, satisfying, and sleek as a bullet.' From the *San Francisco Examiner and Chronicle*: '[SHATTERED] mounts to a crash climax that has elements both of satisfaction and tragedy. This one is genuinely tense.' From the *Long Beach Press-Telegram*: 'The author is an exceptionally gifted stylist... SHATTERED is the work of a fine craftsman, a storyteller of great talent.'

* * *

SOFT COME THE DRAGONS. New York: Ace Books, 1970.

Opening sentence of the title story: 'And what will you do when the soft breezes come and the dragons drift in to spread death?'

Comments: This was one half of an 'Ace Double Novel,' with the author's DARK OF THE WOODS on the reverse. This was a collection of his earliest short stories, all science fiction. Some of these still hold up, though written when he was as young as twenty and twenty-one. The best of them will undoubtedly turn up in a new collection sooner or later.

* * *

STARBLOOD. New York: Lancer Books, 1972.

Opening sentence: Timothy was not human.

Comments: This straight science-fiction novel was written when the author was twenty-four, and was based on his novella titled 'A Third Hand.' This is one of Koontz's lesser science-fiction efforts and will no doubt be kept out of print through the life of copyright.

* * *

STAR QUEST. New York: Ace Books, 1968.

Opening sentence: Jumbo Ten was pulling out of the ranks.

Comments: This was the author's first novel, written when he was twenty-one. It is a science-fiction pulp novel, immature in style, yet it is packed with an array of original ideas and concepts, as well as some twists on long-established science-fiction gimmicks that make it interesting in its own way. This book will never see print again during the life of copyright, as it is not up to the author's current standards and is not a good candidate for revision.

* * *

STRANGERS. New York: Putnam, 1986.

Opening sentence: Dominick Corvaisis went to sleep under a light wool blanket and a crisp white sheet, sprawled alone in his bed, but he woke elsewhere – in the darkness at the back of the large foyer closet, behind concealing coats and jackets.

Comments: This is a key novel in the author's oeuvre. With a cast of *twelve* major characters and an enormous number of supporting and walk-on characters, STRANGERS is the largest novel the author has written to date, yet it is nearly as headlong in its pace as anything he's done at half its length. Though the novel deals with as many issues and themes as it does characters, it is primarily an exploration of the nature of friendship in all its permutations – man to man, woman to woman, woman to man, old to young, interracial, and finally even alien to human. Ginger's friendship with the old black magician and hypnotist, Pablo Jackson, is one of the book's more obvious statements about the power of good will and kindness to overcome all differences between people. The title fits the story so well, in so many ways, on so many levels of complexity, that any number of academic papers could be written on that aspect of the novel alone. The author's talent for salient detail, for imagery, for descriptions of the natural world that would become increasingly obvious in later books is here in full flower, resulting in a novel that, in spite of its size and density, is nearly as visual as a motion picture.

It must have been satisfying for Koontz when his idol, John D. MacDonald, praised the book without reservation: 'I thoroughly enjoyed STRANGERS. You can't call this merely spooky. It is a contemporary novel of manners and morals and politics and freedom. This is a book with a capital B!' Other reviewers were equally impressed, such as the *Library Journal* critic: 'An almost unbearably suspenseful page-turner. His ability to maintain the mystery through several plot twists is impressive, as is his array of believable and sympathetic characters. With its masterful blend of elements of espionage, terror, and even some science fiction, STRANGERS may be the suspense novel of the year.' From the *New York Times*: 'The plot twists ingeniously . . . an engaging, often chilling book . . . tough to put down.' From the *Wichita Falls Times*: 'Dean Koontz is a master storyteller. He has absolutely amazing knowledge of his subject matter, whether it be religion, military weapons, medicine, or an understanding of human nature. STRANGERS is absolutely enthralling.'

* * *

STRIKE DEEP. As by 'Anthony North.' New York: Dial Press, 1974.

Opening sentence: Lee Ackridge was two blocks from home when a sudden flurry of snowflakes struck his face and melted on his skin.

Comments: This was the first and last novel under the North pseudonym. The publisher went so far as to create an entire false biography for the writer, in order to present STRIKE DEEP as a major first novel by a new talent in suspense. The jacket flap biography claims: 'Anthony North lived in Washington for years and is intimately acquainted with the workings of the Pentagon. He now lives in Jamaica with his wife and four children.' This was one early, if not the first, novel about computer terrorism by hackers; though the term 'hackers' was not yet in use. Disaffected veterans of Vietnam, one of them the son of the Chairman of the Joint Chiefs of Staff, cooperate in a plot to steal the nation's most sensitive defense secrets and sell them to a foreign power. In the end, the lead finds himself incapable of treason and at odds with the other conspirators. The book is well-paced and involving. In considering the issue of computer security and the vulnerability of electronically-stored information, STRIKE DEEP was years ahead of its time – although much of the computer detail is now dated. The author may consider revising it, updating the technical information, and republishing it under his real name if he can find the time.

Publishers Weekly called it 'a lean, exciting thriller' and went on to say: 'As the ingeniously planned heist goes into execution, the FBI, a Russian spy, [the lead's girlfriend], and a number of minor characters get drawn into a swirl of events that move toward a violent and unusually satisfying conclusion. It's fun to read and as a first novel distinctly promising.'

* * *

SURROUNDED. As by 'Brian Coffey.' New York: Bobbs-Merrill, 1974; London: Arthur Barker, 1975.

Opening sentence: The slim, tousle-haired man entered the lobby of the Americana Hotel, leaving the cacophony of the Seventh Avenue traffic behind him.

Comments: This was the second of five novels published under the Coffey pseudonym, and the second of three featuring the same protagonist – Michael Tucker – an educated, gentlemanly, but thoroughly tough professional thief who stole only from other criminals or, in this case, from merchants who would be covered by an insurance company. See BLOOD RISK for additional information.

From *Publishers Weekly*: 'Plotted like an expert chess game. What happens as cops and robbers try to outsmart each other is handled with ingenuity and finesse.' From *Library Journal*: 'The mechanics are most interesting. The problems of suitable hardware and reliable personnel are thoroughly gone into, and the robbery is excitingly brought to a successful conclusion.'

* * *

TIME THIEVES. New York: Ace Books, 1972; London: Dobson, 1977.

Opening sentence: First, there was a purple-black emptiness the texture of moist velvet, clinging to him like the pulsing membrane of a living heart.

Comments: This was written when the author was twenty-five and is one of his earlier straight science-fiction novels, though it has a contemporary setting. The central premise is intriguing, the pace

303

fast, and the surprises plentiful. The author intends to revise the novel – which is short – for inclusion in a collection of stories one day, though it is not yet on his schedule.

* * *

TWILIGHT. As by 'Leigh Nichols.' New York: Pocket Books, 1984; London: Published as THE SERVANTS OF TWILIGHT by Fontana; 1985, reissued as by Dean Koontz by Headline, 1991.

Opening sentence: It began in sunshine, not on a dark and stormy night.

Comments: This was the fourth of five novels published under the Nichols pseudonym. It was later reissued under the author's real name and his original, preferred title, THE SERVANTS OF TWILIGHT. This is one of the best of the Nichols books. The author's intention was to see if an unadulterated chase story could be successfully sustained at major-novel length. Most readers would agree that Koontz carried it off. The pace and high suspense are unrelenting.

However, the novel operates on more complex levels than just the chase, and its central concern – that it's a mistake to judge the message by the messenger – is quirkily explored and leads to a stunning climax. If you haven't read the novel yet, stop here. If you have, then you know that the crazy old woman, Grace Spivey, is every bit as right as she is crazy, and sweet little Joey is, in fact, the monster she believes him to be. This revelation, at the end of the novel – much clearer to the reader than it ever is to the main characters – comes like a physical blow, a very real shock. Yet, when the reader reflects on the story, he sees that the surprise has been well prepared for and that the clues were there from the start.

The original Pocket Books cover is dreadful and one of the worst misrepresentations of a novel in which any publisher has indulged. The artwork features a handsome couple in a romantic clinch, against a windswept backdrop. Any browser would imagine that it was a typical genre romance. On the *back* cover, a child with a rotting skull for a face is shown clutching a cross that has just been struck by lightning. While the front of the book sells a romance novel, the back sells a crude horror story – and the novel is neither.

THE SERVANTS OF TWILIGHT was later published by Dark Harvest in an illustrated trade hardcover and in a limited edition in two states – a 52-copy lettered version (A to Z) and a 450-copy numbered version.

* * *

TWILIGHT EYES. Plymouth, Michigan: The Land of Enchantment, 1985; expanded version: New York: Berkley Books, 1987; London: W. H. Allen, 1987, reissued by Headline, 1990.

Opening sentence: That was the year they murdered our president in Dallas.

Comments: The author's broad knowledge of carnival life and culture, which was exhibited to a minor extent in THE FUNHOUSE, is on full display in this novel. This milieu has been frequently used as a backdrop to horror and science-fiction stories, but usually it has been an outsider's idea of what carnivals are all about; TWILIGHT EYES portrays the *real* inner world of the carnival and the psychology of carnies perhaps better than any American novel, regardless of genre, has ever done. It reveals to us a culture with traditions, mores, and attitudes that are more colorful than the bright lights and razzle-dazzle of any midway. The heavily ornamented prose gives Slim MacKenzie (the narrator) a distinct voice, and it is also perfectly suited to a story about a carnival; the flamboyance of language and subject are matched.

Thematically, the novel explores mankind's awareness that he is somehow an outcast in his own world, largely due to his capacity for evil. The shape-changing goblins might be seen as a symbol of the dark side of humanity; and the previous civilization alluded to in the end of the novel, said to have been destroyed by nuclear war in ages past, might easily be regarded as a symbol of Eden, of paradise lost. The Sombra Brothers Carnival functions, in many ways, as a retreat for those who are weary of the world and who are seeking the life of a closed and structured community – rather like a traveling monastery.

TWILIGHT EYES was originally published in a 120,000-word version by The Land of Enchantment, heavily illustrated with pencil drawings and full-color paintings. The trade hardcover and both states of the limited, signed edition – a twenty-six-copy lettered edition and a 250-copy numbered edition – have become much sought after by collectors. Subsequently, the author remained haunted by the story and wrote a continuation of 80,000 additional words prior to

305

the publication of the Berkley paperback. The book had originally ended with this line: 'But that is another story.' Koontz added two words – 'Which follows' – to link the old and new material. The only hardcover appearances of the full text in the English language were a British edition by W. H. Allen, and later another British edition by Headline.

* * *

THE VISION. New York: Putnam, 1977; London: Corgi, 1980, reissued by Headline, 1990.

Opening sentence: 'Gloves of blood.'

Comments: This bridging book in his career sits between his first genre-bridging efforts in NIGHT CHILLS and his first major success with WHISPERS. Koontz has written: 'The book is very heavy on dialogue. The style, while recognizably mine, is leaner and more clipped than in most of my books. When I was casting around for an idea, it occurred to me that most horror novels are written, to one degree or another, in a dense style, and that it might be fun to see if one could be done in almost minimalist prose, where every word and image counted, rather as if Dashiell Hammett had set out to write a horror novel.' In the end, it didn't turn out to be exactly a *horror* novel, though in parts it is certainly horrifying.

From the *Durham Herald*: 'Suspense that's almost discomfiting in its intensity. The characters are so fully dimensioned that they lift the book from the thriller genre to the rarefied atmosphere of the mainstream novel.' From the *Florida Times-Union*: 'The tension never lets up, building page by page to a nail-biting, hair-raising finale.'

* * *

THE VOICE OF THE NIGHT. As by 'Brian Coffey.' New York: Doubleday, 1980; London: Robert Hale, 1981, reissued as by Dean Koontz, Headline, 1990.

Opening sentence: 'You ever killed anything?' Roy asked.

Comments: This was the fifth of five novels published under the Coffey pseudonym, and the best of the five. It is a key novel in the author's oeuvre, because it is the first in which he portrays young people with the depth and power long evident in his adult characters. In subsequent books, he frequently creates teenagers, pre-teens, and children of unusual complexity: Such as Laura Shane, Thelma and Ruth Akerson, and all their friends at the orphanage in LIGHTNING; Chrissie in MIDNIGHT; Regina in HIDEAWAY; and, not least of all, Charlotte and Emily Stillwater in MR MURDER. VOICE is also important because, in its lean but hallucinatorily vivid prose, one can see the author experimenting with language to a greater extent than he had ever done previously, and one can see the results of that experimentation – still ongoing – in everything he has written since, especially in his ability to tell a story with a large cast and canvas in fewer words than one might expect. When reissued under the author's real name, THE VOICE OF THE NIGHT was a number-one *New York Times* bestseller in paperback.

From the *Houston Chronicle*: '[The author] has packed this terrifying novel with hair-raising suspense from cover to cover. Not a word is misspent, not a page is wasted as the colors of psychological horror are artfully applied to what might have been a simple story of the adolescent discovery and disillusionment that forces us all to grow up. He has caught and crystallized the entire character of doubt, knowledge, and self-awareness that we all have faced, with a skillful nostalgia devoid of the usual sentimentality.' From the *Chicago Sun-Times*: 'A fearsome tour of an adolescent's tortured psyche. Knee-knocking suspense.'

* * *

THE WALL OF MASKS. As by 'Brian Coffey.' New York: Bobbs-Merrill, 1975.

Opening sentence: In 1519, Hernan Cortez landed at Veracruz, Mexico, with a Spanish army at his command; but when Michael Tucker arrived there on Monday, September 2, four hundred and fifty-five years later, he didn't even have a handgun.

Comments: This is the third of five novels under the Coffey pseudonym and the third of three featuring the same lead character, Michael Tucker, who is a professional thief. For more details, see BLOOD RISK and SURROUNDED.

From the *Detroit Free Press*: 'THE WALL OF MASKS is exciting, fast-moving, and has a dynamite climax involving a double cross, a deadly car accident and a nice touch of Robin Hood.' From *Library Journal*: 'A smashing adventure. The action is full of surprises [including] a boat chase on the Gulf of Mexico in the teeth of a hurricane, culminating in a mass shootout.'

* * *

WARLOCK. New York: Lancer, 1972.

Opening sentence: In his cluttered study on the west end of the house, Sandow sat at a desk which was strewn with archaic texts whose pages had yellowed and cracked with the passage of much time.

Comments: This early science-fantasy novel, written when the author was twenty-five, is an adventure story involving a great trek across a future world that is much changed from our own because of a war that has all but obliterated the past and any memory of it. In quality, it fits in the middle of Koontz's science-fiction career. Because it is not equal to his later standards, it will probably not see print again, though it might one day be revised for inclusion in a story collection.

* * *

WATCHERS. New York: Putnam, 1987.

Opening sentence: On his thirty-sixth birthday, May 18, Travis Cornell rose at five o'clock in the morning.

Comments: This is a key novel in the author's oeuvre. More than any other work to date, it embodies *all* of the major themes with which he is obsessed: The healing power of love and friendship; the struggle to overcome the past and change what we are; the moral superiority of the individual over the workings of the state and large institutions; the wonder of both the natural world and the potential of the human mind; the relationship of mankind to God; transcendence; and how we sustain hope in the face of our awareness that all things die. This book contains the quintessential Koontz love story, in which two people, both damaged but with their individual strengths, find that they can be more complete and more alive together than either can be alone; love, in any of the author's novels, is expressed not merely in romantic or sexual terms, but as a condition with broad emotional effects and with a profound involvement of the intellect. In Travis and Nora, from WATCHERS, Koontz achieves a depth of insight into loving relationships that he sometimes equals in later work but never (as yet) surpasses.

This is the author's personal favorite of his books to date (with MR MURDER a close second). In this excerpt from a letter to Bill Munster, he makes several points that are best made in his own words: 'I believe that we carry within us a divinely inspired moral imperative to love, and I explore that imperative in all of my books. Indeed, that is the case with WATCHERS, a theme to which I even posted signs, such as those embodied in the epigrams that are used at the start of Part Two. ("Love alone is capable of uniting living beings in such a way as to complete and fulfill them, for it alone takes them and joins them by what is deepest in themselves" – Pierre Teilhard de Chardin. And "Greater love hath no man than this: that he lay down his life for his friends."' – The Gospel According to St John.) We have within us the ability to change for the better and to find dignity as individuals rather than as fragments of one mass movement or another. We have the ability to love, the need to be loved, and the willingness to put our own lives on the line to protect those we love, and it is in these aspects of ourselves that we see the face of God and through the exercise of those qualities that we achieve a godlike state. My books are about the great value of the individual ... about the loving relationships between mates, friends, relatives ... and I am, of course, a thoroughgoing optimist, a believer in people and the future. I think my optimism makes my fiction considerably different from that of anyone I can name in the dark-suspense arena, where misanthropy of one degree or another seems to color most of what else is written.'

For the clearest statement of optimism that the author has ever made within a novel, one need look no farther than chapter seven, subchapter six, of WATCHERS, in which these words appear: 'Although the constant shadow of certain death looms over every day, the pleasures and joys of life can be so fine and deeply affecting that the heart is nearly stilled by astonishment.'

From the *Los Angeles Daily News*: 'Convincing characters, good dialogue ... written in prose of a literary quality that puts most bestselling authors to shame.' From the *Cleveland Plain Dealer*: 'WATCHERS is so well crafted that it is nearly everything one could wish for in a modern suspense novel ... unrelentingly suspenseful. His style is a model of clarity, his prose so smooth that it goes down like apple juice while his plot carries the delayed punch of hard cider. First-class entertainment.' From *Kirkus Reviews*: 'His best ever, an imaginative and unusual blend of suspense and sentiment. A fable about love and trust . . . with echoes of *Frankenstein* and *The Island of Dr Moreau*.' Finally, from the *Baltimore Daily Record*: 'Characterization is Koontz's unexpected gift. He made me genuinely care about his characters. I had to keep reading. I had to make sure everything would turn out all right. WATCHERS reads less like a thriller and more like a novel, a novel that is capable of making us cheer for the characters and fear for them and ultimately take them into our hearts.'

* * *

A WEREWOLF AMONG US. New York: Ballantine, 1973.

Opening sentence: Morbidly curious, the squint-eyed customs official examined the two holes in Baker St Cyr's chest.

Comments: This is a science-fiction novel set on another world but could as easily have been set on Earth in the not-terribly-distant future. It ranks in the top third of the author's science-fiction work, and he intends to revise it one day, most likely for inclusion in a collection.

* * *

WHISPERS. New York: Putnam, 1980; London: W. H. Allen, reissued by Headline, 1990.

Opening sentence: Tuesday at dawn, Los Angeles trembled.

Comments: This is a key novel in the author's oeuvre. WHISPERS and THE KEY TO MIDNIGHT were his first two attempts at stories with large canvases and interwoven webs of complex psychology, and this was the more successful of the two. In this book he took cross-genre writing much farther than in NIGHT CHILLS or any previous work; the blend of police-procedural, psychological suspense, love story, and even minor elements of horror reads smoothly and engagingly. In THE VISION, California had served as backdrop; however, in WHISPERS, California's culture, history, and landscape are center stage through so much of the novel that, as the

310

author has noted, the locale almost becomes another character. Following WHISPERS, Koontz has used California as the primary setting for most of the novels that constitute his finest work; he has made southern California, in particular, as much his own as it was ever Raymond Chandler's. This novel is also a landmark in his career, because it marks the apex of his faith in Freudian psychology as the map by which characters' motivations are traced and explored; subsequently, novel by novel, he moves toward an apparent belief that the human mind functions far more complexly than Freud ever theorized; at the same time he seems to believe that the explanation of human evil is simpler than Freud proposed yet more mysterious. Ultimately, Freudian theory can be used to excuse any behavior because each man or woman is the helpless victim of the experiences and traumas that he or she has survived; that flight from responsibility clearly troubles the author and, as a theme, powers two of his best novels to date – DRAGON TEARS and MR MURDER.

From novelist John D. MacDonald: 'A solid piece of work, good craftsmanship. The shelves fit together and the hinges work. WHISPERS is all I ask of a book and precisely what I find less of with each passing year.' From the *Birmingham News*: 'With a style that sweeps the reader along beautifully . . . WHISPERS stands tall above the shock-for-shock's-sake tales so current.' From novelist Elmore Leonard: 'A winner . . . fascinating. A hell of a job, a thoroughly engrossing story about real people in a frighteningly bizarre situation.'

* * *

WINTER MOON. New York: Ballantine, 1994; London: Headline, 1994.

Opening sentence: Death was driving an emerald-green Lexus.

Comments: This novel began as a revision of INVASION, originally published under the pseudonym of Aaron Wolfe. However, it is so different from the book that inspired it, a separate listing is not only justified but required. While not as complex as Koontz's novels of the past decade, WINTER MOON seethes with the concerns that are common to all of his better works, and the characters of Jack and Heather McGarvey are well-realized and different from other Koontz characters in numerous ways. It will be interesting, for instance, to see whether some of the blue-collar concerns of the people in this story are carried forward to future novels by the author as yet one more ingredient of his unique mix. Though the novel has a science-fictional premise at its core (the one major element carried over from INVASION), its depiction of daily life in contemporary Los Angeles is harrowing and thoroughly convincing. Because Koontz takes risks with this piece, it is interesting as a monitor of his evolution as a writer; and it belongs among the top third of his body of work. See INVASION.

2. Short Fiction

'Altarboy,' *Infinity Three*, edited by Robert Hoskins. New York: Lancer, 1972.
'Beastchild,' *Venture Science Fiction*, August, 1970.
'The Black Pumpkin,' *Twilight Zone*, December, 1986.
'Bruno,' *The Magazine of Fantasy and Science Fiction*, April, 1971.
'Cosmic Sin,' *The Magazine of Fantasy and Science Fiction*, April, 1971.
'The Crimson Witch,' *Fantastic Stories*, October, 1970.
'A Darkness in My Soul,' *Fantastic Stories*, January, 1968.
'Dreambird,' *If*, September, 1968.
'Down in the Darkness,' *The Horror Show*, Summer, 1986.
'A Dragon in the Land,' *Venture Science Fiction*, August, 1969.
'The Good Ship Lookoutworld,' *Fantastic Stories*, February, 1970.
'Graveyard Highway,' *Tropical Chills*, edited by Tim Sullivan. New York: Avon, 1988.
'Grayworld,' *Infinity Five*, edited by Robert Hoskins. New York: Lancer, 1973.
'Hardshell,' *Night Visions 4*, Arlington Heights, Illinois: Dark Harvest Press, 1987.
'In the Shield,' *If*, January, 1969.
'The Interrogation,' *The Horror Show*, Summer, 1987.
'Killerbot,' *Galaxy*, May, 1969.
'Kittens,' *Readers and Writers*, 1966.
'Miss Attila the Hun,' *Night Visions 4*, Arlington Heights, Illinois: Dark Harvest Press, 1987.
'A Mouse in the Walls of the Global Village,' *Again Dangerous Visions*, edited by Harlan Ellison. New York: Doubleday, 1972.

'Muse,' *The Magazine of Fantasy and Science Fiction*, September, 1969.

'The Mystery of His Flesh,' *The Magazine of Fantasy and Science Fiction*, July, 1970.

'Night of the Storm,' *Continuum 1*, edited by Roger Elwood. New York: Putnam, 1974.

'Nightmare Gang,' *Infinity One*, edited by Robert Hoskins. New York: Lancer, 1970.

'Ollie's Hands,' *Infinity Four*, edited by Robert Hoskins. New York: Lancer, 1972. Revised for *The Horror Show*, Summer, 1987.

'The Psychedelic Children,' *The Magazine of Fantasy and Science Fiction*, July, 1968.

'Shambolain,' *If*, November-December, 1970.

'The Sinless Child,' *Flame Tree Planet*, edited by Roger Elwood. New York: Concordia, 1986.

'Snatcher,' *Night Cry*, Fall, 1986.

'Soft Come the Dragons,' *The Magazine of Fantasy and Science Fiction*, August, 1967.

'Temple of Sorrow,' *Amazing Stories*, January, 1969.

'Terra Phobia,' *Androids, Time Machines and Blue Giraffes*, edited by Roger Elwood and Vic Ghidalia. New York: Follett, 1973.

'A Third Hand,' *The Magazine of Fantasy and Science Fiction*, January, 1970.

'To Behold the Sun,' *The Magazine of Fantasy and Science Fiction*, December, 1967.

'Trapped,' *Stalkers*, edited by Ed Gorman and Martin H. Greenberg. Arlington Heights, Illinois: Dark Harvest Press, 1989.

'The Twelfth Bed,' *The Magazine of Fantasy and Science Fiction*, August, 1968.

'Twilight of the Dawn,' *Night Visions 4*, Arlington Heights, Illinois: Dark Harvest Press, 1987.

'The Undercity,' *Future City*, edited by Roger Elwood. New York: Trident Press, 1973.

'Unseen Warriors,' *Worlds of Tomorrow*, Winter, 1970.

'Wake Up to Thunder,' *Children of Infinity*, edited by Roger Elwood. New York: Franklin Watts, 1973.

'We Three,' *Final Stage*, edited by Roger Elwood and Barry N. Malzberg. New York: Charterhouse, 1974.

'Weird World,' *The Horror Show*, Summer, 1986.

'Where the Beast Runs,' *If*, July, 1969.

3. Book-length Nonfiction

HOW TO WRITE BEST-SELLING FICTION. Cincinnati: Writer's Digest Press, 1981; London: Poplar Press, 1991.

Comments: This title has been out of print for years, although it was well reviewed and used widely in creative-writing classes in its day. The author wrote it to replace *Writing Popular Fiction*, which he felt was outdated. He removed this title from print, too, because he felt that it had become outdated in some regards, as well. He hopes to revise it for republication some day – but the reality is that his time is so filled with the writing of fiction, now, that he might never get to it.

* * *

THE PIG SOCIETY and THE UNDERGROUND LIFESTYLES HANDBOOK. Los Angeles: Aware Press, 1970.

Comments: These two books, while bearing the author's by-line, are not the books he wrote. His manuscripts were bastardized; much of his material was removed; 40 percent of the book in the first case, 70 percent in the second case, consists of material added by the publisher without the author's consent. Koontz does not consider these titles to be a legitimate part of his bibliography.

* * *

WRITING POPULAR FICTION. Cincinnati: Writer's Digest Books, 1972.

Comments: This book was written when the author was still in his twenties. When he felt that it became outdated, he took it off the market and replaced it with *How to Write Best-Selling Fiction*.